Town and Country

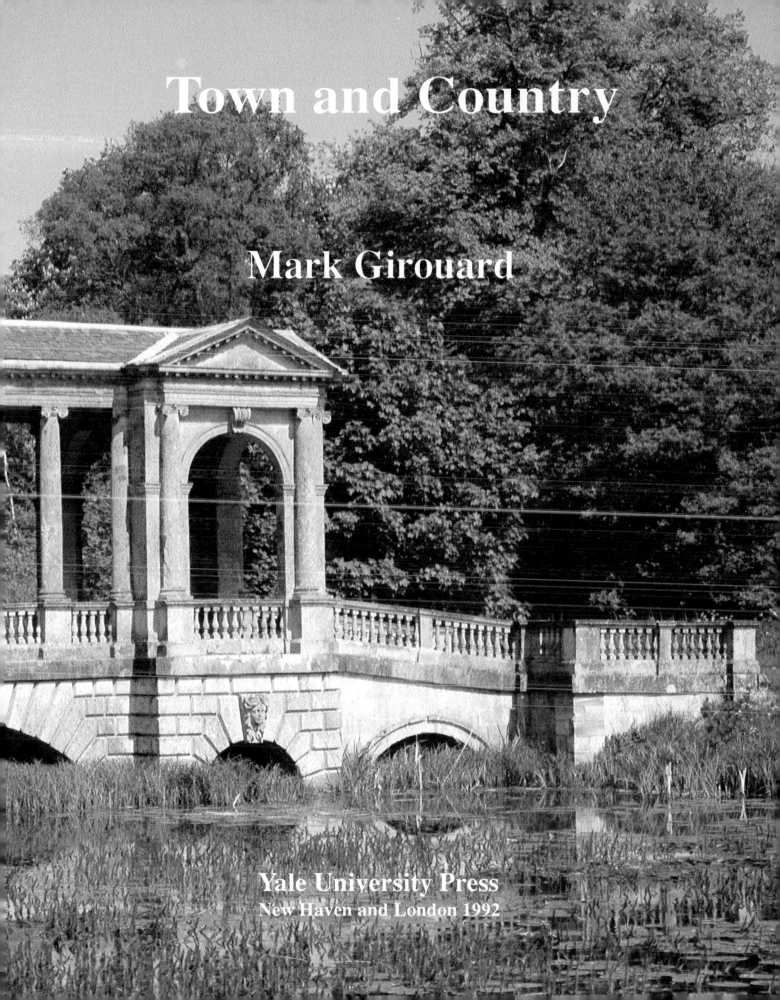

Town and Country

Mark Girouard

Yale University Press
New Haven and London 1992

Designed by Dorothy Girouard

Set in Times New Roman by Dorothy Girouard, London
Printed in Hong Kong through World Print Ltd.

Library of Congress Cataloging-in-Publication Data

Girouard, Mark, 1931 -
    Town and country : essays- on buildings, places, and people / Mark
Girouard.
        p.   cm.
    Includes bibliographical references and index.
    ISBN 0-300-05185-9
    1. Architecture - - England - - Miscellanea.   2. Architecture - - Ireland -
    Miscellanea.   I. Title.
NA961.G55   1992   92-54168
720 ' .941 - - dc20   CIP

(Half-title page)   Looking from the portico of the house to the Triumphal Arch, Stowe, Buckinghamshire.
(title page)   The Palladian Bridge, Stowe, Buckinghamshire.

CONTENTS

ACKNOWLEDGEMENTS

I am grateful to I.P.C.Magazines Ltd. and Cross River Press Ltd. for allowing me to make use of copyright material; to James Miller, Ian Lumley, Peter Day, the Duchess of Devonshire, Laurence Banks, Julian Walton, Katharine Bulbulia and Michael Gallagher for help in various ways; to Peter Burton and Harland Walshaw for the pleasure of their collaboration on the photographs; to Faith Hart for her skill as an editor; and above all to Elizabeth Manners without whose constant and unfailing help the book would never have achieved publication.

1. (right)   Where the author works.

INTRODUCTION
Something of Myself

I began to notice buildings at the age of five or six, on my daily walk from Upper Berkeley Street in London, where I lived, to Hyde Park, where I relieved hours of boredom by searching the litter-bins for discarded cigarette packets, in the hope of finding cigarette cards in them. The walk had three markers. First came the rusticated stucco quoins on the National Provincial Bank, at the corner of Edgware Road and Connaught Place. These took my fancy because they each looked like a mass of wriggling worms. A block of flats on Bayswater was intriguing because it was in the course of construction, and only the mounting cage of rust-red steel so far existed. The final landmark was a tall spiky drinking fountain at the point where we entered the park. This, I learnt much later, was a gift to London from the Maharaja Meerza Vijiaran Gajipataran Manea Sooltan Bahndoor of Vijianagram.

Out of London I visited my mother's relatives, who lived in country houses dotted over England and Ireland, and my father's grandmother, who was one of the dozens of widows dusting their husbands' medals in grace-and-favour apartments at Hampton Court Palace. When we stayed with her my sisters and I slept in a room in the Tudor part of the palace, separated by a garden from her rooms in the Wren building. Going out-of-doors to get to bed was interesting, but so was the contrast in colour, shape and even smell between the two kinds of building.

On a visit to my great-aunt at Chatsworth I was hauled every evening along the gallery of the Painted Hall, on my way from the nurseries to be shown to the grown-ups. The experience of a succession of lusciously gilded balusters passing by me at eye-level lies like a truffle in the recesses of my memory. When I was a year or two older my parents claimed that I looked at a Victorian insertion in a row of Georgian houses and said 'that house spoils the row'. I have no recollection of this, but at least I remember that I never got bored of building with bricks, assembling meccano, or making sandcastles, and that I spent hours poring over the illustration of Celesteville in *King Babar*.

It was not till I was eleven or twelve that I moved on from collecting stamps or spotting wildflowers and became consciously interested in architecture. In spite of past experiences and future developments, my interest did not start with country houses. My mother had been killed in a traffic accident, my great-aunt had taken us in, and I was spending the holidays on the edge of the park at Chatsworth. The house was occupied by a girls' school, but between terms I was free to bash out Chopsticks on the school pianos beneath the Verrio ceilings, or catch frogs in the Canal Pond, and try to make pets of them. The building, as such, did not especially interest me. Architecture meant Norman, Early English, Decorated, Perpendicular, and expeditions to churches. I drew my first plan when I was twelve and a half, in a letter to my father. It was of the parish church in Chesterfield, and was keyed to show dates. The result was fairly crude, and less entertaining (if that is the right word) than two sectional

2

drawings which I produced a year or so earlier, as my contribution to the war effort. These were inspired by diagrams in the *Illustrated London News*. They showed two versions of a giant vacuum cleaner, designed to hoover up the enemy, and fire them out again in the form of black-puddings, used as cannonballs, and red-hot glue, made from the bones of melted Germans.

I am grateful to Osbert Lancaster for first expanding my architectural horizon. My father owned his two cartoon histories of architecture, *Pillar to Post* and *Homes Sweet Homes*, and gave me his history of an imaginary seaside resort, *Progress at Pelvis Bay*. I loved them. They supplied me with endless new styles to spot, and took me from the Middle Ages right on to Pont Street Dutch, By-pass Residential and beyond. They also showed me that the vagaries of architecture could be entertaining. Moreover, from *Pelvis Bay* I learnt that one could spot architects as well as buildings; I went carefully through it and wrote 'Sir Septimus Ogive' under each drawing of that High Victorian purveyor of memorial fountains and municipal Gothic.

Spotting and classifying buildings acted as a seed-bed, out of which unexpected flowers of aesthetic enjoyment began to grow. An early experience was in the parish church at Melbourne in Derbyshire. Its huge stone columns walloping down the nave filled me with awe; 'solid Norman', I rightly described it in a letter, and 'solid' was perhaps my first attempt at aesthetic description. Then, when I was thirteen, my father took me for a walk round Chichester. Here, for street after street, the same architectural language was used with many gentle variations, always modest and always satisfying. I doubt if I analysed it at the time; but a day among the quiet red-brick of its eighteenth-century houses left me happy and excited.

A revelation came when I was fifteen and read Sacheverell Sitwell's *British Architects and Craftsmen*. I had learnt a good deal from the series of books on architecture, designed for the general public, which Batsford published after the war, but the Sitwell book — also Batsford — was in a different class. I came across it in the school library, and read it at a sitting; I gave it to my father that Christmas, shovelling all the money I had out of my pockets and paying the last portion with a couple of postage stamps.

I was reading Shelley at the time. Sitwell became my architectural Shelley. I found that one could get drunk on architecture as well as poetry. I moved from:

> Arethusa arose
> From her couch of snows
> On the Acroceraunian mountains

to: ' ... and the shivered, rooky battlements, black as rooks, and the whole building, Bolsover Castle, entire, dead, dead, as the Mayan rooms of Uxmal or Chichen Itza, and as remote from us, but with a ghastly poetry that fires the imagination, that can never be forgotten, and that never cools'. Both set me in a fever. From *British Architects and Craftsmen* I went on to Sitwell's two books on Baroque architecture. Goodbye to Norman, Early English, Decorated and Perpendicular; I became a convert to the Baroque.

I was helped in this by the Duke of Wellington. He was an old friend of my father's, an idiosyncratic mixture of humour and pomposity. He loved looking at buildings, and when we went to stay with him, took us round the countryside to see them in a brown and yellow Rolls Royce, singing extracts from John Betjeman as he drove. As a young diplomat in Rome, not yet a Duke or likely to become one, he had collected seventeenth and eighteenth-century books on architecture. He gave me the freedom of his library, and let me take the books up to bed with me, and read them into the small hours. I remember with especial vividness Le Pautre's luscious books of ornament, and the series of Baroque altarpieces in Pozzo's two volumes on perspective. In return, I designed Baroque water-closets and sent them to him from school. His reply, pointing out rather tartly, as was his way, how I had misused the Orders, was my first lesson in the grammar of classical architecture.

At about this time, I read Nikolaus Pevsner's *European Architecture*. There was no analysis in Sitwell (and not much accuracy, as I was later to discover). Pevsner showed me that one could dissect buildings, as well as enjoy them, that dissecting made them more, not less enjoyable, and that sections, plans and elevations were not just dry records of fact but keys to an expanded world. In his description of a walk up the Baroque staircase at Bruchsal, plans, photograph and text fused together; spaces interpenetrated, darkness opened up into a celebration of light; reading it inspired me to design Baroque staircases myself, with little success.

Buildings played more and more of a part in my last years at school. I walked to Rievaulx Abbey across the Yorkshire Moors, and to Fountains Abbey through the park and formal gardens of Studley Royal. I walked to Castle Howard, toiling doggedly along its interminable avenue towards an obelisk that never seemed to get any nearer. When I was fifteen my father took my sister and me on holiday abroad. We travelled through France to Collioure down by the Pyrenees, looking at buildings on the way there and back. I was especially excited by the soaring, needle-thin columns in the Dominican church at Toulouse — the other end of the scale from Melbourne — and by the experience, as much aesthetic as religious, of serving early mass beneath the Baroque reredos which glittered in the dim light at one end of the church at Collioure. Back in England I bought engravings, and books both new and old. My first purchase of an early book on architecture was of William Wrighte's *Grotesque Architecture or Rural Amusement*, which I bought for, I think, five shillings in a second-hand bookshop in York. Next came a battered copy of P.F. Robinson's *Ornamental Villas*, and then, in my last term and more ambitiously, the two folio volumes of Leoni's translation of Palladio. I also acquired three of Zocchi's eighteenth-century engravings of Florentine villas, which I still have, and a set of aquatints from Pyne's early nineteenth-century views of *Royal Residences*, which I framed and hung in my room at school, and which have long since disappeared.

My writing about buildings was confined to letters, for architecture played no part in the curriculum of my school — or pretty well any other, I suspect, then and all too often today. In my letters there does appear to be an advance in my comment on Castle Howard aged fourteen: 'I do not like it so very much as a whole, but I like bits of it', and my description of the Castle Howard Mausoleum, two and a half years later: ' ... in the most beautiful local stone with plenty of restrained but magnificent decoration in the right places, a nice echo and the wind making a splendidly sad sound'. There is a feeling for the ambience of a building as well as its architecture here, which may have owed something to John Piper. If so, this was a bonus from my Sitwell period, for I had come to his drawings by way of the four volumes of Osbert Sitwell's memoirs. In these years, too, I grew to love the wild confusion and murky splendour of the tombs in Westminster Abbey; they had an overpoweringly evocative quality, some of which was drained away when the Abbey was tidied and freshened up in ensuing decades.

I also learnt the power of architecture to console. Our house study was in the modest old part of the school, sandwiched between hefty chunks of public-school Gothic; in one corner of it, hemmed in by desks and obscured by a coat of chocolate-coloured paint, was a pedimented eighteenth-century doorcase of some splendour. When school was getting me down, I found I could get comfort just from looking at this; and every time I walked along the corridor outside the study, I used to crane my head to glance up the curving staircase to more and similar doorcases, out of bounds to me, on the landing above. I was helped in the same kind of way when I started on my National Service, and spent four months at Eaton Hall in Cheshire. I was an inept soldier, and it was a bitterly cold winter. We paraded in front of the house before breakfast every morning; the rifle butts froze to our bare hands; the sergeant-major bellowed orders; I was kept going by the silhouette of Waterhouse's Gothic mansion, sparkling in the frosty light like an enormous pincushion.

I left Eaton Hall to spend eighteen months with the Royal West African Frontier Force in Nigeria. With the doubtful exception of the buildings in sandcastle style to be found in Hausa towns and villages, architecture of any significance left my life. Apart from writing a long poem on the tombs in Westminster Abbey, I gave it little thought. But I did at least learn the lesson that the thick mud walls and thatched roof of the round hut in which I lived happily for part of my time in Nigeria were much pleasanter to be in than the new Public Works bungalow into which I was removed in the cause of progress.

Architecture came back in the four years at Oxford that followed. I was reading Greats, which for me was a mistake; what I value from those years is the friends I made, stayed and travelled with, the parties I went to, the books I read, and the buildings that I saw. I started to collect architectural books again. I travelled in Greece, France, Belgium and Italy — and ultimately, after my last half, in the Near East. I drove or walked to churches or houses all round Oxford. I broke into Ditchley, which was standing empty in those days, and wandered with friends through room after room filled with frescoed ceilings, magnificent plasterwork, towering chimney-pieces, and nothing else. I skated on the lake at Blenheim down below the silhouette of Vanbrugh's towers. I and my room-mate Thomas Pakenham removed some of the Georgian Gothic fittings from the derelict church at Hartwell, and installed them in our rooms on Folly Bridge, where for all I know they still are. Above all, I got to know Hardwick Hall, where my great-aunt was now living, as one can only know a building where one goes to stay for long periods, and has the freedom to wander for hours by oneself through its huge sun-soaked rooms, up and down its heroic staircase and out to the turrets and vistas of its roof.

In Greece I waded across the Alpheus to the lush Corinthian splendours of

Olympia and up into the mountains from Andritsena to the temple at Bassae. In the public library at Andritsena, I was intrigued to find an excellent collection of eighteenth-century architectural books, left to the little town by some long-dead citizen. I went to stay with my friend Erkinger Schwarzenberg in Tuscany, and found that by mistake I had come a week too early. To fill the gap, I walked with rug and knapsack from hill-town to hill-town, sleeping in small hotels or on the ground. I arrived as it was getting dark on the outskirts of Montepulciano, and went to sleep on a herb-scented terrace on the edge of the town; I woke up to find Antonio da San Gallo's S. Biagio looming above me in all the dazzling purity of its Renaissance geometry. In Syria a lorry gave us a lift across the desert from Maan to Palmyra. In the intervals of sleep in the ruins, we walked barefoot over the cool sands among the moonlit columns, and did not realize that the black shapes scuttling in the silver light were scorpions.

I decided that I wanted, if possible, to earn a living by studying, looking after or preferably writing about buildings. I was encouraged by Rupert Gunnis, a friend whom I owed to the Duke of Wellington. This lovable, large, loud-voiced Edwardian bachelor lived in a house at Tunbridge Wells which was crammed from attics to cellar with objects, books and pictures; he was working on his pioneer *Dictionary of British Sculptors* and was an endless source of stories of the pleasures and perils of his hunt for monuments, busts and source-material all over England. Through him I appreciated for the first time that one could work back, not only to contemporary published sources, but to the original documents — and that such documents were there in shoals, waiting to be discovered.

I was accepted as a Ph.D. student by the Courtauld Institute in London. I did not have much difficulty in my choice of a subject for a thesis. The RIBA owned the drawings made by Robert and John Smythson in the late sixteenth and early seventeenth centuries. They had never been properly researched or catalogued; Elizabethan architecture in general was full of unexplored areas; there was a probable connection between Robert Smythson and Hardwick, and a certain one between his son John and Hardwick's neighbour, Bolsover Castle. I briefly considered working on James Wyatt, and then plumped for the Smythsons.

I found myself, for the first time, off the receiving end and having to research, select, judge, and put together an architectural study for myself, to learn how to interpret drawings, look at and for documents and read Elizabethan handwriting, to tour with a purpose rather than for pleasure, and to try to relate Elizabethan architecture to its background. I had the enthralling experience, common to all historians, of watching a coherent picture gradually emerge on an all but blank canvas. I experienced the thrills and disappointments of the chase; perhaps the most exciting moment came when I was working at Hardwick through Bess of Hardwick's own account books, and found the payment to Robert Smythson and his son that clinched the former's connection with the house.

I wrote my thesis with an eye to publication, and a determination that it should be easy to read. My models were the lucid and elegant prose of my examiner, John Summerson, pioneer of Elizabethan studies as of so much else, and my old love, Sacheverell Sitwell: a rash combination, no doubt, but I got a lot of fun out of my

Sitwellian purple passages, most of which survived in the book into which the thesis ultimately developed. For better or worse, I can trace the mixture in my writing today

I now had to find a job. Posts for architectural historians were hard to come by in the 1950s. During or even before my thesis I had put in for a vacancy in the Ancient Monuments department of the Ministry of Works, innocently giving the Duke of Wellington and Rupert Gunnis as my references. These gentlemanly amateurs cut no ice with the Ministry; but they did cut ice with *Country Life* and combined with the backing of the Courtauld to get me a job in its architectural department, when Gordon Nares, the youngest of its three architectural writers, unexpectedly died in 1958.

I stayed on the staff of *Country Life* for eight years, and have written on and off for it ever since. My main responsibility was to write my share of the weekly country-house articles, on which much of the reputation of *Country Life* is based. This involved a good deal of visiting. At the Earl of Carnarvon's Highclere, I was fed on my own, separate from the servants but also from the Earl and his house-party, whose cheerful chatter I could hear in the next-door room. But for the most part working on the articles involved staying in the houses in the pleasantest possible circum-stances, with a job to do which interested both me and my hosts, and the excitement, on occasions, of finding designs and documents which had not been looked at since they were drawn or written. The houses were of all dates, types and sizes, and I was expected to write about contents and family history, as well as architecture. I was not confined to England, or to country houses, although they were my main staple. I had to learn to write to a deadline, and therefore to work through and absorb material under pressure. I had to be readable.

Inevitably, I began to specialize. Victorian country houses, and Victorian buildings generally, were still unfashionable and unexplored. I had been intrigued by Victorian architecture since schooldays, when I hung a large coloured lithograph of the Albert Memorial above my bed, and designed imaginary Victorian buildings in a sub-Osbert Lancaster manner. In Oxford I kept glass domes of wax fruit and knitted flowers in my rooms. It was all a bit of a joke, and a bit precious, as was common enough at the time, but gradually became serious, so that my increasing discovery and appreciation of Victorian architecture was one of the pleasures and excitements of my late twenties and early thirties.

They were shared with the other enthusiasts who joined together in 1958 to form the Victorian Society. We were a dedicated but amateurish crew, led by the Society's secretary Peter Fleetwood-Hesketh. He fed us on whisky in his flat in Great Ormond Street, as he walked on tiptoe through the piles of papers on the floor, peering through his lorgnette for the letters which eluded him, and talking in the high-pitched highly accented drawl which was unique to the Heskeths. We worked, literally night and day but without success, to save the Euston Arch and the Coal Exchange. We produced annual reports, large portions of which I wrote myself. We sat on committees, a form of activity for which I have never had any aptitude: 'Dear little Mark', commented John Betjeman; 'So good, and never says a word'. At this period he enjoyed teasing me by ringing up *Country Life* and asking the operator if he could speak to his 'little godson' (I was not his godson).

In 1966 I decided to qualify as an architect. After eight years at *Country Life*, I was, I suppose, getting bored. I had, in fact, thought of becoming an architect on and off since boyhood. But 'Mark cannot draw' said the family, and then were reassured when Sir Patrick Abercrombie, meeting my step-grandfather in his club, told him 'Christopher Wren could not draw. In spite of this good news I had opted for architectural history. But the hankering remained. I was too young to have experienced the first fervour of the Modern Movement, but old enough to have my share of post-war idealism. We were going to build a new world. Inspired by such feeling, Thomas Pakenham and I, when we became victims of compulsory purchase in our post-university pre-marriage years, had chosen to be moved from a crumbling terrace on the banks of the Paddington Canal to the top floor of one of a group of tower blocks on the GLC's Bateman Estate in Kennington.

I enrolled at the Bartlett School of Architecture in University College, London. Under Lord Llewellyn-Davies, this had acquired a reputation as the progressive school of the moment. I had gone to the wrong place. Llewellyn-Davies was a formidably able and persuasive man, but as head of an architectural school he was a fraud. Those were the days of Harold Wilson's 'white heat of the technological revolution'. Llewellyn-Davies had moved into a school which still bore the imprint of Sir Albert Richardson, thrown out the models of the Parthenon and drawings of the Orders, brainwashed what members of the existing staff he allowed to remain, and set out to teach architecture as a science.

But even within the limits of this debatable concept the Bartlett image of those days was a bogus one. Llewellyn-Davies was a front man, with little interest in the day-to-day working of the school, and none at all in the students. In spite of all the trumpet-blowing, the technical side of architecture was very badly taught. As a mature student eager to learn a new discipline, I tried to go along with the Bartlett ideology instead of questioning it. It was a great mistake and I can see the disastrous results by going through my portfolio. My first projects, however amateurishly executed, are much more interesting and inventive than my later ones. However, I stuck it out for five years; I scraped through Parts I and II of the RIBA examinations; then I went back to architectural history.

Five years is a long time. On looking back, I find it hard to say what I got out of them. I acquired some understanding of how buildings were put together, and how they worked, as well as how they looked. I learnt to draw — not very well, and with little encouragement at the Bartlett, for drawing, in those pre-computer days, could not be treated as a science. I experienced the traumas and shared companionship of studio-life in an architectural school. As part of the course, I spent six months on a building site, which I much enjoyed, and six months in the fossilizing architects' department of the ILEA, which deeply depressed me. I passed much of my time with people ten to fifteen years younger than I was. I discovered that architects were, on the whole, better company than architectural historians. I met my wife, introduced to her by my friend and fellow-Victorian, Peter Ferriday, in the bar of the Devonshire Arms at Notting Hill Gate. All in all, I suppose I got out of a rut.

My second book, *The Victorian Country House*, was projected while I was still at *Country Life*, and based on articles which I had written for it, but was completed (no easy job) while I was an architectural student. It came out the year that I left the

Bartlett, was well received, and much more widely reviewed than my first one. I followed it with a book on Victorian Pubs, and with *Sweetness and Light*, on the so-called 'Queen Anne' style of the 1870s and 1880s. The first of these was partly a tribute to many hours spent in bars with Peter Ferriday and other friends; partly an exercise in detection, which tried, with some success, to document buildings which had previously been thought of as vernacular architecture beneath the level of documentation; and partly a move to develop the approach which lay behind my introduction to *The Victorian Country House*, by looking at pubs in terms of who used them, how they worked, and how they were financed, as well as just as visual objects. *Sweetness and Light* moved up the social scale to study the ideals and life-style of the progressive or 'artistic' middle classes in late-Victorian society, in terms of books, gardens, furniture and decoration, as well as architecture.

In 1975 I was asked to give the Slade lectures at Oxford in the following year. I chose 'Life in the English Country House' as my subject. I cannot now remember how easy the choice was, or what other subjects I considered, but my experience and writing in recent years had put me in a position to go back to old pastures, look at country houses from a new point of view, and relate the way they had been lived in to their architecture.

My daughter Blanche was born while I worked on the first lecture, writing against the clock in green hospital overalls at the foot of my wife's bed. She was removed from her cradle to attend the last one (six years later she was to write a polemic 'Boring Old Buildings, or why I hate Architecture'). The lectures went down well in Oxford, and, expanded and part rewritten, were published as a book in the following year.

Life in the English Country House was easy and enjoyable to write, and correspondingly easy to read. Obvious though its approach now seems, nothing like it had been written before. It was much my most successful book. It relieved me from financial anxiety for several years, and enabled me to set something aside for old age. But I have mixed feelings about it, common, no doubt, to all authors in a similar position. Endlessly interesting although country houses are, I resent being thought of just as the man who writes about them. When people come up to me and say how much they enjoyed my book, I resent the certainty with which I know what book this will be — and am correspondingly delighted if I turn out to be mistaken. I am depressed by the mixture of snobbery and nostalgia which forms so large an element of the country-house cult today. There is no more ghastly bore than a country-house bore. Poised, as a Londoner with country-house connections, between town and country, I feel most at home in the former, and it is with towns and cities that my two most recent books have been concerned.

Setting aside *Life in the English Country House*, these and my other books have done well enough to keep me afloat financially — helped by occasional journalism and lecturing, by brief forays into teaching or television, and by a little money of my own. Compared to writers in the real best-seller league, it is a modest achievement. Compared to other architectural historians, it is more unusual. To the best of my knowledge I am the only one who more or less makes a living as a freelance writer. I cannot claim all the credit for this. I must share it with my wife, who designs my books and makes them visually enticing with the eye of an artist, and with my publisher, who produces them to high standards, markets them at reasonable prices, and keeps them in print.

As for my own contribution, anything that I have achieved is based on a passion for architecture. I can think of no other word to use for something which has filled so much of my time, my thoughts and my imagination from so early on in my life. I cannot look through a window, walk down a street, or drive along a road without scanning, absorbing, dating, and mentally commenting on all the buildings which I see. I started with the stucco worms on the bank in Edgware Road, and every year there was more to discover. The search for buildings has taken me twice round the world, given me some of my happiest memories, and brought me some of my closest friends. I never tire of them, because they can be looked at in so many different ways. They have a practical function. They are places in which people live and work from generation to generation, changing them in doing so. They are structures crafted to withstand gravity or the weather. They are complex assemblies of different spaces and materials. They can be works of art. They can be status symbols, advertisements, or statements of beliefs or ideas. They have a relationship with the buildings or the countryside around them, or the spaces in between them. They change and decay, and tug at our emotions by doing so. Most artefacts have some of these qualities, but only works of architecture have all of them.

Some buildings give one a shock of surprise and delight, because they are still alive with the creative explosion which first produced them. A similar shock emanates from any building that is intensely evocative of a person, family or age. Buildings of both types have a quality which can be felt by anyone, but can be deepened and illuminated through knowledge and understanding. And in buildings of all kinds there is a surface to be immediately enjoyed, and layer after layer to be unpeeled as a result of which one can experience the ingenuity, folly, vanity, skill, affection, pride, or adventurousness of all types of people in all kinds of locations.

I find exploring buildings in this way an immensely enjoyable and enlightening experience. It is always, of course, possible to look at one or two aspects in isolation, but curiosity usually drives me on to look for more. I continuously find myself asking, Why. And since all the different aspects are of necessity inter-related, finding out more about one aspect increases ones understanding of the others; working out the relationships is a fascinating task, although not always an easy one.

One result of a life so largely involved with buildings is that I fight to stop them being destroyed or mutilated. It is inevitable that one should fight for what one values and loves, and much of my time has been spent in preservation battles. These have their excitements and their rewards, as well as their disappointments; they have their creative side; but they inevitably have a negative side as well, for of their nature they are involved in stopping people from doing what they want to do.

To write about buildings is more positive, and, for me at any rate, more rewarding. Had I been able to design to my satisfaction, I would have been an architect; as it is, I am an architectural historian. And my main reason for writing is not a desire to instruct, change, improve or even entertain other people; it is not to make money, although the need to make money acts as a useful stimulus; it is because I get fulfilment from the process of creation which writing involves.

10

An architectural historian's relationship to buildings is similar to that of an actor's or a producer's to a play, a conductor's or a musician's to a musical composition. He has to interpret them, and to make his interpretation accessible to others. This involves creation, even if on a lower level of creativity than that open to an architect, a dramatist or a composer. Research, besides being intensely enjoyable, is also creative, in so far as it

2. View from the author's window.

involves starting with a more or less blank canvas, and gradually filling it with a coherent picture. Moreover, one has to adjust one's personality and point of view, in order to put them in sympathy with people of different periods and backgrounds; and since the potential for research into any building is virtually infinite, one has to decide on a strategy and a line of approach, knowing that it can never be more than partial. Then comes the final, far more traumatic, but if it goes well endlessly satisfying act of assembly, the selection and rejection of material, the attempt to present a building, a town or a movement clearly and convincingly to others, and, since one cannot and should not suppress one's own personality, to present them in a way that is seasoned with one's own reactions and warmed by one's own enthusiasm. So, finally, the book or article emerges.

Although my main work lies in my books, I have published a good deal outside them, in the form of articles, reviews, introductions or contributions to joint publications. Some of this has arisen out of work on the books, or been incorporated into them, but enough is left over for it to seem worth publishing a selection in a less scattered form. I work on an *ad hoc* basis: one subject leads to another; ideas, themes or hypotheses occur to me, and I follow them up. Sometimes they lead me into wider fields than just architecture, sometimes away from architecture altogether, but it is from buildings that I start, and to buildings that I return. This pattern appears in the articles that follow. Such collections can never hope to have a unity, but I have grouped them in two sections round the two poles between which I move; the town and the country, especially the country house. In between I have put a section of articles on Ireland. Having an Irish mother,and numerous Irish relatives and friends, I have written a good deal about Irish buildings, but always in the form of articles. I cannot pretend that these have made more than a sporadic contribution to Irish architectural history, but I have included some here as a memento to the pleasure which I had in writing them. The houses described are all those of relatives or friends, and the city of Waterford was where most of my Irish expeditions began and ended.

3. (right) Roofscape in Whitby.

4. (right)   Portrait of Sir William Temple, engraved for Birch's *Heads of Illustrious Persons* in a frame designed by H.F. Gravelot.

1 COFFEE AT SLAUGHTER'S?
English Art and the Rococo

This essay starts in a café and moves on to a pleasure garden, a way of passing the time much favoured by most of the people whom it is about. In my case this apparently frivolous programme conceals, I am afraid, a more ponderous aim, which is to trace the launching and popularisation of a style. But the style in question was the exceedingly unpompous one of the rococo; and in any case, as places for artists to breed in, cafés and pleasure gardens are as good as, if not better than, academies and the houses of the great.

The café in question was Old Slaughter's Coffee-House in St Martin's Lane, long ago closed down, but in its day, as Vertue put it, 'a rendezvous of persons of all languages and nations, Gentry, artists and others'.[1] It was to the mid-eighteenth century what the Café Royal was to the 1890s. In its pleasantly bohemian purlieus Fielding used to imitate Roubiliac's accent for the entertainment of the company;[2] Roubiliac, after a convivial evening there, invited a stranger home for the night but forgot to tell him that he would find a dead negress in his bed;[3] and Clermont, the monkey-painter, overhearing Hubert Gravelot make some snide remarks in his direction about 'stupid silly blockheads or bunglers in Art', crossed the room and slapped him on the face.

This incident was witnessed by Grignion the engraver, little more than a boy at the time and apprenticed to Gravelot. Sixty years or more later he told it to Joseph Farington, who wrote it down in his diary.[4] Gravelot, said Grignion, 'was accustomed to go to Old Slaughter's Coffee-House, to meet Roubiliac and others'. After the face-slapping, 'at his own house Roubiliac and others urged him to go again to the Coffee House and return the blow he had received ... but his spirit was too timid'. Who the others were is made clear from a number of eighteenth-century sources. In the late 1730s and the 1740s there was a particular gang of artists who used to frequent Slaughter's Coffee-House and one another's company. They were a closely knit group, who exchanged ideas, influenced one another, and gave one another a leg-up at every possible opportunity. Young, cheerful and rebellious, they chafed against the Palladian dictatorship so long imposed by Lord Burlington and his friends. Leading members of the group were Hogarth, Gravelot, Roubiliac, Francis Hayman, George Michael Moser, the chaser and enamellist, and Yeo, the medallist; Henry Fielding, David Garrick and Martin Folkes, the antiquary and scientist, were habitués from outside the immediate world of the arts; other members, including the young Gainsborough and the architect James Paine, will appear in the course of the essay. Depending on whether one looks at them socially, geographically or artistically, one might call them the Slaughter's Coffee-House set, or the St Martin's Lane set, or the St Martin's Lane Academy set.

Though not, apparently, the companion one would choose in a fight, Hubert François Gravelot was a figure of the first importance in the history of English art. If any single person can be said to have introduced the rococo to England, it was he. He came to England from Paris, young and unknown, in 1732. In 1733 Vertue jotted down in his notebook: 'A very curious pen and writes neatly ... if he here continues he will be *rara inter aves*'.[5] He did here continue, and by 1741 Vertue could write of him as 'Mr. Gravelot whose drawings for Engravings and all other kinds of Gold and Silver works shows he is endowed with a great and fruitful genius for designs, inventions of history and ornaments. He is a man of great industry and diligence, causes himself to be well paid for his works and deserves it.'[6] In the intervening years he had built up a reputation already great and still growing. He was and is best known as an illustrator and decorator of books. He introduced the sophistication and gaiety of the French style to an English audience; he made a speciality of combining delicate illustrations with elaborate and very decorative rococo frames. Charming examples of the latter occur in the illustrations of royal tombs he made in 1735 for the book published the next year as *Heads and Monuments of the Kings*. These are, I suspect, the earliest important English examples of rococo design; and it is, incidentally, amusing to see

16

how to the more elaborate of the Gothic tombs, which clearly appealed to him, he managed to impart a gentle rococo flavour.

Gravelot's highly decorative rococo frames (the earliest engraved in 1738) to the portraits in Birch's *Heads of Illustrious Persons* (Pl. 4) were also much admired in their day. So were his superb rococo decorations for John Pine's *Tapestry Hangings of the House of Lords* (1738) and his light-hearted illustrations to Sir Thomas Hanmer's edition of Shakespeare, published in 1743-4. In the latter he collaborated with Hogarth's boon companion, drunk and sober, Francis Hayman. Hayman learned much from Gravelot and continued to work in his manner after Gravelot had returned to France in 1746. So, with some charm though considerably less talent, did another prolific book illustrator and habitué of Slaughter's, Samuel Wale.

5. The Rotunda or Music-Room at Vauxhall Gardens, London (*c.* 1743-9), from the engraving after Samuel Wale.

Gravelot's achievements in spheres other than book illustration were perhaps even more important, though harder to trace. What, for instance, were the 'other kinds of Gold and Silver works' for which, according to Vertue, he made drawings? The evidence to identify these is lacking, but it was in the mid-1730s, shortly after his arrival in London, that silversmiths such as Paul de Lamerie first began to experiment with the rococo style. Pye, in his *Patronage of British Art*, says that he also made designs for joiners and cabinet-makers.[7] He was a teacher as well as a designer. He had, at one time, his own drawing school off the Strand. And as early as 1745 he was a leading member of the institution known as the St Martin's Lane Academy.

This Academy had been founded by Hogarth in 1735, on the basis of the casts and other paraphernalia left to him by his father-in-law, Sir James Thornhill.[8] Originally it was concerned only with figure drawing, but later it moved to larger quarters, in what had been Roubiliac's studio off St Martin's Lane, and its programme became more ambitious. Unfortunately, its papers, if they ever existed, have disappeared, but Vertue gives a few details, including a list of the principal members in 1745. These included 'Mr Hayman (History Painter & c.), Mr Gravelot (designer), Mr Moser (chaser), Mr Roubiliac (statuary), Mr Yeo (seal engraver)'.[9] The Academy was, in fact, run from Slaughter's Coffee-House; or perhaps it would be more accurate to say that the Slaughter's gang frequented the coffee-house because it was conveniently round the corner from their Academy.

It has, I think, never been pointed out that if one moves up the river to Vauxhall Gardens, one finds the whole Slaughter's–St Martin's set at work. Roubiliac made his reputation — and gave English sculpture its first rococo injection – with his statue of Handel, installed in Vauxhall Gardens for the season of 1738 (Pl. 8); he also contributed statues of Harmony and Genius as a setting for Handel, and possibly a statue of Milton. In the years around 1740 the supper-boxes at Vauxhall were decorated with a series of paintings executed mainly by Hayman (Pl. 6), though with the collaboration of both Gravelot and Hogarth (Pl. 7). Hayman never improved on his best Vauxhall

17

paintings; and their rococo gaiety was echoed in the enchanting decoration of the Rotunda (Pl. 5), designed, according to Vertue, by George Michael Moser and installed between 1743 and 1749.[10] The elegant rococo medals used as tickets of admission for Vauxhall were for a long time attributed to Hogarth, but are now generally ascribed to Yeo.[11] Gravelot and Hayman designed, in 1737 and 1738, vignettes and decorations for the music sheets of the immensely popular Vauxhall songs (Pl. 8); the words for many of these were written by John Lockman, a poet and translator from the French who, incidentally, had 'learnt to speak French by frequenting Slaughter's Coffee-House'.[12] After this list it comes as no surprise to find, in 1751, Gravelot's protégé, Samuel Wale, making the set of engravings of Vauxhall that have preserved its appearance for posterity.[13]

The link between the St Martin's Lane set and Vauxhall is provided by Hogarth, who was a personal friend of Jonathan Tyers, the proprietor of the Gardens. Hogarth is said to have suggested to Tyers the idea of the *ridotto al fresco* that saved the Gardens from bankruptcy in 1732; and Tyers presented him and his party with a perpetual free pass to Vauxhall

18

6. (top) Francis Hayman's *Milkmaid's Garland* (or *Humours of May Day*), one of the series of paintings by him installed in the supper-boxes at Vauxhall.
7. Terracotta bust of William Hogarth, by L.F. Roubiliac, 1740.
8. (next page) Song-sheet for Vauxhall Gardens, incorporating a view of Roubiliac's statue of Handel, by Gravelot.

Gravelot inv.
The Words by Mr. Lockman.

G.Bickham jun.r sc.
The Musick by Mr. Gladwin.

The Invitation to Mira,

REQUESTING

Her Company to Vaux Hall Garden.

To the Right Hon.ble the Lady FRANCES SEYMOUR, These four Plates are humbly Inscrib'd.

Affettuoso.

Come, Mira, Idol of ÿ Swains (So green ÿ Sprays, The Sky so fine) To Bow'rs where

heav'n-born Flora reigns, & Handel warbles Airs divine. & Handel war . . . . bles Airs divine.

Come, ev'ry sprightlier Joy to taste,
That rural Art & Nature boast:
Fly thither with ÿ Lightning's haste,
And be ÿ universal Toast.

A scene so beauteous can't be shown,
Tho' thou shoud'st ev'ry Realm survey,
As all, wher'er thou com'st must own;
Thy Graces claim the highest sway.

in gratitude. So it is not surprising that Vauxhall was, to such an extent, a St Martin's Lane design job. As a result it became perhaps the most complete and convincing expression of the rococo in England, and as it was also frequented by the whole fashionable world, its influence in popularising rococo design must have been considerable. It was rococo not only in its decoration, but in its whole concept: its gaiety, its alfresco meals, its music and its illuminations. Even the fact that 'Haycocks, and Haymakers sporting' are mentioned in a description of 1751 as one of the pleasant prospects from the gardens might be said to express a rococo attitude to nature. One tends to think of it as a rather more successful version of the Battersea fun-fair; but as an instrument of stylistic propaganda it is more comparable to the 1951 Festival of Britain, or the Barcelona Exhibition of 1929.

A prominent feature of Vauxhall was the building known as the Prince's Pavilion, built especially for the accommodation of Frederick, Prince of Wales, and his friends. Its portico was festooned with red curtains, and decorated with crystal chandeliers and 'three little domes with gilt ornaments'; inside, it was 'embellished with Busts, Looking-Glasses, a Chandelier & c.'[14] Prince of Wales feathers were also incorporated in the decoration of the Rotunda, and proudly surmounted the ogee dome of the semi-outdoor dining-room known as the Tent, an elegant piece of blue-and-gold frivolity supported on twenty columns festooned with flowers. Pavilion and Tent were erected between 1738 and 1742, as part of a deliberate campaign to attract the patronage of the Prince of Wales.

But in 1738 the Prince's relations, never at any stage good, with his father George II reached the point at which the two were no longer on speaking terms. The Prince became still more what he had always been to some extent — the centre of the political opposition; and all that was most gay and lively socially tended to pivot round him rather than the elderly respectability of his father. The fact that he patronised Vauxhall (of which he was the ground-landlord) automatically gave it an opposition flavour, though it would be a great exaggeration to say that only the opposition frequented it. But it is not coincidence that the first full-length description of Vauxhall appeared in 1742 in the *Champion*, the opposition newspaper; and that Fielding, who was for a time editor of the *Champion*, went out of his way to give Vauxhall a puff in his novel *Amelia*.[15] Nor is it, I think, coincidence that Fielding was Hogarth's friend, and a Slaughter's Coffee-House man; or that the *Champion* praised Gravelot's Shakespeare designs in 1741; or that the *Champion*'s successor, the *Remembrancer*, consistently publicised Roubiliac.[16]

By the 1730s and 1740s Palladianism, as established by Lord Burlington and William Kent, was to all intents and purposes the official government style. The Palladian architects — Kent, Flitcroft, Ware and Vardy — monopolised the Board of Works; the Prime Minister, Sir Robert Walpole, lived in one of the grandest of Palladian houses, embellished for him by Kent and the favoured Palladian sculptor, Rysbrack; and Kent and Rysbrack were equally patronised by George II and his consort. The St Martin's Lane set was, for a number of reasons, conspicuously anti-Palladio and anti-Burlington. They had little interest in the classical tradition; they were alive to new movements in France, the rococo in particular, which was anathema to the Palladians. Gravelot is supposed to have published caricatures of both Walpole

(*The State Coach*) and Burlington (*The Funeral of Factions*).[17] And Hogarth had for many years been in open enmity with Lord Burlington — an enmity which had a personal as well as a stylistic basis, for his father-in-law, Thornhill, had been ejected from the post of Serjeant-Painter by Lord Burlington in favour of Burlington's protégé Kent. Hence Hogarth's attack on Burlington in his famous cartoon *The Man of Taste* (1731); to which Kent effectively retorted by having Hogarth shut out from the Chapel Royal when the latter wished to attend it for the profitable purpose of making engravings of the marriage of the Princess Royal in 1734.

In the situation thus very roughly sketched in, new artistic developments were more likely to take place in opposition rather than in government circles and it was among the opposition that the St Martin's Lane

9. Chimney-piece, probably sculpted by Henry Cheere, formerly at Woodcote Park, Hertfordshire.

set would tend to look for patronage. To a certain extent they found it, although more from the Prince of Wales's friends than from the Prince of Wales himself. It is interesting to look at Roubiliac's early career in this light. His statue of Handel set him on the road to success, but by no means established him. For the next seven years he had to support himself mostly on provincial commissions for monuments and portrait busts of fellow-artists and his own immediate circle — Hogarth, for instance, in 1740, Handel in 1739, Tyers about 1738. But before 1742 he had obtained what were, for a young sculptor making his way, the enviable plums of four portrait-sittings from Alexander Pope, by then the undisputed monarch of English literature. He gained these commissions, I suspect, because Pope in the last years of his life was friendly with the opposition and had made new young friends among the entourage of the Prince of Wales, including Lyttelton, the Prince's secretary, and Warburton, the Prince's chaplain.[18] In 1745 another opposition commission, of the first importance, fell to Roubiliac: the monument in Westminster Abbey to the Duke of Argyll, arch-opponent of Walpole; with it Roubiliac initiated a series of magnificent monuments in the abbey, and finally established his reputation.

It is worth remarking that when Lyttelton inherited Hagley, in Worcestershire, from his father in 1751 he built a new house there and filled it with rococo plasterwork and furniture as elaborate as any in England (Roubiliac did a bust of his wife in 1748). Chesterfield House in London had interiors of advanced and dazzling French rococo;

21

and Chesterfield (whom Roubiliac sculpted in 1746) was Lyttelton's friend and for many years the leading politician of the opposition. Less well known are the equally French rococo interiors of Woodcote in Hertfordshire, and Belvedere House at Erith, both built for the Prince of Wales's treasurer, the Earl of Baltimore. In 1749 the Prince of Wales himself was parading up and down the Thames beneath Belvedere in a Chinese barge rowed by Chinese boatmen; in the same year he built an Indian temple at Kew.[19] Tyers responded promptly to his patron's fancy; by 1751 the Chinese Pavilions were up at Vauxhall, and rococo chinoiserie was all the rage in fashionable society.

The architect of Chesterfield House was Isaac Ware. Ware was ostensibly an arch-Palladian; he had been put on the map by the Burlington circle and it was to Burlington that he dedicated his translation of Palladio in 1738. When he published his own *Book of Architecture* in 1756, he included a few rococo designs, among them a ceiling from Chesterfield House, but appeared to do so unwillingly and with many qualifications, as a concession to fashion. But this Palladian image of Ware begins to dissolve when one finds that, besides Chesterfield House, he was probably responsible for the equally rococo interiors of Woodcote (Pl. 9) and Belvedere.[20] Moreover J.T. Smith, in his *Life of Nollekens* (1829), specifically heads an interesting section on the Slaughter's Coffee-House set: 'Isaac Ware and his companions'.[21] Ware ran the St Martin's Lane Academy jointly with Hogarth in 1738, and possibly in 1739 and 1740;[22] Roubiliac sculpted him in or before 1740 and again about 1755. Intriguingly enough, Ware would appear to have been, by Burlingtonian standards, a fellow-traveller. We are back where we started, in Slaughter's Coffee-House; and it is time to look in more detail at some of the artists who strolled in and out of its rooms.

Two important older men and a number of younger ones need to be added to the group. The older men are Henry Cheere, the sculptor, and Thomas Hudson, the portrait painter. Although Cheere was not in the innermost circle of the group — he seems never, for instance, to have been a member of the St Martin's Lane Academy — his affiliations with it were close. Roubiliac had worked for him when he first came to London; their relations continued friendly after Roubiliac set up on his own, and Cheere seems to have helped his old employee to get commissions. Both his son, Charles Cheere, and his assistant — in the end virtually his partner — Richard Hayward, were members of the Academy. Hogarth and Hayman were on friendly terms with him and accompanied him to France in 1748.[23]

It was probably under the influence of the Slaughter's group that the tombs and chimney-pieces which came so prolifically from his workshop developed, in the course of the 1740s, unmistakable, if gentle, rococo characteristics. They are among the prettiest products of the mid-eighteenth century, usually constructed of a combination of different coloured marbles and gaily decorated with putti, garlands of flowers, trophies of shells or (in the case of the chimney-pieces) tablets of animals (Pl. 10), cherubs at

22

10.   Detail from a chimney-piece at Picton Castle, Pembrokeshire, supplied by Henry Cheere about 1750.
11. (right)   Sir William Courtenay and his family, painted by Thomas Hudson in 1756.

play, or rustic scenes. Cheere's chimney-pieces are, on the whole, based on traditional Palladian designs, though set in a livelier and lighter key; but there are one or two executed by him in out-and-out rococo, notably one formerly at Woodcote in Surrey, a house probably designed by Isaac Ware, whose rather ambivalent position in the Slaughter's Coffee-House circle has already been discussed.[24]

The second eminent figure on the periphery of the group was Thomas Hudson. Hudson went with Hogarth, Hayman and Cheere to France in 1748; he owned the original modello for Roubiliac's Vauxhall statue of Handel; Roubiliac sculpted two caryatid figures to adorn his fireplace; and he accompanied Roubiliac and Hayman to Italy in 1752.[25] He had a gift for money-making which Hayman, Hogarth and Roubiliac (who died bankrupt) lacked; until displaced by his former pupil Reynolds, he was the most popular and prolific portrait painter in England, and he died rich, with a house in London and a country estate at Twickenham. Although there is a certain stiffness about even the best of his portraits, they have on occasion an element of rococo gaiety which can be very charming — as for instance in the immense family group of Sir William Courtenay and his family at Powderham Castle, painted in 1756 (Pl. 11).

In 1755 Courtenay had decorated the staircase at Powderham with plasterwork that remains one of the most elaborate expressions of the rococo in England. The conjunction of an important Hudson painting with rococo plasterwork is not, I think, accidental; it underlines the fact that patrons with a leaning towards rococo tended to patronise the Hogarth circle. And one gets the impression that the members of the circle loyally got one another commissions whenever they could. The most impressive example of this, Hogarth's netting for his friends commissions for almost all of the decorations at Vauxhall, has already been dealt with. Another interesting context where several members of the circle are found together is that of Grimsthorpe and the

Dukes of Ancaster. Roubiliac supplied the monument for the 2nd Duke, who died in 1742; in 1745 the 3rd Duke bought three pictures by Hogarth, *Sophonisba*, and two of the *Times of the Day* sequence, *Morning* and *Evening*; Hudson painted a superb portrait of his wife; Cheere supplied chimney-pieces in the 1750s; and at the same time a series of rooms were given rococo decoration of great charm and liveliness.

The circle had a loyal and useful friend in the person of Dr Martin Folkes. Folkes mixed conveniently in a number of different circles.[26] Though very much an urban figure, he was by origin a country gentleman, with a substantial estate in Norfolk; and he had numerous grand friends, the Duke of Montagu among them. He was a scientist and antiquarian, who became President of both the Royal Society and the Society of Antiquaries. He was a philanthropist, an active vice-chairman of the Foundling Hospital in its formative years. He was a regular frequenter of Slaughter's Coffee-House, and had married an actress. This social scientist and bohemian gentleman was painted by Hogarth and Hayman, and sculpted by Roubiliac (Pl. 12) as one of the four friends of whom busts were commissioned (probably at Folkes's instigation) by Lord Pembroke. In 1749 he obtained for Roubiliac the commission to carve the superb monument to the Duke of Montagu which he himself is said to have designed; this commission led to another, for the equally fine monument to the Duchess.[27] Folkes had no doubt also got Hogarth the commission to paint a conversation piece of the Duke and Duchess some years earlier. Moreover, one cannot help feeling that his good services were in part responsible for the considerable number of scientists and doctors of whom Roubiliac did portrait busts and Hogarth portraits.

It is interesting to investigate some of the younger men who were pupils or assistants of those already dealt with, or who studied at the St Martin's Lane Academy. By far and away the most famous of these was Thomas Gainsborough. Precise documentation of his early career is lacking, but he is said both to have been a student at the Academy, and to have worked under Hayman and Gravelot.[28] All three traditions appear convincing when one studies his early work. The relationship between, in particular, his early portraits and the portrait groups painted by Hayman has often been commented on; and the two overmantel pictures he supplied to the Duke of Bedford

24

12.   Bust of Martin Folkes, by Roubiliac.

(Fielding's patron) in 1755 are among the highlights of rococo painting in England (Pl. 13). His early friend and sitter, Joshua Kirby of Ipswich, was another habitué of St Martin's Lane circles, who lectured to the Academy on perspective in 1752, and published his lectures in 1754, together with an introductory plate by Hogarth. The subscribers' list to Kirby's *Perspective* marks with an asterisk the members of the Academy, and is the first (indeed, the only) reasonably full list of its members. Characters already discussed who appear in it are Charles Cheere (Sir Henry Cheere's son), Gwynn, Hayman, Hayward, Hogarth, Moser, Wale and Yeo. Also in the list are two interesting young men, William Collins and James Paine.

William Collins is an artist who could do with further research. He was a pupil of Sir Henry Cheere, and there is evidence for thinking that he carved some of the decorations for Cheere's chimney-pieces. He was a friend of both Gainsborough and Hayman. He was a plasterer as well as a sculptor, supplying, for instance, in 1755, a large plaster relief of the Marys at the Sepulchre for Magdalene College, Cambridge (Pl. 14). This is a rococo work of considerable charm and distinction; equally attractive is the slightly later oval relief of Pan and the Graces in the dining-room at Burton Constable. At Burton Constable and also at Warwick he was associated with the architect Thomas Lightoler, who had published very competent designs for rococo interiors

25

13. Detail from Gainsborough's *Woodcutter Courting a Milkmaid* (1755) at Woburn Abbey, Bedfordshire.

as early as 1742, in Morris and Halfpenny's *Modern Builder's Assistant*.[29]

James Paine is much better known than Collins; Hardwicke's comment is generally familiar, that 'Paine and Sir R. Taylor divided the practice of the profession between them until Robert Adam entered the lists'. Paine's background was entirely non-Palladian. He himself acknowledged his debt to the instructions of Thomas Jersey, 'a man of genius', who was Gibbs's clerk of the works for the Radcliffe Camera.[30] This Gibbs connection has not been commented on; nor have his affiliations with the Slaughter's circle, undeniable though they are. He studied as a young man at the St Martin's Lane Academy and 'attained considerable skill in drawing the human figure as well as ornament'.[31] His St Martin's Lane training comes out clearly in the decorations which he installed about 1740 at Nostell Priory. These are among the earliest examples of rococo plasterwork in England, and are probably a direct result of the teaching of Gravelot. In 1744 Paine was given the commission for the Mansion House in Doncaster. He published his designs in a splendid folio volume in 1751, with his portrait on the title-page, engraved from a painting by his friend Hayman. The book shows sumptuous schemes of decoration (Pl. 15), containing both wall paintings and rococo plasterwork; one cannot help feeling that Paine intended the paintings to be a valuable commission for Hayman, who had ambitions in that direction. But, if so, the economy of the town corporation prevented him, for the decorations were only partially carried out.

In 1754 Paine, rich from his northern practice, built a large house for himself in St Martin's Lane, exactly next door to Slaughter's Coffee-House. In a small house (or pair of houses) at the bottom of the garden he installed two friends and fellow-members of the Academy, Samuel Wale and John Gwynn.[32] About this time (and possibly earlier, though documentation is lacking), he employed William Collins, who executed for him sculpture in the pediments at Sandbeck (about 1760) and Worksop (1765), and medallions at Kedleston (1761).

14. Relief of the *Marys at the Sepulchre* by William Collins (1755), in the chapel of Magdalene College, Cambridge.

It is satisfying to be able to tie up James Paine and Isaac Ware with the Slaughter's set; for they both played an important part in introducing what Christopher Hussey was, I think, the first to analyse perceptively as the rococo phase of English architecture. In comparison with architecture on the Continent, this phase might not seem rococo at all; but it is none the less the peculiarly English expression of a movement common to the whole of Europe. In England the Palladianism of Lord Burlington's generation was not abandoned but it was liberalised; experiment and eclecticism took the place of the search for the ideal; it became possible once more to admire Wren, Vanbrugh and even the Gothic; imagination (or 'fancy' as they called it then) was stressed at the expense of authority. Approval of what Isaac Ware termed 'variety of figures'[33] led to the prolific reintroduction of the bay window; and bay windows were combined with swept or Venetian windows and eyebrow pediments to produce, particularly in some of Paine's work, effects of rocking, almost fluttering, movement.

In this architectural framework one frequently finds fittings or decorations which can be described as rococo in the straightforward Continental sense. Ware's interiors at Chesterfield House and Woodcote, Paine's at Nostell and Doncaster Mansion House, have been referred to. But what about the furniture, the silver, the china with which the rooms were filled, and which were often more obviously and extravagantly rococo than the rooms themselves?

In contrast to the Slaughter's Coffee-House set — whose links and friendships with each other stare one in the face once one starts to look — the craftsmen form a separate, if related, group. Among them were figures who played an important part in

15. James Paine's only partially executed design for the Banqueting Room in the Mansion House, Doncaster.

the history of English rococo: silversmiths like Paul de Lamerie, craftsmen-designers like Matthew Lock, Thomas Johnson and John Linnell. Indeed, the craftsmen adopted the rococo with greater and longer-lasting enthusiasm than the artists and architects. Yet I suspect that initially the latter — in particular the Slaughter's group — played an important part in passing the rococo virus on to the former. This, however, is hard to prove. Almost all manuscript evidence has disappeared; and the craftsmen moved for the most part in a different social milieu, the activities of which, unlike those of the artists, are largely ignored by the diaries, anecdotes and journalism of the times.

The key figure in this artist-craftsman relationship was undoubtedly Gravelot. His stay in England — 1733 to 1746 — covers the seminal period of English rococo, the years in which, for instance, silver succumbed to the new style, and the first rococo pattern-books appeared. Vertue says that Gravelot designed for silversmiths. Pye's statement in his *Patronage of British Art* that he also designed for joiners and cabinet-makers, though made one hundred years after the event, is in accordance with all that is known of his career. We know, too, that he kept a drawing school of his own,[34] and by at any rate 1745 was involved with the St Martin's Lane Academy. 'De English,' he is said to have remarked to Basire, the engraver, 'may be very clever in deir own opinions, but dey do not draw'.[35] By the time he returned to France they drew a good deal better.

Were his teachings confined to artists like Gainsborough, Hayman and Wale, or did cabinet-makers, silversmiths and plasterers study under him as well? It seems at any rate likely that they did — in view of his specialist knowledge of the rococo style, and his reputation, underlined by all contemporary writers, for design and ornament. Enough drawings survive by, for instance, Lock, Linnell and Johnson to show that they were very capable draughtsmen. Johnson, in fact, by 1763 was described in Mortimer's *Universal Director* as 'Teacher of Drawing' as well as 'Carver'. Where did such men — cabinet-makers, not artists, by training — learn to draw? I would suggest that Gravelot, teaching both in his own school and at the St Martin's Lane Academy, did much to improve standards of draughtsmanship and to spread the knowledge of rococo ornament and methods of composition among the craftsmen. And perhaps one should bracket with Gravelot

28

the name of George Michael Moser, already mentioned as a member of the Slaughter's set, and the designer of the decor for the Music Room at Vauxhall.

Moser was a German Swiss, a chaser (and later an enamellist) by profession. He worked originally for a cabinet-maker called Trotter in Soho, and one suspects that much of the chased ornament on high-class eighteenth-century furniture and silverware was due to him, for he had the reputation of being the best chaser of his age. Such work would have been lost in the identity of the cabinet-maker or silversmith who commissioned it; but he made and signed watch-cases under his own name, and a number of these survive. The relevance of Moser to this section of the essay is that he, like Gravelot, kept a drawing school of his own, in association with others and apparently as early as the 1730s,[36] and taught at the St Martin's Lane Academy. That he was a capable draughtsman is shown by a sheet of his watch-case designs (Pl. 16), now in the Victoria and Albert Museum. With his Continental connections, his training and reputation as a craftsman, his activities as a designer and teacher, and his friendship with artists, he had a finger in many pies and was admirably equipped to disseminate the rococo style.[37]

Moser and Gravelot published no pattern-books. We are at an earlier stage, the stage of direct contact between master and pupil rather than dissemination by printed works. It is, of course, a much harder stage to document. But at least one suggestive drawing by Gravelot survives, an ornamental design in the British Museum (Pl. 17). It is suggestive not so much for its conventional rococo apparatus of shell-work and S- and C-curves as for the hissing swan, the dogs and fox, the reeds, grass and sprays of leaves with which it is embellished. For these, and similar flora and fauna, riot and sprout lavishly in English rococo furniture and decoration, and help to distinguish it from equivalent productions on the Continent. Did these peculiarly English attributes of applied rococo art stem from the inventions of Gravelot?

Unfortunately any papers of the St Martin's Lane Academy have disappeared, and there are only partial lists available of who became members or who (not necessarily

29

16. (left) Designs for watch-cases, by George Michael Moser.
17. Design for ornament, by H.F. Gravelot.

members) attended the classes. But at any rate one important furniture-maker can be associated with it. This is John Linnell, who appears in the very haphazard list of the Academy (which does not distinguish members from students) printed by W.H. Pyne, under the pseudonym of Ephraim Hardcastle, in *Wine and Walnuts* (1823).[38] Linnell worked to begin with in partnership with his father, William, who had maintained a prosperous workshop in Berkeley Square from about 1730, and took over the firm on his father's death in 1763. I can find no evidence that he ever became an actual member of the St Martin's Lane Academy, but it seems likely (on the strength of Pyne's reference) that he studied there as a young man. A large number of Linnell's designs are preserved in the Victoria and Albert Museum (Pl. 18). The earliest of these are emphatically, and on occasion extravagantly, rococo.

It seems reasonable to assume that Linnell acquired his knowledge of the grammar of the rococo from the Academy classes, probably from Gravelot or Moser. And, geographically at any rate, other cabinet-makers were in an admirable position to do so as well — or perhaps to employ clever young men from the St Martin's Lane Academy as designers. For St Martin's Lane was the centre of the furniture-making industry as well as the art world. Vile and Cobb, William Hallett and Thomas Chippendale, perhaps the three leading firms of the mid-eighteenth century, all had their workshops in it; so did the enigmatic, but probably important, firm of Channon and Son; and almost all the other cabinet-makers of any distinction were within easy reach. In Slaughter's Coffee-House the two worlds must surely have met and mingled.

There are shadowy but suggestive associations between two cabinet-makers and two individual members of the Hogarth circle. William Hallett and his family were painted by Hayman posed in a group before the elegant villa that Hallett had built on the site of the great palace of Cannons (Pl. 19).[39] And there seems to have been some kind of link between James Paine and Thomas Chippendale — both with Yorkshire backgrounds. Paine was the only architect who subscribed to Chippendale's *Gentleman's and Cabinet-Maker's Director*; his house in St Martin's Lane almost directly fronted Chippendale's workshop; a series of designs by him (now in the Victoria and Albert Museum) for a cabinet warehouse may have been made for Chippendale; and the Earl of Northumberland, to whom the *Director* was dedicated in 1754, was perhaps Paine's most important patron in the 1750s.

Apart from this possible connection with Chippendale, Paine was responsible for establishing an important school of rococo craftsmen in the north of England. Roubiliac was a friend of Sprimont, the French manager of the Chelsea porcelain factory, and

18. Design for a chimney-piece, by John Linnell.

may have modelled for it.[40] Gainsborough's friend William Collins was both sculptor and plasterer and may have formed a link between the Slaughter's set and the world of stucco. The whole business of the connection between artists and craftsmen at this period deserves further research; at the moment there is not enough evidence available to allow more than suggestions. The routes by which a style spreads are innumerable and it would be stupid to make too sweeping claims for the Hogarth set; yet I do not think it would be too sweeping to say that it was they who first set the rococo style rolling. By the mid-1750s it had rolled far and wide, and its spread had passed outside their control. They found themselves rather in the position of Ruskin, when capitals from Venice greeted him from every public house; S- and C-curves danced before their eyes from every tradesman's card and every headstone in country

graveyards. But in the 1750s they themselves were developing away from the rococo. This, I think, helps to explain Isaac Ware's disapproving attitude in his *Architecture*, first published in 1756; though it was also without doubt fomented by the fact that the rococo came from France, and that 1756 was the first year of the Seven Years' War.

An interesting sample of the taste of the set at this time is presented in *The Present State of the Arts in England*, published in 1755 by Jean André Rouquet, a French painter and enamellist who had settled in England, where he became an admirer of Hogarth's. It has been convincingly suggested that the unknown 'Ricquet', who according to the 1762 *Description of Vauxhall* did the chinoiserie decoration for the central of the Chinese pavilions, was in fact Rouquet. Rouquet praised all the people and institutions one would expect: Hayman ('master of every qualification that can form a great painter'); Roubiliac; Moser ('whose abilities really deserve the attention, and the approbation of his profession'); Sprimont and the Chelsea pottery; Gravelot ('his easy

31

19. William Hallett and his family, by Francis Hayman.

and fertile genius was a kind of oracle, to which even the most eminent occasionally applied'); Vauxhall and Tyers ('a man of an elegant and bold taste ... born for undertakings of this kind'); the St Martin's Lane Academy ('this institution is admirably adapted to the genius of the English').[41] But he flatly condemns what he calls 'Contrast'. By this he means the rococo principle of asymmetric design, the invention of which he ascribes to Meissonier: 'By a fruitful imagination, joined to great skill in his profession, and the assistance of novelty, he oftentimes excited admiration for those bold and inconsistent compositions.' Regrettably, this 'taste so ridiculous and whimsical ... has reached as far as England'.[42]

Probably neither Ware nor Rouquet would have been so censorious ten or fifteen years earlier. Nevertheless, this quotation does spotlight the problem — already touched on earlier — of just how far the members of the Hogarth set can be described as rococo artists. There would seem to have been different shades of opinion among them: Gravelot, so to speak, on the left, the belligerently English Hogarth on the right. The rococo in its narrowest sense — a distinctive type of ornament and method of composition — never won unconditional acceptance from the group as a whole, though they were certainly both intrigued and influenced by it. Many members of the group were too insular and inhibited to surrender themselves unconditionally to its allurements. Their patrons were equally guarded: with few exceptions they were not prepared to do more than leaven their inherited Palladianism with a little French gaiety. There was never the same wholehearted abandonment to the rococo that one finds in Germany. Even such English ornament as can undeniably be described as rococo is more often than not symmetrical: the wild infectious gaiety of irregular design was seldom allowed to spread further than the silver, the furniture and the china.

What all members of the group shared was an attitude of mind. They turned away from authority and back to nature — material nature, not the ideal nature of the Renaissance. They were interested, not in what Palladio or Aristotle had done or said, but in what they saw with their own eyes. Fielding made fun of the three unities; Hogarth steadfastly ignored all earlier treatises in his *Analysis of Beauty*; Ware complained that 'the modern architects too strictly and scrupulously follow these antients';[43] Paine could remark iconoclastically of Palladio: 'Experience daily convinces us, that the houses built by that great master, are very ill adapted to our climate, still worse to our present mode of living, and consequently are not proper models for our imitation.'[44] In this liberated atmosphere it was easy to turn to the immediate and the unpompous. The corsets and candlesticks with which Hogarth illustrates his points in the *Analysis*; the squirrels and foxes peering among the oak leaves of rococo decoration (Pl. 20); Gainsborough's cottages and peasants; Tom Jones, with all his human failings; Roubiliac's sitters, in their unbuttoned shirts and nightcaps: all these express a similar frame of mind.

Yet similar frames of mind need not add up to a style. Pulled in different directions by their inherited disciplines, by the seductions of the rococo, by the charms of a new liberty, which let them roam in Chinese and Gothic as well as classic pastures, the artists and architects of the Hogarth set leave one with the impression of a synthesis never fully completed. English baroque and English Palladianism on the one hand, or English neoclassicism on the other, all present a clearer image than what — for the

20. (right) A detail on the staircase of Powderham Castle, Devon, 1755.

lack of a better phrase — one is forced to call English rococo.

The reason for this was partly, perhaps, the changing conditions of patronage. English art was drifting, with neither artists nor patrons in command. The artists of the previous generation had revolved around Lord Burlington and a few other noble cognoscenti. Their sources of income were derived almost entirely from the patronage of individual members of the upper classes, and it was the upper classes who set the pace. The middle years of the eighteenth century saw important changes. Hogarth made his income largely from the sale of his engravings — bought by a, for the eighteenth century, large and predominantly middle-class section of the community. Hogarth's friend Fielding wrote for a similar audience. The boom in book illustration provided a steady source of income for artists such as Gravelot, Hayman and Wale. Although architects and sculptors were still largely dependent on upper-class patronage, Roubiliac exploited a profitable new line in portrait busts of doctors, scientists, clergymen and dons, and in monuments to military heroes. Impresarios such as Tyers, book publishers and print-sellers such as John and Paul Knapton and Hogarth's friend John Pine, as well as the more prosperous goldsmiths and cabinet-makers, provided increasing opportunities of employment to artists and designers. At the Foundling Hospital — with the affairs of which many of the Hogarth set were intimately connected — artists found somewhere where, for the first time in England, they could exhibit their productions to the public.[45]

It is not surprising that these developments made them increasingly independent and conscious of their status — or what they thought ought to be their status — in the community. One result of this was an increasing criticism of aristocratic patrons, in particular for their habit of ignoring living English artists in favour of the Old Masters. Both Hogarth and Roubiliac, for instance, violently expressed this feeling at the time of the exhibition of pictures held in Spring Gardens in 1761 — the first public art exhibition in England to be held under the auspices of artists alone. Roubiliac wrote satirical French verses

33

against the 'Prétendu Connoisseur qui sur l'Antique glose'; while Hogarth designed a tailpiece for the catalogue, representing a dead tree being watered by a monkey dressed up as a connoisseur (Pl. 21).

Another almost inevitable result was a growing agitation for a state academy — an artistic trade union subsidised by the state which would give artists a status, a training and an independence which they could not derive from their own amateurish academy in St Martin's Lane. Hogarth himself — probably through hurt pride, for he regarded the St Martin's Lane Academy with the fondness of a father — refused to have anything to do with the idea. The rest of the set were violently in favour, and this difference of opinion erected, in his later life, an unhappy barrier between Hogarth and his friends. When, in 1755, a committee of twenty-five artists was set up to consider the formation of an academy, Hayman was its president and Moser, Roubiliac, Hudson, Grignion, Cheere, Ware, Paine, Wale, Gwynn, Yeo and Pine were among the members. This represents virtually a complete roll-call of the Hogarth set, apart from the gaping absence of Hogarth himself. The scheme came to nothing owing to a row with the Society of Dilettanti, which had originally sponsored it but wanted the artists (or so the artists thought) to play too subservient a part. The Dilettanti represented aristocratic, as opposed to artistic, taste; the fact that they were mixed up with the scheme, and that the association was a failure, shows with accuracy the increasingly (but not yet fully) independent state of English artists at the time. They were in a betwixt-and-between position, and the result, however interesting, was a betwixt-and-between art.

The Royal Academy finally came into existence in 1768. By then, however, many of the old circle — Hogarth, Ware and Roubiliac, for instance — were dead. The survivors were treated with honour: Hayman became a founder member, a visitor and ultimately librarian; Moser became the first Keeper; Wale the Professor of Perspective. But the driving force of the new academy derived from a completely different group, the circle of Chambers and Reynolds. Neoclassical winds were blowing through the country, and the rococo withered beneath them.

21. Hogarth's tailpiece illustration to the catalogue of the picture exhibition held at Spring Gardens, London, in 1761.
22. (right) The figure of Justice (today, minus her scales) on the parapet of the Stamford Hotel, Stamford.

2 THE BAITING OF BURGHLEY:
Politics and Architecture in Stamford

A bird or a balloonist hovering above Stamford in the early nineteenth century would have looked down on an epitome of English tradition and beauty. The town itself was an island of golden stone, opening through medieval walls into a sea of cornland or green fields. Out of this island rose the towers and spires of five medieval churches, of the same beautiful stone, dug from quarries in the vicinity. And from the southern edge of the town parkland stretched to the spires and towers of Burghley House, an Elizabethan Camelot set into a Georgian paradise by the genius of Capability Brown.

All was not as golden as it seemed, however. There was enough poverty, overcrowding, faction, brutality and resentment in the little town to keep it on a simmer, which, between intervals of somnolence, erupted every now and then into violence. The surrounding fields acted as a stranglehold, making it impossible for the town to expand. And the position of Burghley House was ambivalent. Was it Camelot? Or was it the castle of the Dragon King, who held the town in thrall? For those who saw it in the latter role, it became the object of a series of political assaults,

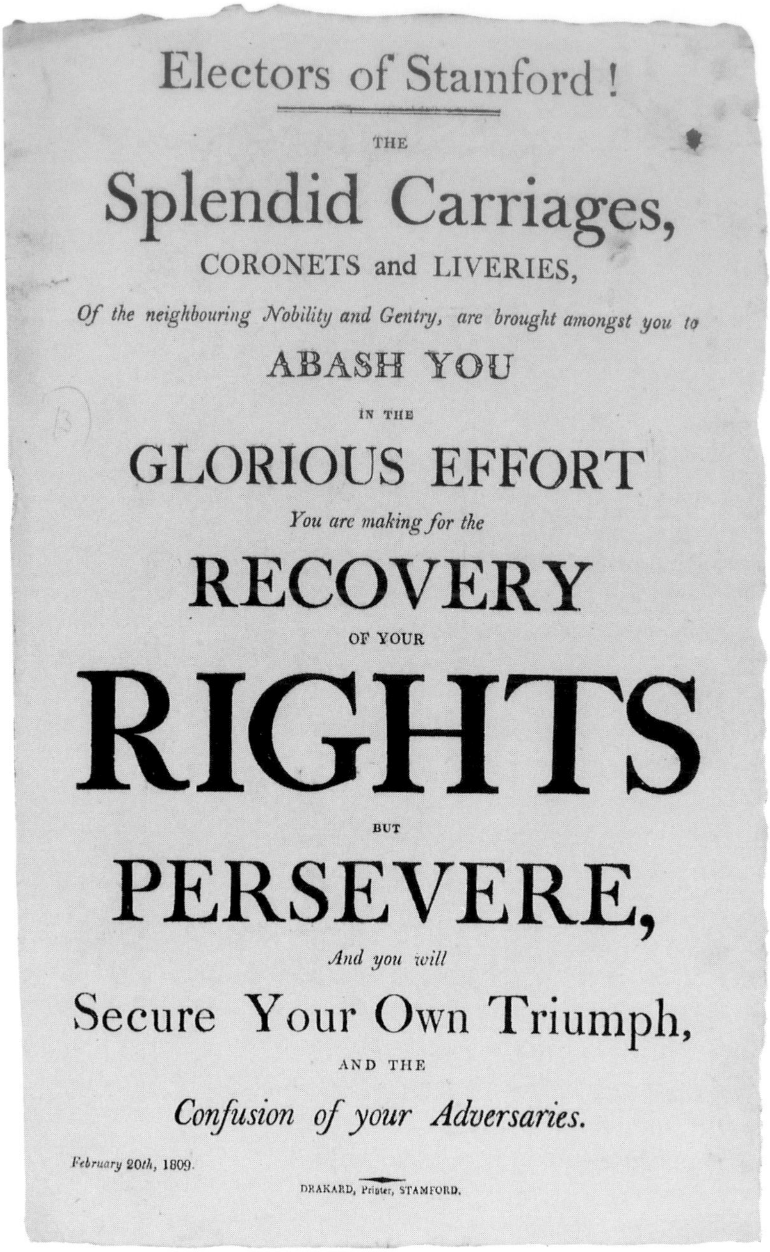

Electors of Stamford !

THE

Splendid Carriages,

CORONETS and LIVERIES,

Of the neighbouring Nobility and Gentry, are brought amongst you to

ABASH YOU

IN THE

GLORIOUS EFFORT

You are making for the

RECOVERY

OF YOUR

RIGHTS

BUT

PERSEVERE,

And you will

Secure Your Own Triumph,

AND THE

Confusion of your Adversaries.

February 20th, 1809.

DRAKARD, Printer, STAMFORD.

designed to rescue or capture the town from the Cecil family.

Stamford was not a pocket borough in the extreme sense of the word, one of those once-thriving medieval towns which had decayed to a huddle of houses, owned by one person, from which half a dozen voters emerged to vote for their two Members of Parliament as their landlord directed. The cloth trade which had made it rich in the Middle Ages had decayed. But it was still a staging post on the Great North Road, a distribution centre for the goods which came up its canalised river, a market town, and the home of prosperous masons who worked the quarries around it, and of the even more prosperous attorneys who looked after the affairs and ran the estates of the numerous rich landowners in the surrounding countryside. All who paid the poor rates had the right to vote, which, in the early 1800s, produced about 650 voters in a town of about 4,000 inhabitants.

But by 1800 Stamford seemed securely in the pockets of the Cecils, Earls — and, from 1801, Marquesses — of Exeter. They were lords of the manor, and owned a large percentage of the town (and, since voting was still public, they knew who voted for whom). They owned the wasteland around Stamford, controlled most of the charities and appointed most of the clergy. Few of the town's shopkeepers were prepared to lose the custom of the Cecil family and the huge household at Burghley. The last contested election had been in 1734. From then on the Lord Exeter of the day nominated the two candidates of his choice.

An election in 1784 was described as follows: 'No-one ever opposes those who are honoured with his recommendations ... the principal agent of Lord Exeter waits upon the mayor, hoping he will fix the day of election agreeable to his lordship's desire, which being done ... the whole town is canvassed in two days, by the candidates, the mayor and corporation with such gentry as choose to honour them with their company, and the whole business ends with the utmost good nature and harmony.'

36

23.   Poster printed by John Drakard for the 1809 by-election in Stamford.

This comfortable situation disguised growing resentment among some voters. It erupted in 1809, and again in 1812, first in a by-election and then in a general election, both of which were contested. A disparate trio led the assault: John Drakard, a radical Stamford printer, who was warm-hearted, hot-headed and instantly opposed to anything he felt was unjust (he was the publisher, incidentally, of what is still the best history of Stamford); Joshua Jepson Oddy, a failed Russia merchant from the City, who was prepared to have a go against high odds for a seat in Parliament; and Colonel Gerard Noel Noel, a flamboyant local landowner, who had fallen foul of the Cecils and joined Oddy as opposition candidate in the general election. In support were a group of discontented attorneys, bankers and merchants, who formed a committee of what was known in the town as the Blue Party — for, confusingly, supporters of the die-hard Tory Cecils were known as the Reds.

Oddy on his own got nowhere in 1809, despite a barrage of posters emerging from Drakard's press (Pl. 23), street parades 'attended by music and a forest of flags', blazing tar-barrels at night, and inflammatory speeches from the windows of the George and Angel Inn, where the Blue committee had its headquarters.

37

24. Looking down St Mary's Street to the Stamford Hotel.

By the time Noel joined him in 1812 two new features had enlivened the election: the *Stamford News* and the Stamford Hotel. The *Stamford News* was started up by Drakard at the end of 1812, and for the next twenty-two years was one of the liveliest radical newspapers in England, and an obstreperous rival to the *Stamford Mercury*, which supported the Burghley interest. The *News* was often in trouble. An article entitled 'One Thousand Lashes', attacking flogging in the Army, had landed Drakard with a fine and eighteen months in prison, from which he emerged just in time to take part in the 1812 election.

The Stamford Hotel was Noel's contribution. In 1810 he bought the Black Bull Inn on St Mary's Street, and rebuilt it as a magnificent classical palazzo, which he used as his headquarters in the 1812 election. The architect was James Linnell Bond, who was rebuilding Noel's country house at Exton for him at the same time. The hotel was the grandest building in Stamford (Pl. 24). It far outshone the modest town hall where the Burghley-dominated corporation officiated. Its great enfilade of Corinthian columns rose well above the roofs of the surrounding houses and was surmounted by a statue of Justice and her scales, which feature prominently on the Stamford skyline (Pl. 22). It was even visible from the park at Burghley — proclaiming, as Noel explained, that 'when the Marquis of Exeter opposes the Noel interest in Rutland, Justice calls for retaliation in the Borough of Stamford'.

It was a grand gesture, but Drakard's *History of Stamford* thought it was a great waste of money. What was needed in a borough like Stamford was not gestures but property: opposition-owned houses, the tenants of which would have the right to vote and who would vote against Burghley. And indeed, despite the Hotel and the *News*, the posters and the speeches, the processions and the music, Burghley romped home triumphant. Oddy dropped out at the last minute and Noel limped in a bad third.

After the poll he paraded bravely through the town, sporting 'a handsome Spanish head-dress with blue and yellow feathers'. He gave a banquet for his supporters in the hotel, but it was for a Red victory that 1,500 people cavorted in a ball at the assembly rooms until four in the morning, and 'many continued to reel and waltz until some time after'. As usual, after contested Stamford elections, there was a petition against undue influence exerted by Burghley and, as usual, it failed. The Stamford Hotel stood empty and unfinished, and Noel retired to Exton, a sadder and considerably poorer man.

There was not to be another political assault on the Burghley interest until 1830. In March 1818, however, Drakard attacked the young Marquess of Exeter in the *News* for his behaviour: 'in our borough (or, as he calls it, his borough) ... The last month has witnessed the parade of your Lordship and a Captain Percy about our streets, for hours each day, at times on horseback, and at others condescendingly on your feet ... Is it not enough, that your lordship must turn window-peeper, but, if a female chance to be within reach of your optics ... she must be nodded too, leered at, and probably disgusted by a wink from nobility, followed by a blown kiss from your lordly lips.' Lord Exeter launched a libel case, but dropped it before it came to court.

He had emerged from a long minority to prove himself the worst card in Burghley's powerful political hand, not so much because of any window-peeping or leering as because of his conviction of his God-given right to do what he liked in and with

Stamford. Small in body and small in mind, it was perhaps the fact that his mother was a farmer's daughter (the 'cottage countess' celebrated by Tennyson) that made him behave like a caricature aristocrat of the old régime, one who was not prepared to make the slightest concession to the times, or pay any consideration to public feeling in Stamford.

His resulting unpopularity must have played a part in the Cecil interest's political defeat in 1831. Charles Tennyson (first cousin of the poet), who came a good third in the general election of 1830, was successfully elected in the next year's by-election, following the dissolution of Parliament in 1831. 'The day is your own,' the posters proclaimed, 'the Victory is achieved, the Fetters of Slavery are broken, the upheld Rod of Iron has dropped from the Hand of Despotism, on view of the enlightened spirit of a Tennyson.' The Cecils took the election results very hard. Indeed, Lord Thomas Cecil, the other successful candidate, fought a duel with Tennyson on the strength of it.

A number of other factors contributed to Tennyson's victory. He had a brilliant political manager, in the person of Joseph Parkes, a solicitor from Birmingham who played a key role in radical politics of the era. The election had been called by the Whig party in an atmosphere of national excitement when the Reform Bill, passed in the Commons in 1830, had been vetoed by the Lords. Whether or not the Bill would become law depended on its results. Another interesting factor was that Richard Newcomb, the editor of the Red *Stamford Mercury*, had defected to the Blue party.

Newcomb was to become one of the most prominent figures in Stamford. He was an able man, but not, one suspects, a likeable one. Reading about him, one is reminded of Mr Bulstrode, the sanctimonious banker in *Middlemarch*. His father, also Richard, had become part-owner of the *Stamford Mercury* in 1785, and sole proprietor in 1797. He took his son into partnership in about 1815; by 1830 the younger Richard was running the business, although his father did not die until 1843.

He was an energetic manager and editor. He doubled the size and greatly increased the circulation of the *Mercury*. In 1820 he bought a nearby paper-mill and wharf at Wansford, with a house adjoining which he used as a country retreat from Stamford. The mill made paper of very high quality, for use in the *Mercury* or for sale; *The Times* was sometimes printed on it. And in 1829 he set about getting rid of Drakard and the *Stamford News*.

His method was ingenious. Drakard rented his premises from Stamford Grammar School. In September 1829 the school's properties came up for re-renting, by open auction. Newcomb bid up Drakard, and more than doubled his rent as a result. Drakard — as, knowing his character, was inevitable — violently attacked Newcomb in the *News*. Newcomb sued him for libel and £1,000 damages. He won his case, and, although he was awarded only a farthing's damages, the combination of increased rent and legal costs was enough to finish Drakard. The *News* ceased publication in 1834, and Drakard left Stamford.

At the time of the libel case, Drakard and the *News* had a good deal to say about Newcomb's relationship with Burghley. He was 'held at Burghley House in more unsavoury odour than an open opponent ... the high Tory party believe him to have demeaned himself towards them after the manner of the viper in the fable, which

stung the child which nourished it.' Whatever the background to this, in the 1830 election Newcomb came out into the open, and voted against Burghley for Tennyson. For the rest of his life he led the Liberals and the Blues in the town against the Tory Cecils and the Reds, and the *Mercury* never had a good word to say about Burghley.

Like Noel, he underlined his change of politics with an architectural gesture. In his case it involved his own house, not a hotel. In 1842 he bought a disused quarry at the end of Scotgate, and on it built the lush classical villa known as Rock House (Pl. 25). Compared with Burghley, it was small beer; but it was still the biggest and most pretentious house in the town. It became the nucleus of a cluster of Newcomb buildings at the end of Scotgate, all but one probably by the same unknown architect: a terrace of ten houses, known as Rock Terrace; two shops with an arch in between them, leading to the Rock House stables and coachhouses, in another disused quarry; Rock Cottages, a row of little houses, with access from the quarry edge at the back (Pl. 26); and the slightly earlier Clock House, which closed the vista down Scotgate on the way out of the town.

But, unlike Noel, Newcomb was politically sharp, and these building were all designed (filling up waste ground where possible) to contain Liberal voters, as well as to wave a Liberal–Newcomb flag. They formed part of a formidable portfolio of property which Newcomb gradually assembled in Stamford. This included two more new buildings, in the form of two handsome shops, built in 1849 to either side of the beginning of a new street projected by Newcomb to join High Street to Broad Street, and never completed. But mostly it was made up of old property, scattered all over the town. When the holding finally came under the hammer in 1919, it was sold in fifty-four lots — among them the Stamford Hotel, which Noel had disposed of in 1845.

It was ironical, however, that the effect of the Reform Act of 1832 was to strengthen the hold of Burghley on Stamford. Under the Act, the boundaries of the borough were enlarged to include the part of the town across the river known as St Martin's; and this adjoined Burghley, almost all belonged to Burghley, and voted solidly for Burghley. As a result Tennyson refused to stand a second time, and it was not until 1847 that the Stamford Blues felt able to contest another election.

In the intervening years, Newcomb occupied himself with increasing his circulation and his property, engaging in local government, and baiting Burghley. In 1837 the Liberals won a great victory in the municipal elections, even though 'the conduct of the Marquess of Exeter's steward has been such as has excited disgust and indignation wherever it has been observed'. In 1842 (a foretaste here of P.G. Wodehouse's Sir

40

25. Rock House, Scotgate, Stamford, from which Richard Newcomb conducted his campaign against the Burghley interest.

Gregory Parsloe-Parsloe) Lord Exeter was accused of cheating to enable his sheep to win the championship at the Agricultural Show.

In the same year, Queen Adelaide came to Burghley, and Lord Exeter gave a party for the Stamford schoolchildren in her honour; but only Church of England children were invited. Disgusted at 'the hideous visage of faction in the full glare of hatefulness and wickedness', Newcomb and others organised a Nonconformist beano on the river meadows, where 'much greater enjoyment was assured than is ever found in the hall of any proud nobleman'.

In 1837 Newcomb played a controversial part in the suppression of bull-running in Stamford. Every year since the thirteenth century a bull had been released in the streets of Stamford (Pl. 27), and baited by the more adventurous or drunken of its inhabitants. It was the great annual event, an opportunity for letting off steam. The 'lower order of the people', according to a report in 1805, were 'bull-mad', and candidates at election time amused the electorate with an extra running.

But then the fledgling Society for the Prevention of Cruelty to Animals began to agitate against the event. In 1809 Gerard Noel was rash enough to announce that if he were elected he would endeavour to 'purge the town of so foul a stain upon its fame as the annual bull-running'. He soon realised that he was committing political suicide, and by election year the issue had been quietly dropped.

By the 1830s, however, the tide was running much more strongly against bull-running. The SPCA and the attitudes behind it were more powerful; and all over

41

26. Rock Cottages, built by Newcomb on the edge of an old quarry at the back of his stable yard.

England society was polarising for or against any kind of popular festival at which local communities went wild together: on the one hand, a mainly Nonconformist and Liberal lobby attacking them as excuses for drunkenness and immorality; on the other hand, a Tory, Old English lobby, defending them as tradition-sanctioned recreations, which helped bring the classes together.

In Stamford this meant Burghley and the Reds for bull-running and Newcomb and the Blues against it. With the support of the central government, Newcomb and his fellow magistrates tried to put down bull-running in 1837, and failed, and tried again in 1839 and succeeded — but only by bringing in dragoons and London police (Pl. 28). Bull-running was not an issue on which to fight an election in Stamford. But in 1847, when the feelings aroused in 1839 had died down, Newcomb (who was mayor in that year) and the Blues felt able to put up John Rolt, a London lawyer, as their opposition candidate, and to whip up feeling against Burghley, on the grounds that Lord Exeter was stopping the new main-line railway coming through Stamford, and would kill its trade as a result. So once again the processions marched, the bands played, the printing presses whirred, and posters and lampoons showered down on the town. Newcomb, according to the Reds, was on the make, and his wife a dipsomaniac:

> To aggrandize himself he's striving
> THAT'S the real game he's driving

42

27. Bull-running in Stamford, from an anonymous painting of *c.* 1820 now in the Town Hall.

And any expense he'll gladly bear
So he may sign himself the Mayor
... And the late Mayoress, such a creature
With spirits stamped on every feature
... He leads a party here called 'Blue',
A riotous low, vagabond crew

The Blues riposted: Red agents, they said, were making 'twilight visits to those voters who may be deemed susceptible of a particular kind of influence'. Or, as a versifier put it:

Of vacillating voters there's full many a one
Who, good judges, ne'er refuse a Burghley bun.

And Burghley won again.

Newcomb died in 1851. In his will he left a legacy for the erection and endowment of schools 'for the inculcation of sound and useful learning and true religion, without priestly or sectarian bias, free of charge to all boys whose parents reside in Stamford'. His nephew and residuary legatee, Robert Nicholas Newcomb, had the bequest annulled on a technicality. Seven years later he backed a public appeal for subscriptions for new

28. Dragoons and police march into Stamford to suppress the bull-running in 1839. Newcomb's Clock House is in the background, and the town prostitute is spitting at the dragoons on the right.

ELECTORS
STAMFORD.

If you love the *abuses* which exist in Church and State :

If you love *Slavery* and unjust usurpation :

If you are Enemies to *Civil* and *Religious Liberty* :

If you respect not your *King* and hate the *Constitution* :

Then Vote for CECIL & CHAPLIN.

But if not, then hasten to Vote for your REAL Friend---& unflinching Supporter,

C. TENNYSON, Esq.

schools in Stamford. In the same year he jilted his fiancée, the rector's daughter at Wansford, on discovering that she was an epileptic. Feelings ran high, and the *Lincolnshire Chronicle* (and its lawyer, in the subsequent libel case) had a field-day.

Nephew Newcomb was parodied: 'I invite you, the people of Stamford, to subscribe your guineas, willingly, cheerfully and liberally; I have pocketed all my uncle's money.' He had, it was reported, been burnt in effigy on the village green at Wansford: '... the mob laughed and jeered, while the flames leapt upward.'

Never a dull moment, in and around Stamford in those days, one might say. And yet, on reflection, it was probably because the days were so appallingly dull in small provincial towns in the early and mid-nineteenth century, that occasional scandals, elections and carnivals provoked such excitement. For a high proportion of the electorate, one cannot help feeling, an election was a free party, an excuse for a lively time, for blood and thunder (Pl. 29), for cheering and booing, for accepting drink and presents from both sides, for making promises accordingly — and then going to the polls and voting once again for the Burghley candidate.

44

29. Poster for the 1831 election.
30. (right) A self-portrait of John Chubb (1746-1818), whose watercolours brought life to Bridgwater and its inhabitants in the late eighteenth century.

3 COUNTRY-TOWN PORTFOLIO:
An Artist in Bridgwater

What was life like in a small town in the eighteenth century? What were the feuds, the jealousies, the excitements and the gossip? What was the hierarchy, and how did it operate? What did the people who walked in the streets actually look like? For country-house life in this period a mass of evidence is available. Wherever a house has remained in the possession of one family, its possessions, including letters, diaries and sketchbooks, are likely to remain in it too, at least until they reach the safe haven of a county record office. But in country towns, where it

was rare for one family to live in the same house for more than two or three generations, personal evidence is much harder to come by. Often the historian has to rely on statistics, on rate books, poor law papers, local government records, and so on. They supply the skeleton which careful analysis and creative sympathy can raise to life; but it can be uphill work to do so.

Occasionally, however, a diary, a collection of letters, or a sketchbook throws a shaft of vivid, even if partial, light on to one town at one period of time. Such is the case with John Chubb (Pl. 30) and Bridgwater in the last decades of the eighteenth century. Chubb lived all his life in the town; all his life he was sketching and drawing the town itself, and even more the people who lived in it or visited it. Several hundred drawings and watercolours by him survive (and more, one suspects, may come to light); and a collection of letters to or from him, and of poems by him, helps to round out the portrait.

In the mid-eighteenth century Bridgwater had a population of about 3,000. Earlier in the century the manor had been bought by the Duke of Chandos, who tried to promote Bridgwater as a manufacturing town, by starting up a glass factory, a distillery and a soap works. His scheme failed, and in 1734 he sold the manor in disgust. But Bridgwater remained what it had been before he arrived, a modestly prosperous market town and port. Presiding over the market-place was the medieval market cross, octagonal and vaulted like those that survive at Chichester and Salisbury; in 1689 it had been hung with heads of rebels defeated at the Battle of Sedgemoor, just outside the town. Down on the quay, boats unloaded wine from Spain and France, butter from Ireland, or timber from Norway and the Baltic, and loaded up with West of England cloth.

In the mid-eighteenth century Chubb's father, Jonathan, prospered in Bridgwater as a merchant specialising, as his trade card put it (Pl. 31), in 'Wines and Rum, Deals, Fir Timber and Spars, Dutch Oak and Mahogany, Staves and other Copper timber', and in addition having a share in a brass-foundry and metalwork business. His house was on Vicar Lane, the street leading down to the bridge across the River Parrett, and had a back entrance and warehousing on the quay. Here he and his family could watch the river as it sank at low tide to a thin ribbon in the soft shining mud, and listen to the

46

31. The trade card of Chubb's father, Jonathan.

Parrett's equivalent of the Severn Bore, as it suddenly lifted up the beached boats and filled the river with a rush and roar of water. John Chubb drew the scene by the family house when the river was full: the bridge, the little boats above it, the arched entrance by which goods were handled from the lower quay to the upper, and a genial figure who might be Jonathan Chubb himself, smoking a pipe in a chair by one of his own barrels (Pl. 32).

John Chubb was born on 9 May 1746. By September 1749 he could 'tell most words and read properly almost any of Gay's fables and can write the Alphabet but not words'. By December 1750 he could 'read English especially verse better than one half of the Parsons and other men who are supposed able to read. Knows a great many Latin words and can read Greek.' The information comes from Jonathan Chubb's notebook, a curious mixture of family dates, lists of the prices of brandy, rum, ribbons and deal, exchange rates in Norway and elsewhere, two pages of pithy 'Rules' for the conduct of life, and quotations, mainly from Shakespeare, arranged alphabetically under headings such as Absence, Advice, Ambition and Adultery.

The small-town merchant who had his son taught Latin and Greek was also able to write a letter to him almost entirely in Latin. This was when John, at the age of thirteen, went to stay in London with his uncle, Charles La Roche, who had a shop in Cheapside. Many letters passed between him and his father, mother and sisters. John adored London, and wrote enthusiastically to his 'Honoured Papa' that 'if it were not to see you, my dear Mama and sisters, I should never wish to see Bridgwater more. I cannot perceive how a person who has any spirit ... can bear to live in the country.'

47

32. The quay at Bridgwater by the Chubbs' house. The seated figure may be Jonathan Chubb.

He would have liked to settle in London, and considered various options — of being a merchant, a doctor, a cornet in the Dragoons, but above all a painter or 'limner'. His father was unenthusiastic about all his suggestions, but especially the last one. John sent six reasons why a limner 'seems to please me most', of which the first was 'because it is a very genteel business', the fifth 'because the painting is pleasant to the painter' and the sixth 'because one has the pleasure of looking at pretty ladies'. His father countered these three and all the others. Painting 'is generally regarded as an ungenteel or mean business ... The pleasure of composition greatly abates when we labour at it for bread ... The looking properly at one pretty lady is better than a thousand.'

Jonathan Chubb clearly combined pride in, and affection for, his son with deep distrust of the big city, and of what its effect would be on John. He stressed the pleasures of life in a country town, and made it clear that John would not be expected to drudge all day at an office desk, but could live a gentlemanly life 'having leisure for the delights of the finer arts, and amusing yourself with painting, music, poetry and composition'.

In effect, that was what John did. He listened to his father, came back to Bridgwater and lived there for the rest of his life. His father, who did not die until 1805, ran the business; John's connection with it seems to have been little more than marginal. In lists of parliamentary voters, his father is always described as 'merchant', but John first as 'son of Jonathan' and then as 'gentleman'. He drew his self-portrait as a gentleman amateur, lounging in elegant clothes, with palette and easel (Pl. 30). At one stage he may have taken drawing lessons; if so, it is not known from whom. He seems to have drawn profusely all his life. In the intervals he amused himself with writing verse, seldom for publication, and never as good as his drawings.

But this clever, frustrated, lively and, one suspects, delightful man had one other interest, besides 'painting, music, poetry and composition'. He became deeply involved in local politics. His political beliefs seem to have derived from his father. He supported the radical wing of the Whigs, distrusted the powers of the Crown and the Church, fought for Wilkes and Liberty, worshipped Charles James Fox, and welcomed the French Revolution.

As early as 1770 a song written by him was being sung at the celebrations at Taunton when Wilkes was released from prison. Bridgwater was the first town in England to petition for the abolition of the slave trade and Chubb was probably behind the petition. In the 1780s he managed the Whig interest in Bridgwater, with the support of one powerful local family — the Percevals, Earls of Egmont, of Enmore Castle — and against the interests of another — the Earls Poulett, of Hinton St George. He was involved in election after election, almost always without success, for the Pouletts carried great weight in Bridgwater. As he wrote proudly in a letter he left behind for his children: 'I have uniformly through a long course of years ... combatted tyranny and oppression, and struggled on every occasion to defend and preserve (alas to little effect) the freedom and beauty of the true English constitution against the instant encroachments of arbitrary power and corruption.'

Chubb's politics broadened his horizon and brought him friendship with two famous men, Fox and Coleridge. He first came into contact with Fox in 1780, when Bridgwater joined other constituencies in petitioning for the reform of the House of Commons. He persuaded Fox to stand for parliament in Bridgwater in the same year, apparently as a

failsafe measure in case Fox was not elected at Westminster; in fact Fox sailed home at Westminster and came bottom of the poll at Bridgwater. Despite this débâcle he and Chubb maintained a warm relationship; in 1785, for instance, when Fox was travelling in the west with his mistress, he wrote inviting Chubb to dinner — but not in Bridgwater, for the sake of the proprieties.

Coleridge got to know Chubb in 1797 or 1798, when he was trying to find a cottage in which John Thelwall, journalist, agitator and supporter of the French Revolution,

33. The (north) gate at Bridgwater.

could retreat from publicity. As Coleridge put it: 'By his particular exertion in the propagation of those principles which he holds sacred ... he has become, as you well know, particularly unpopular thro' every part of the kingdom.' Chubb failed to find a cottage, but a friendship started which was still going in 1810 when Thomas de Quincey went looking for Coleridge, and found him staying with the Chubbs at Bridgwater. He was standing under the arch on the quay, shown in Chubb's watercolour. 'He was in a deep reverie,' as de Quincey described: ' ... the sound of my voice, announcing my own name, fast awoke him; he started, and for a moment seemed at a loss to understand my purpose or his situation; for he repeated rapidly a number of words which had no relation to either of us.'

With a sharp eye, a genial wit and a skilled brush Chubb set out to put on to paper the people of Bridgwater and its neighbourhood. In addition he drew a number of town views (Pl. 33) and landscapes, often of considerable charm; but it is on his people that his reputation must rest. Although it seems likely that examples of his work were acquired by friends and neighbours in Somerset, and may still survive, almost all the known examples belong to his descendants, and are either in the possession of the family or on loan to the Admiral Blake Museum in Bridgwater.

50

34-37. Bridgwater people. George Beale, merchant; George Cass, printer; John Pine, watch-maker; and Charles Smith, attorney.

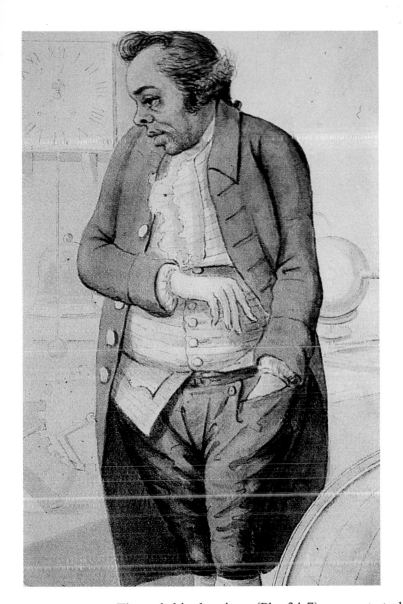

Through his drawings (Pls. 34-7), one gets to know Matthew Luff, poulterer and fishmonger, with his coop of hens and his bag of fish; ingratiating 'Pussy' Woodham, the barber; big-bellied, self-important Samuel Thomas, the schoolmaster, with his shirt bursting out between his trousers and waistcoat; even bigger-bellied George Beale, merchant and mayor, hands cocked in pockets, standing on the quay among his bales and sacks; villainous John Hicks, described as of 'doubtful occupation'; Charles Smith, gentlemanly attorney; little Mr Philpotts, merchant and maltster, mysteriously wrapped in plaid; and George Cass, printer and bookbinder, who was perhaps of radical inclinations, like Chubb himself, for he is tearing up a Bible to provide backing for his books. The drawing of John Pine, watchmaker, captioned 'a local bore of pseudo-scientific inclination', brilliantly suggests the loose lips, self-absorbed manner and limp hands of the vintage bore.

One of the biggest and liveliest of the drawings shows Lord Perceval, eldest son of Lord Egmont (Pl. 38). He is dressed in the height of fashion, and seated at the reins of his phaeton, with a lap-dog on his lap and a favour in his hat. The drawing probably dates from 1790, when Perceval stood unsuccessfully for Bridgwater as a supporter of Charles James Fox.

38. Lord Perceval goes electioneering.

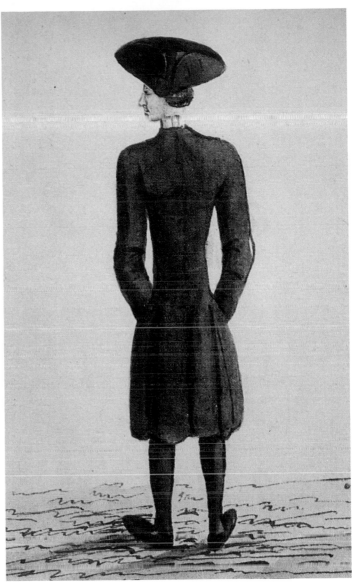

A good many of Chubb's drawings have a political background, and contain political references that further research would probably elucidate. One caricature features 'G.R.', 'T.P.', and 'J.H.', apparently preparing an address to parliament. T.P., on the right, is Thomas Pyke, a rich Bridgwater brass-founder who 'dealt in brass' and had an ambivalent political relationship with Chubb. J.H. who 'dealt in cloth' is presumably a tailor or draper. G.R. is George Rowley, a clergyman whom Chubb especially disliked and must have considered brazen (Pl. 41).

Chubb was no friend to the clergy; his critical attitude was shared by his father, and went with the family's radical politics. He drew clergymen in considerable numbers, among them the Rev. John Coles, the Tory vicar of Bridgwater from 1742 to 1785; he was famous for his knobbly cudgel, which he carried everywhere and is said to have used on those of his parishioners who displeased him. The tough old man makes a striking contrast with timorous, out-at-elbows little Parson Sealy, vicar of the poor living of Wembdon (Pls. 39, 40). Chubb had a soft spot for Sealy, who was one of the few Church of England clergy who shared his political views. He features in

53

39, 40. Contrasting clergymen. The Rev. John Coles, Vicar of Bridgwater, and (right) Parson Sealy of Wembdon.

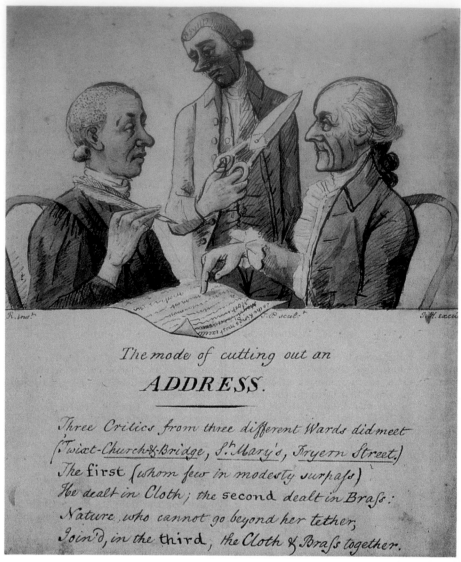

The mode of cutting out an

ADDRESS.

Three Critics from three different Wards did meet
(Twixt Church & Bridge, St. Mary's, Fryern Street.)
The first (whom few in modesty surpass)
He dealt in Cloth; the second dealt in Brass:
Nature, who cannot go beyond her tether,
Join'd, in the third, the Cloth & Brass together.

'The Visitation', much the best of Chubb's poems. It describes the bishop's official visitation to the local clergy in 1785, and is full of verse portraits, mainly unflattering. Chubb has the bishop address Sealy:

> Quoth my Lord, I'm in doubt, you're so like a church mouse,
> If you live in the poor, or the parsonage house
> ...Then Sealy replies, as he sprawls out his feet
> And twists like a spare-rib of port on a spit,
> But if ev'ry good clerk must appear in good case,
> Or a plenty of grease prove abundance of grace,
> My preferment like me must remain ever lean
> While Stambr'y next year shall, at least, be a Dean.

Chubb seems to have continued to like 'looking at pretty ladies'; at any rate, he drew them in large numbers. These female sitters are mainly unidentified, for his drawings of them, unlike those of men, are seldom captioned. He married Mary Witherell of Wells, had three children — two sons and a daughter — and died in 1818.

54

41. A political caricature in need of elucidation.
42. (right) Christ Church, Spitalfields, in the early nineteenth century.

4 LOCAL GOVERNMENT IN SPITALFIELDS

Few people penetrate to the vestry of Christ Church, Spitalfields. It is on the first floor of the tower, behind the portico (Pl. 42), and is approached by handsome wooden staircases, to north and south. It is a large room, and an imposing one (Pl. 43). Its walls are part panelled, part lined with ashlar. At either end bolection moulded fireplaces are surmounted by lists of donors to parish charities, painted on the stonework. The room's most impressive feature is

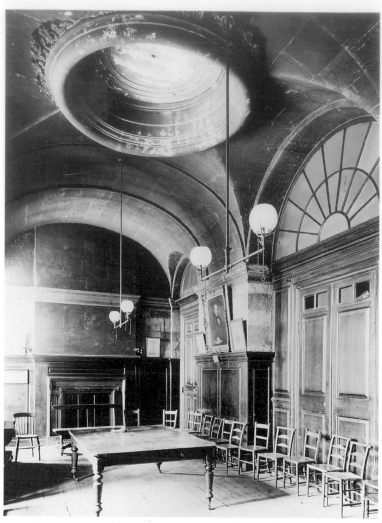

43. The vestry, on the first floor behind the portico at Christ Church.

44. (right) Model of Spitalfields Market House, on the head of the churchwarden's staff, Christ Church.

its ceiling. This takes the form of stone vaults made up of three compartments, a quadripartite vault in the middle and barrel vaults to north and south. The four ribs of the quadripartite vault rise to a circular roundel, carved with flowers and foliage. The carving is in stone, but is inspired by similar roundels on contemporary plaster ceilings — a curious example of a superior material imitating an inferior one.

A room of this pretension was clearly not intended just as a depository for surplices, or even for meetings of the parish council, as such an institution is understood today. Its use is amply documented in the vestry minutes, now in the Bancroft Road branch of Tower Hamlets Public Library. In the eighteenth century Spitalfields, like other town parishes in London and elsewhere, was administered from and by its Vestry. Christ Church was effectively the town hall of Spitalfields, as well as the parish church.

To this the reservation has to be made that the parish of Christ Church, although large, did not include the whole of Spitalfields. Small sections of it formed part of two curious domains, the Liberty of Norton Folgate, and the Precinct of St Mary Spital. The former included Spital Square, Elder Street and most of Folgate (then White Lion) Street — the richest corner of Spitalfields, in fact. It was extra-parochial, and had its own government, all in eight acres. It had its own court-house, charity school and workhouse. It cleaned itself, lit itself, and paved itself. From 1759 it was run by a group of thirty trustees, and patrolled by the constable, beadles and watchmen whom they appointed. The watchmen were based at four sentry boxes, in Elder Street, Folgate Street, Blossom Street and Spital Square. The Liberty also had its own Anglican place of worship. This was a long-demolished chapel erected as a proprietary chapel by Sir Charles Wheeler in 1693. It was in Church (now Nantes) Passage — to confuse matters, just outside the Liberty.

Oddities such as the Liberty of Norton Folgate were common enough in eighteenth-century England. But, in general, local government in areas which were not boroughs was divided between three authorities, the county, the manor and the vestry. In many places, of which Spitalfields was one, the manor had ceased to be of much significance, and the county and vestry were the operative partners; in Spitalfields, for instance, the constable and headboroughs, who had been manorial officers, were appointed to the vestry. There were no county councils; the counties were run by unpaid Justices of the Peace meeting at Quarter Sessions and on the Grand Jury at the Assizes, and by a very small paid staff. In the eighteenth century Spitalfields was in Middlesex. The equivalent of a county hall was, until the 1780s, a converted private mansion in St John's Lane, and after that the imposing new Sessions House, which still stands on Clerkenwell Green.

The Justices combined administrative and judicial functions. Individual Justices committed malefactors for trial, and collectively tried and sentenced them at Petty and Quarter Sessions. But in addition they licensed public houses and were responsible for the building or repair of prisons, roads and bridges, paying for the necessary work by means of a county rate. Maintenance of roads in each parish was supervised by an overseer of the roads, who was appointed by the Justices from a short list drawn up by the relevant vestry.

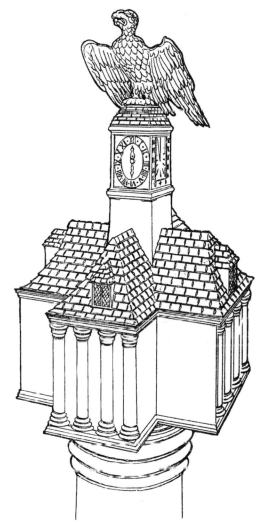

The vestry of Christ Church took over the functions and much of the organisation of what had been known as the hamlet of Spitalfields. Minutes of its meetings are also preserved at Bancroft Road. Until Christ Church was constituted a separate parish in 1729, and Hawksmoor's great church was built, Spitalfields formed part of the enormous parish of St Dunstan's Stepney. This was originally divided into four hamlets, Ratcliffe, Limehouse, Poplar and Mile End; further subdivision created five more, including the hamlet of Spitalfields, which was formed in 1662.

The ratepayers of each hamlet elected a churchwarden, constable, headboroughs, scavengers, who were responsible for cleaning the streets, and overseers of the poor. These officers each served the hamlet for one year, unpaid. Having served, they could continue to come to hamlet meetings and vote there; this larger body formed the hamlet vestry, also known as the 'ancient or ruling persons of the hamlet'.

The area over which they presided was a good deal more than a hamlet in the usual sense of the word. By the 1680s Spitalfields was already largely built up, to the line of Brick Lane and a little beyond it. It was thickly populated, mainly with weavers and members of allied trades; most of these were occupied in the production of woollen cloth, for the silk industry did not take over in Spitalfields until the eighteenth century.

Hamlet meetings were held in a modest and long since demolished building in Crispin Street, known as the town or town hall. There is one physical survivor from hamlet days, in the form of what is now the churchwarden's staff of Spitalfields. This dates from the late seventeenth century and is surmounted by a model in miniature of the original market house in Spitalfields, which was built in 1684 (Pl. 44). The market house seems a curious choice for the decoration of hamlet insignia, for the market was run and owned by private individuals, on the basis of a royal patent, and the hamlet had little, if anything, to do with it. The explanation probably lies in the minutes of a hamlet meeting held on 10 October 1710. They recorded the purchase of a staff with silver head from Thomas Wright, who had been beadle in the hamlet from 1693 to

1709. It was to be handed over from churchwarden to churchwarden for the use of the hamlet. The staff appears to have been Wright's personal property, and it seems possible that he had also served as the constable or overseer in charge of the market.

The new parish of Christ Church was created by an Act of Parliament of 1729. The text of the act was the result of discussions between the Commissioners for Fifty New Churches and a committee set up by the hamlet. The structure of government which ran the parish was similar to that which had run the hamlet, but there were a number of changes. There were two churchwardens, instead of one. The hamlet vestry had been made up of all past and present officers, including scavengers and headboroughs; the parish vestry contained only present and past churchwardens and overseers of the poor — or those who had been elected to these posts and paid a fine to be excused. This was a significant change, for, unlike the scavengers and headboroughs, the churchwardens and overseers had always been chosen from the richer members of the parish. Moreover, while hamlet officers had been elected by the ratepayers, parish officers were appointed, and the gaps in the vestry filled, by the members of the vestry. In short, government of Spitalfields changed from being conducted on a reasonably democratic basis to government controlled by a self-perpetuating body of the richer parishioners.

The parish churchwardens seem of necessity to have been members of the Church of England, but the overseers did not have to be. A substantial number of them were in fact Huguenots. Although some of these may have joined the Christ Church congregation, and others have belonged to Huguenot congregations in communion with the Church of England, it seems likely that others were not. In any case it is clear that Christ Church, at least in its important secular role, was by no means divorced from the life of the Huguenots in the parish, and that substantial numbers of them came up its stairs to vestry meetings.

The composition of the parish government was complex. At the head was the actual vestry, made up of the two churchwardens, the four overseers of the poor and perhaps seventy or eighty vestrymen. Their meetings were recorded and necessary paperwork done by a vestry clerk, a permanent official paid £30 a year; he was appointed

45.   4-6 Fournier Street, house of Peter Campart, master-weaver and treasurer of watch and lamps at the vestry.

by the vestry and not a member of it. From their own numbers the vestry appointed two treasurers, twelve auditors, who did the annual audit, and, from 1753, thirty governors of the workhouse, who were appointed for a year only. They also appointed one constable, nine headboroughs and four scavengers, who were unpaid, not members of the vestry and served for a year only. In addition they appointed the following paid servants: the vestry clerk, two beadles (paid £30 and £12), eighteen watchmen, a lecturer, a surveyor of highways, a master and mistress of the workhouse, a lamplighter, an engineer, a pew opener, an ale-conner, four collectors of watches and lamps, and a joint bellman, cryer and blower for making public announcements through the street (the latter job was sometimes combined with that of junior beadle). The parish also had a paid parish clerk, organist, sexton and surgeon-cum-apothecary. These seem to have been elected by the ratepayers, rather than by the vestry, although the vestry set up and supervised the elections.

The vestry's secular income came from rents from its own considerable property; from fines levied on ratepayers refusing office, which amounted to a sizeable sum; and from the poor rates, scavenger rates, and

watch and lighting rates. There was a treasurer of rents and fines, and, from 1738, a treasurer of watching and lighting, both appointed by the vestrymen from their own members. The two treasurers were the officers who carried most weight in the vestry, because theirs were long-term rather than annual appointments, unlike all the others, from that of churchwarden downwards.

The treasurer of rents and fines was John Peck until 1748 or 1749, when he died and was replaced by Thomas Jervis. The treasurer of watch and lamps was Peter Campart until 1752, when he was succeeded by John Sabatier. John Peck was the son of Edward Peck, a rich dyer who, being both a vestryman and a member of the Commission for Building Fifty New Churches, had acted as the chief go-between to the hamlet and Commission when the parish was formed and the church built. His family was given a free pew, in appreciation of his services, and his monument, erected by John, is the finest in the church. The Peck family lived in a big house in Red Lion Street, long since demolished. Jervis was a silk-thrower, and his house in White's Row still survives (Pl. 46). Campart was a Huguenot weaver, and lived in 4-6 Fournier Street, then as now one of the finest houses in the parish (Pl. 45). Sabatier,

59

46. White's Row, home of Thomas Jervis, silk-thrower and treasurer of rents and fines at the vestry.

another rich Huguenot weaver, lived at 16 Princelet Street until 1755, and then in a house later remodelled as a public house (now the Ten Bells), at the west end of Fournier Street.

Apart from these, a dozen or so vestrymen occur again and again in the vestry minutes, attending meetings or sitting on various bodies, trusts or committees; together with those already named they formed the inner group which ran the parish. Among them were Samuel Worrall, who built many of the new houses in the district and whose own house still survives in what was probably his building yard, between Fournier and Princelet Streets; and Nicholas Jourdain, a mercer and director of the French Protestant Hospital, who lived in one of the two finest houses in Artillery Lane — not the one with the magnificent shopfront, but its neighbour.

In the adjacent parish of Bethnal Green the vestry continued to be elected by the ratepayers, many of whom were immigrants who spoke little or no English. By the end of the eighteenth century a Tammany Hall situation had arisen, and the parish was run by one man, Joseph Merceron, and his family; he owned all the beer shops in the parish and packed vestry meetings with his supporters, who shouted down opposition. The small self-perpetuating oligarchy of Spitalfields was never dominated by one person, and its rule in the eighteenth century does not seem to have been corrupt, though it was probably inefficient. Serious charges of corruption were first raised in the 1820s, when the church was restored; it was claimed in the local press that the vestry was giving the work to its own members, and borrowing the necessary funds from them at excessively high interest.

Vestry meetings took place approximately every fortnight, and were attended by between twenty and fifty people. A good many vestrymen seldom, if ever, came to the meetings, which took place in the vestry room. They were kept warm by the two fireplaces, which from 1751 were fitted with stoves, replaced in 1842 by the existing open cast-iron grates. Some eighteenth-century parish vestries were accused of doing themselves too well at the expense of the ratepayers, but this does not seem to have been the case in Spitalfields. In 1729 the hamlet had laid down that 'no dinner or entertainment whatever be provided at the expense of the town'; by 1830 'refreshments' were being provided at the quarterly meeting to set the poor rate (which took all day), and once a year the treasurer, churchwardens and auditors were given £10 towards a dinner at the annual audit.

Vestry business was divided into four main sections: church business, the poor, cleaning, and lighting and watching. Church business included repair and alterations to the fabric of the church, appointment of church officials and a variety of miscellaneous matters, often of a minor nature. On 31 October 1750, for instance, it was ordered that 'for the future Mr Day take the care of all the surplices and clean the same', and likewise that 'Mrs Rue shall have the care of the plate for the future, and that she clean the same'. On 29 May 1752 it was ordered that one of the beadles was to attend at each end of the church during divine service in order to prevent the boys misbehaving themselves. The vestry also supervised the important business of appointing the lecturer, a clergymen who assisted the vicar, and the organist. Once appointed, however, their positions seem to have been automatically renewed year after year. In April 1748 the vestry reduced the amount of music that the organist was required to

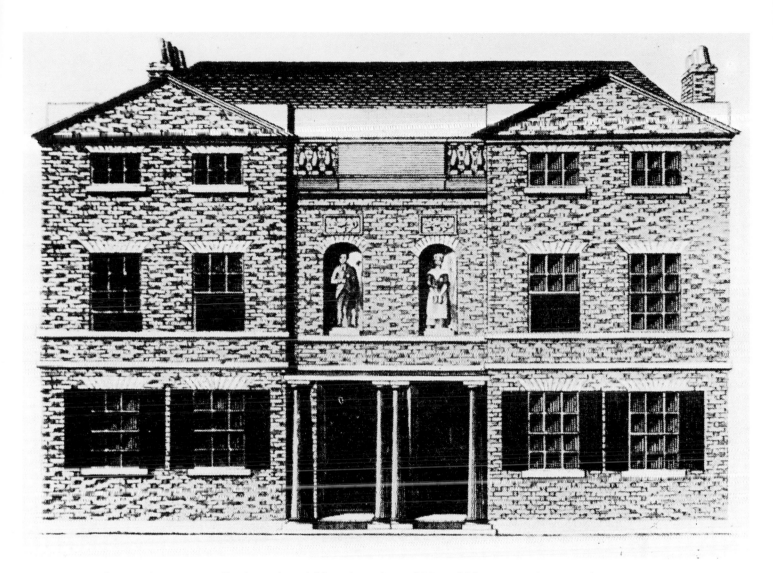

play, and correspondingly reduced his salary from £30 to £20 a year; the organist, William Desanthans, resigned in protest.

Owing to the vestry's curious combination of ecclesiastical and secular authority, all these ecclesiastical decisions were made by a body of mixed Church of England and Nonconformist members. It may be that, when such decisions were under discussion, the Nonconformist members did not participate, but there is no indication of this in the minutes.

Care of the poor was one of the oldest and most important functions of parishes throughout England; in Spitalfields setting the poor rate was a significant quarterly event, and the lists of householders from whom it was collected formed the basis on which all other rates were paid. The rate was collected by the four annually appointed overseers of the poor. It was used to pay the salary of a surgeon-apothecary, whose main business seems to have been setting broken limbs. It paid for outdoor relief and, on and off, for a workhouse. It may have been used to maintain the parish almshouses in Crispin Street, and the parish charity school, which, from 1772 until its demolition in 1851, was a charming building in Red Lion Street (Pl. 47); it then moved to a new schoolhouse in Brick Lane, which still exists.

47. Spitalfields Parish Charity School, in Red Lion Street.

Spitalfields had serious problems of poverty. The Georgian houses which are its pride today were where its richer parishioners lived: silk merchants, master weavers, mercers, superior builders, professional people and so on. They were the filling, which has survived when its setting of far more numerous tenements and cottages has long since disappeared. The latter were largely inhabited by working weavers, all but a small proportion of whom were unskilled, badly paid, and likely to be laid off without compunction when trade was slack.

From 1726 to 1743 the parish workhouse was in Bell Lane. In 1743 it was closed, by unanimous vote of the vestry. Ten years later a new workhouse was built, under a special Act of Parliament passed in 1753. Its site was on what is now Vallance Road, outside the bounds of the parish. It was run by a master and mistress, under a committee made up of churchwardens, overseers of the poor and thirty governors appointed by the vestry out of its members.

In 1754 there was an unsavoury disagreement between the vestry and the governors as to the rations to be allowed to workhouse inmates. The rations originally decided on by the governors were cut down by the vestry. The original Sunday supper allowance, for instance, of four ounces of bread, two ounces of cheese, one ounce of butter and a pint of beer was reduced to one of four ounces of bread (and three for children under twelve) an ounce of cheese, no butter and a pint of beer (and half a pint for children). In December a deputation from the workhouse complained that an allowance of two ounces of bread and one ounce of cheese was inadequate, and humbly prayed that it be increased to the original level. Their request was allowed, but otherwise the cuts seem to have remained. At some stage an attempt seems to have been made to set the inmates to some kind of industrial work. An advertisement or the master in 1773 specified 'a man and his wife, or a single man. They must have no family and thoroughly understand the silk manufacture.'

Street cleaning in both hamlet and parish was the responsibility of four scavengers, chosen annually by the vestry from the ratepayers, and was paid for by a special scavenger rate, which they collected. The hamlet owned its own horses and carts, but under the vestry the service was contracted out to two rakers. These were paid £160 a year each, a substantial sum which suggests that they each employed their own workforce. The service was responsible for cleaning the streets but not for the removal of night soil or household rubbish; for this, individual householders had to make private arrangements with firms of 'night men and rubbish carters'. There was no system for draining sewage. The street drains, where they existed, took surface water only and were installed by the Tower Hamlets Commission of Sewers, a body quite separate from the parish vestry.

The job of scavenger carried no prestige. It often seems to have been imposed on new arrivals to the parish. In 1718, under the hamlet, it was ordered that Mr Jefferies, the ale-conner, 'do attend the two scavengers that can neither read, nor write, nor speak English'. This was for their tour of the hamlet to collect the scavenger rate. In 1753 the beadle was ordered to perform a similar service 'by reason Mr Chiddick cannot read or write, and Mr de Lorme cannot speak English'.

Both hamlet and parish were responsible for lighting and policing (or, as it was called at the time, watching) the area, but fulfilled their responsibilities inadequately.

Policing was the responsibility of the constable and headborough. 'Lamp money' was collected, but it is not clear on what basis. In 1738 the parish obtained a special Act of Parliament, on the grounds that both lighting and watching were ineffective. The Act enabled the vestry to raise a special rate, and laid down its powers. The rate was levied by four collectors of the watch and lamps, appointed annually from vestry members, and was administered by a permanent treasurer.

The watch consisted of twelve watchmen, supervised by the constable and headboroughs. Their headquarters was on the ground floor of the town hall in Crispin Street. Each watchman spent three-quarters of an hour on duty and three-quarters off, throughout the night. They patrolled the parish in pairs on three beats. The aim was 'that every inhabitant may have a watchman at their door every three quarters of an hour'. In 1754 the number of watchmen was increased to eighteen, and six watch stands were set up, distributed through the parish, as in the Liberty of Norton Folgate.

The vestry had no judicial powers; wrongdoers, if apprehended, had to be taken before a Justice (a number of the vestrymen were always also J.P.s). On 29 August 1749, for instance, it was reported that one of the watchmen, Jacob Godfrey, 'was about 2 o'clock on Sunday morning last assaulted and violently beaten on Wheeler Street by a great number of men as he was going his round'. Four of the mob were arrested, carried before a Justice, and committed to prison for trial.

The vestry minutes do not make it clear how the four men were arrested; probably, as was often the case in Georgian London, local residents lent a hand. Street security must have been improved by the higher standards of street lighting introduced by the new Act, even if these were far below those which followed the introduction of gas in about 1820. The parish was lit by 235 lamps, each supplied 'with double spouts and not less than 20 threads of cotton in each spout, and with good oil'. The lamps were almost certainly bracketed to street frontages, rather than set on standards. The lighting service was contracted out; in August 1743, for instance, Moses Smith agreed with the vestry to light the parish for 27 shillings a lamp.

The parish also had its own fire engines, in the form of a 'hand engine' and a 'great engine'. They were kept next door to the charity school and looked after by a parish employee grandly called the 'engineer'. The minutes for 26 December 1753 record 'Mr Robert Day to be engineer of the parish, to take out the engines twice a quarter and play them, to be paid 2 guineas a year, and 10s 6d per fire' over and above what was laid down by the Act of Parliament.

The state of the streets and pavements in Spitalfields was one of the least satisfactory features of the parish. Roads were inadequately maintained by the overseer of the roads, out of the county rate. Pavements, if they existed at all, were installed, maintained and cleaned by the owners of the properties opening on to them. To remedy the situation a further private Act was passed in 1772. But the Act covered much more than roads; it caused a basic shift in the system of local government in Spitalfields. It was for 'paving, cleansing, lighting, watching and regulating' the parish, and also for paving and regulating parts of Brick Lane that were not in the parish. It took over the duties of the scavenger and the watch and lamps committees, as well as of the overseer of roads. The Act empowered the levying of a special paving rate, and the borrowing of £14,000 (later increased to £16,000) on the security of it. The borrowing power was important; improvements both in Spitalfields and elsewhere had been constricted by the inability to borrow adequate sums. All the streets in the parish, and also the main courts and passages, were to be paved, but inhabitants were still responsible for sweeping the footway before their own houses. A clause giving powers for numbering the houses suggests that they had not been numbered before.

Both the descriptive parts of the Act and the prohibitions in it give a vivid picture of the condition of the streets at the time. They describe how the squares, streets, courts and yards of Spitalfields are 'not properly paved, nor sufficiently cleansed, and are in general obstructed by sundry nuisances' — especially Brick Lane, 'a great thoroughfare for carriages, and the only convenient one from the waterside, through White-Chapel to Spitalfields, Mile End New Town, Bethnal Green, Shoreditch, and parts adjacent' (Commercial Street was not formed until the 1850s). The Act gave powers to remove trees, signs, sign-posts, sign-irons, dyers' racks, dyers' scourers and barbers' poles, porches, penthouses, boards and encroaching spouts and gutters. Anyone emptying a boghouse or taking away night soil outside the hours of midnight and four in the morning (or five in winter) could be taken to court. A strengthening Act of 1788 added penalties for slaughtering cattle in streets or public places, keeping swine in the parish, and allowing cattle or swine to wander in the streets. Other street activities prohibited were cleaning casks, hewing wood, shoeing horses, setting up oranges, cocks, pigeons or fowl to be thrown at, making bonfires, letting off or throwing squibs, serpents, rockets or fireworks, exposing wood, coals, greens, fruit or fish for sale, putting up stalls or stools, hanging up beasts, swine or sheep or leaving carriages in the streets.

The responsibility for carrying out the Act of 1772 was not given to the vestry, but to fifty-nine named commissioners, in addition to the rector and churchwardens. Some of the commissioners were grandees who owned substantial areas of the parish but did not live in it, like Viscount Folkestone and Sir George Osborne. But the remainder were local people of repute, most and perhaps all of whom were vestrymen. Meetings were to be held 'in the vestry room or other places'. Meetings of six or more commissioners were empowered to fill gaps, but only with vestrymen or resident proprietors.

The new commission was closely tied up with the vestry, but it was not the vestry; it was an even smaller and equally self-perpetuating body that continued to pave, light, clean and watch the parish until the newly formed Borough of Stepney took over its powers in 1900. The only secular responsibility left to the vestry was care of the poor, and it lost that as a result of the Poor Law Act of 1834. From then on it concerned itself with church affairs only. During the last war the vestry room fell into disuse along with the rest of the church. It has recently had a gratifying resurrection as the office and meeting place of the Friends of Christ Church.

48. (right) Looking up from the harbour to St. Mary's, Whitby.

5 'WHAT A PLACE IS WHITBY GROWN'

Some towns, such as Bath and Nancy, have a perfection which is the result of design. Others have grown unself-consciously to fulfil a particular function which derives from their site. Whitby is in the second class. There is no other town in England so wholly and happily related to its setting, or the setting of which is so obviously the reason for its existence. It grows out of its harbour, and up the surrounding hills, as inevitably as the greenery grows round an oasis. This lovely natural fit makes visiting and walking round it a continual delight. But to say 'fishing' or 'whaling', as many visitors do, and leave it at that, does not do justice to the complexity of its story.

The town was at its peak roughly between 1750 and 1820. It is far older than that, as the three buildings on its skyline (Pl. 48) make clear: the ruins of the Benedictine abbey church, which loom over the town in skeleton majesty from almost every viewpoint; the long low mass

49. Prospect of Whitby town and harbour, by E. Niemann, *c.* 1850.

of Abbey House, next door to the abbey ruins; and the squat comfortable tower and bulk of the parish church, closer to the cliff above the harbour.

The abbey was originally founded in the seventh century, as a double monastery for men and women, was destroyed by the Danes in 867 and refounded, for men only, by the Benedictines in the late eleventh century. It was probably for convenience that the monks built close to the natural harbour formed by the mouth of the River Esk; but it remains mysterious why they chose a sensational but cruelly exposed cliff-top site, in preference to a more sheltered one down by the water. The first non-religious settlement may have grown up on the high ground by the abbey, to service the abbey community and the surrounding farms. A stone cross, the shaft of which stands before the abbey front, was perhaps a market cross. This would explain why the parish church is where it is, next to the abbey and Abbey House but to nothing else, separated by 199 stone steps from the town down by the water. By early on in the Middle Ages, the town's centre of gravity had shifted to the harbour, and the main lines of its present street pattern had been established. Unlike its neighbour, Scarborough, it did not become a borough with its own Members of Parliament and independent corporations. Medieval abbeys were always jealous of any attempts at independence by the towns which grew up at their doorstep. The abbots of Whitby not only owned most of the town but effectively ran it, by means of the manorial court, of which they appointed the steward.

When the abbey was dissolved in 1539, its buildings and most of its lands were acquired by Sir Richard Cholmley, a cousin of the Cholmondeleys of Cheshire. In terms of power and position, the Cholmleys took over where the monks left off. They became lords of the manor of Whitby, and built a house for themselves, next to the abbey and out of its materials. The last portion to be built was the former entrance range, the blocked windows of which now stare in sightless splendour across a forecourt of tangled vegetation. This range was built in the 1670s by Sir Hugh Cholmley, and possibly designed by him as well. In 1663 he had been appointed surveyor-general of Tangiers, during its short period as an English possession. Between 1663 and 1672 he resided mainly at Tangiers, building a great mole round the harbour there with the help of Whitby masons.

The roof of Hugh Cholmley's building was blown off in a gale in 1774, and never replaced. Howsham Hall, near Malton, which came into the family by marriage in the 1770s, became its main residence. The Cholmleys may have preferred a snug inland seat to one exposed to the North Sea gales. But perhaps another reason for abandoning Abbey House was that they were not as great a people in Whitby as they had been. Most of their property in the town had been let on thousand-year leases in the mid-seventeenth century; the powers of the manorial court were gradually taken over by commissions the members of which were appointed by Parliament; and although the Cholmley of the day was always represented on these, they were effectively run by the leading citizens of what had become a booming and self-confident little town.

The abbey was ignored by the town and gradually fell to pieces (the great central tower finally collapsed in 1830). Abbey House was reduced to a shadow of its former self. The town prospered. In 1547 John Leland had described it as a 'great fisher town'. He exaggerated its size: its population was perhaps 1,500 people. But a fishing

68

town was essentially what it was. By 1816 the population had risen to over 10,000, but the town contained only nine fishermen.

The fishing industry had migrated to Staiths, Runswick and Robin Hood's Bay. The Whitby seamen had found bigger fish to fry and gone off after whales rather than herrings. This was only part of the story. The early whalers were adventurous and intrepid people, and it is not surprising that whaling has captured the imagination of the local people and visitors, while the less romantic coal trade has been forgotten. Coal came first at Whitby, however, and was economically more important.

The coal trade was closely connected with the local alum industry. Alum, which was used as a fixative for vegetable dyes, was of the first importance in the textile industry, the main industry of Europe. Up to the end of the sixteenth century, supplies came mostly from mines in Asia Minor and from near Rome, in the Papal States. In about 1590 Sir Thomas Chaloner of Guisborough, near Whitby, discovered alum on his property, and is said to have smuggled alum-workers in barrels out of the Papal States to work it. For two hundred years alum works flourished in the area around Guisborough and Whitby. They brought much prosperity to local landowners, the Cholmleys among them, and to Whitby mariners. Coal for smelting the alum was carried to the alum works from Newcastle and Sunderland, and the refined product was exported out of Whitby to ports all over Europe.

According to Lionel Charlton, whose history of Whitby was published in 1779, Whitby ships first got into the coal business because of the alum, and then expanded and built up a carrying trade all down the coast to London 'whither nobody belonging to Whitby before that time had ever gone without first making their wills'. At any rate, by 1700 Whitby had a useful fleet of ships, carrying goods of all kinds but above all coal: coal for the alum works and even more coal, in bigger ships, to feed the insatiable demands of London. Whitby vessels figured prominently among the swarms of colliers which queued up to take in coal from the Newcastle staiths, and queued up again to unload it outside London's principal dock at Billingsgate: coal was as important as fish at Billingsgate in the eighteenth and nineteenth centuries. In 1702-4 Whitby had the third largest number of ships engaged in the Newcastle coal trade, with 98 ships as compared to Yarmouth's 211 and London's 168. It was in colliers, not in whalers, that Whitby's best-known citizen, Captain Thomas Cook, gained his seafaring experience in the 1740s and early 1750s. When Cook mounted his three expeditions to the South Seas in 1768-79, he insisted on using Whitby-built ships. The shipping industry there had generated a ship-building industry. The first man to build sizeable ships in the town was the elder Jarvis Coates. He was living in Whitby by the 1690s, and some time in the first decades of the eighteenth century constructed two shipyards above the town on the west side of the Esk, near where the railway station is today. Other yards followed, on both sides of the river.

The Coates family built a stone-fronted house which still stands in Baxtergate, next to the post office. It is probably a rebuilding, dating from about 1740, of a house bought or built by Jarvis Coates in 1692. But the two grandest houses of mid-sixteenth century Whitby were built by two rich shipowners, John Yeoman and John Addison (Pls. 50, 51). The first is of brick and dates from about 1760, the second is of stone and was built ten or fifteen years later. Addison was active in the coal trade; Yeoman probably made

his money there but also pioneered the whaling industry, and acquired an alum works in 1764. Both made enough money to buy country houses and estates. In addition Yeoman owned the fields above the town on which the resort end of Whitby was to be laid out in the 1850s.

Yeoman's house stands relatively intact in a cul-de-sac off Haggersgate. Its reticent dignity and generous proportions put it on a line with the houses being built in York by the Yorkshire gentry at the same time. Inside, it retains a fine staircase and much original decoration. Addison's house, at the top of Flowergate (now the Working Men's Club) has been less fortunate. Its side façade was remodelled, and the lower half of its entrance front obscured by additions, when it was converted into an hotel in 1869-70; little is left inside. Old photographs show how grand it was — amazingly grand, indeed, for a remote, if prosperous, Yorkshire port.

Nothing is known about the architects. The style of Addison's house has little in common with contemporary Yorkshire houses. Perhaps the architect came from Newcastle? It seems to relate stylistically (in particular, in its idiosyncratic use of rustication) to Airy Hill (Pl. 52), a fine detached house standing in spacious grounds on a hill above the harbour and town. This was built in 1790 for Richard Moorsom, whose family had pioneered the whaling industry along with the Yeomans.

The Coates house originally backed on to the inner harbour, and was a few minutes' walk from the family shipyards. John Yeoman lived just off the quay of the outer harbour, and had a sideways view down to its waters. The harbour was what Whitby was all about (Pl. 53). It was and is divided into two halves by its bridge, a swing bridge today, a drawbridge in the eighteenth century. The shipyards and dry docks were in the inner harbour, where the ships laid up in the winter months. Like most harbours, it needed constant maintenance and improvement to keep it a working entity. A series of Acts of Parliament, passed from 1702 onwards, set up a body of trustees and from at least 1781, a resident engineer.

The post was filled by a southerner, Jonathan Pickernell, from 1781 to his death in 1812, by James Peacock from 1812 to 1822, and by Francis Pickernell, probably Jonathan's grandson, from 1822 until 1871. Jonathan Pickernell was responsible for

50. (top left) House off Haggersgate, built by John Yeoman, shipowner, c. 1760.

51. (bottom left) House in Flowergate, built by John Addison, shipowner, c. 1780. From an old photograph, taken before the front was altered in the late nineteenth century.

52. (above) Airy Hill, on the edge of the town, built in 1790 for Richard Moorsom, shipowner, and perhaps by the same architect as the Addison house.

53. (left) Looking across Whitby harbour.

rebuilding and extending the west pier and for building the quay along the west side of the harbour, today's Marine Parade. The lighthouse at the end of the pier was added by Francis Pickernell in 1831, in the form of a Doric column (Pl. 54).

Jonathan Pickernell also designed the agreeable little Town Hall, built by the market-place, at the expense of Nathaniel Cholmley, in 1788 (Pl. 55). The open ground floor served as a covered market, the room above for the meetings of the Improvement Commissioners. These were appointed under Acts of Parliament of 1764 and 1789, and under them Whitby reached its apogee.

> What a place is Whitby grown
> Once but a poor fisher town.

So John Twistleton, a local barber, wrote in about 1765, and went on to describe the changes. The plaster and thatch of its houses had given way to red brick or stone, pantiles and sash windows; its ships had doubled in number; its shipowners and sea captains rode in coaches and wore coats decked out with gold and silver lace; it now had masquerades, balls, a playhouse and a Wesleyan chapel.

> So, as you choose, may spend your time
> In carnal pleasure or divine.

Twistleton was writing at the very beginning of a period of great prosperity in Whitby. Its population was about 5,000 when he wrote and had doubled by 1816; by the 1820s it was the seventh port in England in terms of the tonnage of its ships; only London, Newcastle, Liverpool, Sunderland, Hull and Whitehaven exceeded it. Its shipbuilding yards grew and prospered, and supplied ports all round England. Its own ships carried coal from Newcastle down the east coast, imported timber from Norway, exported butter and alum to London and the Continent, and ventured to India and America.

Killing whales and transporting soldiers joined carrying coal as its most profitable lines of trade. The first whalers went out from Whitby in the 1750s, but the great days of the trade were between

72

54. The lighthouse designed by Francis Pickernell in 1831.

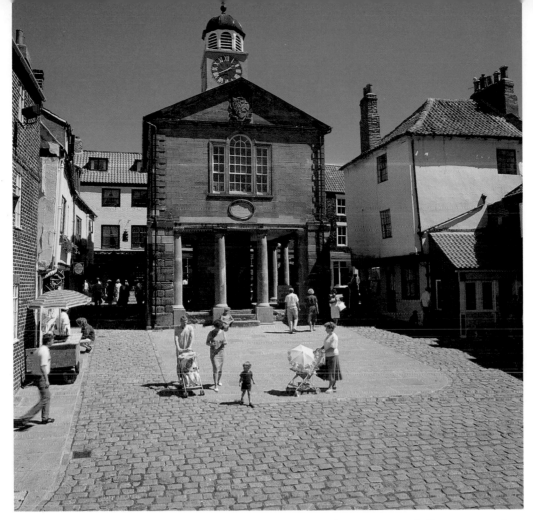

about 1775 and 1815. Whitby never sent out more than twenty whalers a year, less than eight percent of its merchant fleet, but the whalers figured prominently in the life of the town because of the great profits enjoyed by all classes as the result of a successful season, and because, unlike most of the cargoes carried by Whitby ships, the whales came back to Whitby and were processed in the town.

According to Twistleton and others, Whitby ships did best of all by being hired out to the government as transport ships in time of war.

> It was the war, I say, by which
> This place became so vastly rich ...
> Our transport ships, by wind and tide
> Have made our masters swell with pride.

Twistleton is referring to the Seven Years' War of 1756-63. The ensuing American and French wars brought in even more money; looking back from the 1850s, a Whitby historian thought that 'perhaps during the latter years of the [French] war, Whitby, for its size, was one of the richest towns in the kingdom'.

In the seventeenth and eighteenth centuries a large proportion of the town's sea captains and shipowners were Quakers. They lived modestly, dressed simply, and made a lot of money. Their life-style can be savoured today in the unassuming but delightful house in Grape Lane, now beautifully restored as the Captain Cook Museum;

55. The Town Hall, designed by Joseph Pickernell and built in 1788.

it belonged to the Quaker John Walker, to whom Cook was apprenticed, and Cook lodged there in the winter months, when Walker's colliers were laid up. But the Quaker community was periodically split by rows as to whether Quaker-owned ships could carry arms for self-defence. In 1783 thirteen of the most prosperous were expelled from the Meeting. Linskells, Chapmans, Walkers, Simpsons and other Quaker families either left Whitby, or moved to the parish church — and usually to a more expansive way of living.

Although a chapel-of-ease was built down in the town in 1776-8, toiling up 199 steps from the town to the parish church remained Whitby's great weekly ritual, as much social as religious. As the population of the town grew, the church changed and swelled in an effort to keep up with it. Galleries were inserted in 1697, 1700, 1709 and 1758; the north arcade and galleried north aisle were added in 1764; only the Norman chancel survived relatively unaltered.

The Church of England of Georgian days believed that a church should reflect the social order. The parish church became an accurate social map of the town. God and Caesar were represented by its two focal points: the towering three-decker pulpit, and the family pew of the Cholmleys behind it (Pl. 56). The pulpit is still dominant enough, but was even more so as originally erected in 1778, when it terminated the central aisle. The Cholmley pew takes the form of a gallery across the chancel arch, supported on barley-sugar columns and gaily decorated with winged cherubs' heads, all of about 1690.

Pulpit and pew together effectively blotted out the chancel in a way that would be unthinkable today. One should remember, however, that in the eighteenth century the chancel was used only for the communion service. The main service was conducted from the various levels of the pulpit. The vicar in the pulpit was the star performer in a religious theatre, surrounded by his audience in the stalls and galleries. As in a theatre, seats were graded and the better ones were paid for. The poor were in the free seats, stacked round the periphery or at the back of the galleries. The middling people were in plain pews of unpainted oak or painted deal. The upper crust had spacious pews lined with green or red baize, with their names painted on the door. A similar hierarchy catered for the dead. Inside the church, the Cholmleys had elegant monuments of coloured marbles, by the York statuary John Fisher; respectable wall tablets were inscribed with the names of the shipbuilding and shipowning occupants of the larger pews; the rest were out in the churchyard. Here on a great wind-swept, cliff-top sward of grass and stone suspended above the town and harbour, the Whitby dead line up against a backcloth of sea and sky. The inscriptions on the rows of headstones and

56. Inside St Mary's Parish Church.

tomb-chests have been largely effaced by winter gales. Occasional sentences — 'died at sea', 'lost in the storm of 1785', 'lost in Greenland' — survive to show the debit side of Whitby's prosperity (Pl. 57).

One can look down from the graveyard and see how the social make-up of late-Georgian Whitby is reflected in the plan of the town as well as in that of its church. Immediately down below are the harbour and the tangled pantiles of the old town; in the distance the long lines of two terraces snake out of the town into greenery. By 1820 Whitby's upper crust had nearly all moved out of the centre, either to free-standing houses in large grounds outside the town, such as Airy Hill, or into the two terraces. These, unlike the terraces later built for summer visitors, resolutely ignored the sea. They were built along one side of the Bagdale valley, formed by a stream which ran down behind the town into the Esk. The lower terrace was actually called Bagdale, the upper one was originally known as New Buildings, and is now St Hilda's Terrace. St Hilda's was socially as well as geographically more elevated than Bagdale, but both were, and still are, very pleasant places (Pl. 58).

Building started in about 1780, and was completed by 1816. The houses were built in continuous rows, but not to a unified design. Only a few are stone fronted; oddly

57. Looking across the graveyard of St Mary's to the George Hudson terraces on the West Cliff.

enough, although excellent stone was quarried in the Whitby area, brick was the dominant material in the late eighteenth and early nineteenth centuries. Nothing is known about the builders or architects (if any) who built the houses, and not much about the entrepreneurs who laid out and developed the land. Both terraces had unusual formats: handsome gates and gate-piers, long front gardens leading to the houses, back access roads, and occasional stabling and further gardens on the other side of the back roads.

Meanwhile, a very different world was developing in the old town. Although shopkeepers and a few prosperous lawyers and bankers continued to live above their work, for instance, and some agreeable, modest, middle-class houses were erected (Pl. 59), off the main streets the town was transformed to accommodate growing numbers of sailors, dockers, and workers in shipyards, sail-factories and rope-walks, who lived off the harbour, and needed to be near it.

The result was as distinctive, in its own way, as the snug galleried world of the parish church, or the new terraces rising above their gardens. Big old houses were converted into tenements, and their back gardens built over with housing and workshops. All along the

streets archways opened into long narrow yards, with houses on either side looking into them, often built back to back with a similar arrangement in the adjoining yard (Pl. 60). Occasionally, a wider plot became available and was developed a little differently. Prospect Place, above Church Street and the inner harbour, consists of two longish parallel terraces, built very close together along the contour lines; access is by a steep flight of steps, which climb up through the houses and end in a massive stone wall, originally one side of Boulby's rope-walk. The terraces were built in 1816 by Gideon Smales, house and ship carpenter, dealer in timber and tiles, and block, mast and pump merchant.

A detailed plan of Whitby published from a survey by John Wood in 1828 shows how crammed and teeming with humanity it was then (Pl. 61). The yards spread up the steep slopes behind the houses on Church Street, south of the harbour, and all through the old town to the north of it. Many ended, or were approached, by precipitous flights of steps; many were linked at both ends to streets, so that cumulatively they formed an intricate network of pedestrian ways, running all through the town. Exploring what is left of them is one of the pleasures of visiting Whitby. A good deal was demolished as a result of slum-clearance in the 1950s and 1960s. Although the housing that replaced it was designed with considerable feeling for the character of the town, too much went that could have been preserved and brought up to acceptable standards.

Down below the yards, along the water's edge, ships' masts towered above the houses, and their bowsprits and figureheads pushed out over Church Street and the quays; the shipyards echoed with hammering; the whale sheds (the trusses of which were often made of whales' jawbones) stank out the town when the blubber was being boiled down. But Whitby also began to develop another industry and to cater for summer visitors. One common accompaniment of a late-Georgian resort appeared in 1826, when a combined bathhouse and subscription library was opened on Marine Promenade; the top floor accommodated the museum of the fledgling Whitby Literary and Philosophical Society, which had been founded in 1823. The building (today the Harbour Café) was built and designed by John Bolton, who first appears, as a

77

58. (top left) Bagdale and St Hilda's Terrace, where Whitby's upper crust lived in the late eighteenth and nineteenth centuries.
59. (bottom left) Late eighteenth-century houses in Cliff Street.
60. (bottom right) One of the many courts letting off Church Street.
61. The Church Street area of Whitby. Detail from the plan by John Wood published in 1828.

stonemason, in a Whitby directory of 1793. In the 1920s both Museum and Society moved up the hill to the neighbourhood of St Hilda's Terrace, where they still flourish.

But the resort was first effectively put on the map by George Hudson, the great railway promoter. In 1848 he bought land on West Cliff above the town and the harbour, and started to lay it out with a grid of terraces, and a crescent looking out to sea. His architect was John Dobson, of Newcastle. The development was tied up with the coming of Hudson's York and North Midland Railway to Whitby, and the opening in 1847 of an elegant little railway station down by the river. It was badly hit by Hudson's financial collapse in 1849. Only half the crescent and perhaps two-thirds of the intended layout were ever completed. As a resort Whitby never did as well as Scarborough; in the years around 1800 it had been a bigger and more prosperous place than its neighbour and rival, but the population of Scarborough had overtaken Whitby's by 1830, and continued to grow, while Whitby's remained relatively static.

Whitby suffered from the collapse of the alum and whaling industries; chemical dyes and mineral oils made alum and whale oil redundant. Its harbour was too small for big new ships. However, its ship-yards went over from building wooden hulls to building iron and steel ones; the fishing industry had a revival; the tourist industry ticked over; mourning Victorians bought large quantities of Whitby jet, mined locally and worked in Whitby workshops. There are plenty of agreeable Victorian buildings in Whitby, including the delightful Seamen's Hospital on Church Street, an early work of Gilbert Scott (Pl. 62).

Whitby managed to adapt and remain moderately prosperous into this century. Today it is once more at a turning point. Commercial activity in its harbour is down to a trickle, and its tourist season is neither long enough nor paying enough to support it. The town is purpose-built to fit an economy and way of life that no longer exist but have left it with an individuality which is its main asset. It faces a formidable but not impossible challenge: how to put new life into an old frame, and revive its economy without losing its soul.

78

62. The new building of the Seamen's Hospital, built to the design of G.G. Scott in 1842.
63. (right) Cromer, by John Nash, c. 1922.

6 THE BIRTH OF A SEASIDE RESORT

The decline and resurrection of Cromer make a curious story. The double town of Shipden-with-Cromer was a flourishing small port and fishing town in the Middle Ages. Then the sea gradually ate it up. Shipden, which was probably on low ground by the beach, vanished entirely, and its church with it. The crumbling remains of the church survived under water and split open and sank a pleasure steamer in 1888. The sea, having devoured Shipden, started to work its way into Cromer on the higher ground, and the houses gradually tumbled down the tall soft cliffs of chalk and sand. Much of the town, and all its prosperity, disappeared.

Defoe, visiting what he called 'this dangerous coast' in 1724, remarked: 'I know nothing it is famous for except good lobsters.' The great Perpendicular Gothic church, with its noble tower, built for more flourishing days, fell into disrepair and its chancel collapsed. The sea would have got to it in the end; but the town's renaissance in the nineteenth century paid for massive sea walls and breakwaters, and the receding cliff line receded no further. Cromer was left with what remains its dominant image: the church with a cluster of houses round it high up on the cliff edge above the sea, the jetty (and later the pier) and the wide and apparently endless sands (Pl. 64).

It was these sands which put Cromer back on the map. As soon as sea-bathing became fashionable in the late eighteenth century, Cromer was bound to attract summer visitors. Apart from its beaches, the gentle hills, spacious vistas and rich woods of north-east Norfolk made up the kind of landscape that appealed to Georgian eyes; bathing could be interspersed with expeditions in search of the picturesque and visits to the numerous local country houses; the sea itself was far from warm, but then sea bathing in its early days was undertaken for health rather than pleasure.

The attractions of Cromer were offset by the difficulty of getting to it. Until the railway came, Cromer was of necessity frequented almost entirely by Norfolk people, which meant, in effect, by a mixture of Norfolk country gentry and the more prosperous citizens of Norwich. As a result, the nineteenth-century history of Cromer falls into two sections, before and after the railways: three-quarters of a century of modest growth as an old-fashioned fishing village where a small but faithful (and rather rich) clientele built houses or passed the summer; and a far quicker blossoming into a full-scale, and, for various reasons, intensely fashionable seaside resort in the 1880s and 1890s. The population figures (excluding summer visitors) rose as follows: 676 in 1801, 1,229 in 1841, 1,597 in 1881, and 3,781 in 1901.

There are plenty of descriptions and drawings of pre-railway Cromer, and surviving photographs of the 1880s and 1890s show it before the railway boom had made much difference to the centre of the town. The narrow back streets remained — and in some cases still remain; along the sea front were hotels, lodging-houses, and the occasional holiday houses of the gentry, all of the most agreeable, unpretentious character,

64. Looking along the beach to Cromer church and pier.
65. (top right) The entrance to Jetty Street in about 1890.
66. (bottom right) The original Hotel de Paris seen from the old jetty.

with bow and oriel windows looking out to sea (Pl. 65). The oldest hotel was
Tucker's, next to the church, with an extension on the beach. Above the jetty was the
Hotel de Paris (Pl. 66), which originally belonged to Lord Suffield, a big local landlord; its name was presumably inspired by its first manager, Pierre Le François. A
series of ramps led down from the hotel front to the wooden jetty. The original jetty
was built in 1822 and washed away in 1836; a storm in 1837 swept away a bath-house
on the beach, and brought down part of the cliff, and a house with it. This was the last
time the sea got at Cromer; a body known as the Cromer Protection Commissioners
was founded in 1844, and a sea wall, esplanade and new jetty were built, all to be
replaced on a larger scale fifty years later.

Jetty Street, leading from the church to the Hotel de Paris and the jetty, survives
little altered, with rows of wooden oriel windows popping out at irregular intervals to
give the houses in the street at least a glimpse of the sea. A little to the east of the jetty
was a way down through the cliffs to the beach, with a row of agreeable houses looking down on the beach, the original lifeboat house (Pl. 67), and the rows of drawn-up
fishing boats. In the daytime visitors swam from bathing machines, or drove their carriages down to promenade on the broad beaches. In the evening they assembled on the
jetty, gossiped, and watched the sun set into the sea. As the guidebooks put it: 'Servants in livery and all common persons are not allowed at this time ... Smoking is not
allowed on the jetty until after nine o'clock in the evening, at which time ladies usually
retire from their evening promenade ... On Sunday the jetty is, with just consideration,
resigned to the inhabitants of the town.'

Prominent on the beach, generous in the town, friendly with everybody but remaining a tight and self-sufficient entity, were a group of families that provided one of
the most curious elements in the history of Cromer. In 1793 John Gurney, of Earlham
outside Norwich, a Quaker philanthropist and banker and father of Elizabeth Fry, the

82

67.   An early photograph of the old lifeguard station, at the east end of the town.

prison reformer, came to Cromer for a holiday with his ten children. They returned at regular intervals, and their banking and brewing relatives came too. At first they only took lodgings, but soon they began to buy or build houses on the edge of the town or in the neighbourhood.

By the mid-nineteenth century a formidable family clan of rich, philanthropic and intensely worthy Gurneys, Hoares, Barclays, Buxtons and Birkbecks owned at least seven roomy houses in Cromer itself, and two in the immediate neighbourhood. They married each other, bought and rented houses from each other, all had enormous families, and moved around in large loving crowds together. They became one of the great inescapable facts of Cromer life.

The ramifications and intermarriages of the clan are baffling to anyone not born into it, and there is no space to describe more than briefly their main connections, in terms of some of their houses. Northrepps Hall in the next village inland from Cromer was rented from Richard Gurney by Sir Thomas Fowell Buxton, the great anti-slavery agitator, who carried Emancipation through Parliament in 1833. He had married John Gurney of Earlham's daughter Hannah, and his two sons owned Colne House and Upton House on the edge of Cromer. Another of John Gurney's daughters, Louisa, had married her cousin Samuel Hoare; her three sons, John Gurney Hoare, Joseph and Francis, lived along the cliffs on the Overstrand side of Cromer, at North Lodge, Cliff House and Weylands. Further along the road to Overstrand, John Gurney's brother Joseph built a house called The Grove in 1795; and the space in between was later filled by The Warren, belonging to Joseph Gurney's grandson Joseph Gurney Barclay, and Herne Close, built by J.G. Barclay's daughter.

Most of the clan had jobs in London or Norwich, and came to their Cromer houses for the holidays. The Gurneys, Barclays and Hoares were bankers; the Buxtons were brewers. They were all originally Quakers, except for the Buxtons; but in the course of the nineteenth century they almost all became pious and active Anglicans.

Cromer suited them to perfection. They enjoyed opportunities for good works and innocent recreation; rather surprisingly, they were passionately fond of shooting. The broad beaches, decayed churches, rich coverts and poor fishing families in and around Cromer gave all these tastes scope, and the fact that Cromer, as contemporary guide-books put it, 'has not the metropolitan luxuries of Brighton ... there are neither ball-room nor card assemblies here', was not a deterrent. Surviving letters and journals give a full picture of the life they led; it does not change very much between the letters of Ricenda Gurney in 1803 and the journals of Ellen Buxton sixty years later. They swam, they rode, they went on picnic excursions, they held Bible readings, and they did everything together. Ricenda Gurney describes a meeting of the relatives: 'It is an uncommonly pretty sight, such a number of young women, and so many, if not pretty, very nice looking ... the ladies were almost all dressed in white gowns, blue sashes, and nothing on the head; after dinner we all stood on a wall, eighteen of us, and it really was one of the prettiest sights I ever saw.'

In 1863 Ellen Buxton describes a Sunday reading at Cliff House ('It was entirely a family party, 33 in all') and a visit to Northrepps House where 'thirty-three parrots and cockatoos came to our windows, and we fed them with bread and butter'. A taste for exotic birds was a somewhat unexpected characteristic of the otherwise unexotic

Buxtons; an old photograph shows emus grazing on the lawn in front of Colne House. The house itself, like all the houses of the cousinhood, was rambling, comfortable, and absolutely without architectural pretensions.

An account of Hannah, Lady Buxton, the widow of the Liberator, at a family gathering at Colne House in 1867, evokes the atmosphere of the cousinhood. 'On the ottoman seat the Dowager, so diminished in size, delicate, refined, in a rich black silk dress, with a shawl of a thin material bordered with white, very feeble but animated, summoning all to come close by her, her hand clasped in that of her dearly beloved son Foxwell, he so gentle, loving, and cordial with her. Then, on chairs and stools of various heights, the grandchildren grouped round her, and beginning at the youngest, each in turn repeated a portion of Scripture or a hymn. Such a sweet party of young life! The four younger daughters of Catherine, Lady Buxton, dressed in pretty white frocks and blue sashes; first Rachel, eleven years old, with long flowing golden hair; Eva, bright in look and voice; Laura, so gentle and sweet, and Catherine, reserved, shy and retiring.'

Between 1880 and 1914 Cromer became the place to go. Rich upper- and upper-middle-class ladies of those days liked to be what is called 'artistic'; and it became fashionable for these smart artistic ladies to take or send their families to Cromer for the summer. On its broad beaches well-born babies were taken for trips in little goat-drawn carts, and thoroughly 'nice' Kate-Greenaway-looking children in jerseys and straw hats paddled and made castles in the sand (Pl. 68). Kate Greenaway herself was

84

68. Beach life at Cromer in the 1880s.

likely to be there, staying (as did Randolph Caldecott) with the Locker-Lampsons at Newhaven Court; her charming drawing of the Lampson children seems to epitomize the Cromer spirit. In 1885 ten-year-old Winston Churchill was sent there with his governess, and wrote to his mother: 'I am not enjoying myself very much. The governess is very unkind, so strict and stiff.' (A few days later he threw an ink pot at her.) In 1887 the infant Compton Mackenzie looked up from the sands and saw 'a beautiful lady in a beige-coloured dress' sitting next to him: 'she had a note book on her knee, in which, after looking out to sea for several minutes she would write a few words, and then gaze out to sea again'. This was the Empress Elizabeth of Austria, on an English holiday.

Oscar Wilde spent a summer outside Cromer in 1892, writing *A Woman of No Importance* in the intervals of playing golf with Lord Alfred Douglas on Cromer golf links; 'I find Cromer,' he wrote, 'excellent for writing, and golf still better.' Another unlikely habitué of the links was J.M. Barrie, not yet delivered of Peter Pan; in 1892 he presented the golf club with a prize putter, to be competed for annually by his own friends. Behind the crazy façades of the Royal Links Hotel, Sir Henry Irving put on two recitations for smoking concerts while staying in the neighbourhood in 1897. Other people one might run into included the ageing Alfred Tennyson, Lord Curzon, Swinburne, Meredith, the Beerbohm Trees, and Ellen Terry, besides duchesses and countesses in plenty. All these celebrities helped to encourage other visitors; and along the cliffs rose big hotels, gay with balconies, cupolas and bay windows, and

69. The bandstand on the pier.

trim comfortable verandah-caparisoned houses of red brick or flint. Finally the inevitable pier shot out from the beach, one hundred feet of walkway with a pavilion at the end (Pls. 64, 69): 'from this stem like a fair flower the head expands', according to the brochure produced for its opening in 1901. Cromer at this period encouraged this kind of language; as a local paper put it in 1888: 'The contemplation of the undulating peaceful country seemed to beget a desire to pass therein a dreamy restful existence, between the highlands and the deep sea.'

The last passage was written in connection with a sale of building land on Lord Suffield's estate at Overstrand, the village next to Cromer. The sale was elaborately stage-managed: a special train from London for prospective buyers, lunch provided in a marquee when they got there, speeches of welcome from Lord Suffield's brother and other local worthies, and then the auctioneer got down to business. Similar and even more elaborate arrangements were made for the two big sales of Cromer building land held by the Bond Cabell estate in 1890 and 1891. The development of Cromer followed a familiar pattern: the ground-landlords promoted it; the local fishermen, tradespeople and hotel-owners were delighted; and the upper middle classes who had settled there when it was little more than a village were furious.

Cromer was a late starter as a popular resort. 'Had the same spirit of speculation in building', fresh editions of the guidebook re-iterated in the 1860s and 1870s, 'existed here as elsewhere, or the same encouragement, at least, been given to it, it is probable that long ere this Cromer would have risen to considerable importance as a bathing place and fashionable resort ... It has, however, been asserted, and perhaps with truth, that this spirit of improvement has been discountenanced on the ground that the moral welfare of the place was promoted by its comparative obscurity and non-intermixture with the idle and corrupted of cities and towns.' The reference is to the clan of Gurneys, Buxtons, Hoares and Barclays, but they could only have kept Cromer small with the support of the ground-landlord, Benjamin Bond Cabell. This London lawyer and M.P. (with a nice bit of property on the Edgware Road) had bought the Cromer Hall estate, and most of Cromer with it, in 1852 for £65,000. It remains surprising that the Gurney cousinhood failed to take the opportunity of the sale to buy Cromer for themselves; they must have regretted it in later years.

Benjamin Bond Cabell died in 1874, aged ninety-three, and left the property to his nephew John. In 1876 the Great Eastern Railway came to Cromer, to a station not very conveniently situated on high ground above the town. In 1877 the Bond Cabell estate prepared an elaborate scheme to sell off building leases for villas between the station and the sea, and for terraces along the cliffs west of the town. It never got off the ground, perhaps because John Bond Cabell died in 1878. But his young son Benjamin Bond Cabell II became an enthusiastic developer of Cromer before his early death, aged thirty-four, in 1892. At a public meeting held in 1888 to discuss the provision of a town hall for Cromer, he announced that 'he did not share the feeling that Cromer should be kept for the few, but thought that it should be for the many'. This was directed, amongst others, at John Henry Buxton, of Upton House, who had opposed the idea on the grounds that 'Visitors came to Cromer as being a place purely of the country, and not a Brighton or a Scarborough.' In the previous year John Gurney Barclay had made a speech against a proposal for a pier below the Red Lion Hotel, 'which would

bring down upon them a large number of excursionists ... Cromer, for the past quarter of a century, had had a constituency of its own — people belonging to the upper class, who came with their horses and carriages, and spent their money here, staying five or six weeks.'

One can scarcely blame the cousinhood for objecting; the fact that Cromer was a small place was the reason they had settled there to begin with. But there was little they could do about it. The (extremely modest) town hall was built in 1889-90. In 1889 the Midland and Great Northern Railway came in to Cromer Beach Station, immediately behind the cliffs to the west of the town; in 1890 and 1891 Benjamin Bond Cabell sold two big plots of land freehold between the new station and the sea. They were immediately covered with new lodging houses (Pl. 70), and the town acquired four big hotels in quick succession: the Grand Hotel (1890-1) on the West Cliffs, the Metropole (1893-4) and rebuilt Hotel de Paris (1894-5) in the old town, and the Royal Links Hotel (1892-5) by the golf club. But, after all, the 'many' who all this attracted were not many, and of what would have been called at the time 'superior character'.

The smart-artistic atmosphere which Cromer acquired in these decades was due to a number of causes. Prominent among them were two families whom the new railways brought to Cromer from London in the 1880s. In 1883-4 the Locker-Lampsons built Newhaven Court on high ground above the Norwich road out of Cromer. Frederick Locker-Lampson ('One does not notice his affected way of talking when one is used to him', a guest wrote) was financed by a rich wife, and had a very small gift for poetry and a very large gift for friendship; he knew all the best people in society and the arts, and a good many of them came to stay or visit at the Red Lodge. In 1888 Lord Suffield persuaded his and the Locker-Lampsons' friend Cyril Flower (later Lord Battersea, and

87

70. A late-Victorian terrace off the West Cliff.

married to a Rothschild) to buy and greatly enlarge a small house at Overstrand, to the designs of the young Lutyens. The elegantly aesthetic Cyril Flower ('artists are perpetually painting him. Bootmakers call to borrow his boots as models') was a discriminating, not to say compulsive, patron of Burne-Jones and other artists, and he and his wife were as dedicated to entertaining as the Locker-Lampsons. Their house, The Pleasaunce, became the first of a group of summer houses built by smart Londoners at Overstrand. All the best late-Victorian visitors to Cromer visited (or, better still, stayed) at The Pleasaunce and Newhaven Court, and drove inland to see Constance, Lady Lothian, at Blickling and admire her white cattle, white ponies, white pigeons and white peacocks, for this high-born, artistic dowager is said to have allowed only white animals on her estate.

Lord Suffield's Overstrand estate extended to the fringes of Cromer, where he presented the land on which Cromer Golf Links were laid out in 1887-8, and persuaded his friend the Prince of Wales to become its patron. It was a generous gesture but perhaps not entirely disinterested, because the Royal Cromer Golf Club attracted many visitors to Cromer, and a big hotel and the select Suffield Park estate were built in its neighourhood. Clement Scott, the Victorian theatre critic and journalist, has a nice description of Cyril Flower and Lord Suffield, the former 'clad in white samite, as mystic and wonderful as he can be, with a bath towel round his neck, or a camera slung on his back', the latter 'laying out imaginary terraces and Queen Anne villa residences' with his faithful solicitor in attendance.

Clement Scott can himself be included, along with the railways, the ground-land-lords, the Lampsons and the Flowers as one of the reasons for the late-Victorian Cromer boom. His essays on the north Norfolk coast, and the Cromer neighbourhood in particular, were published in one volume in 1886 under the title *Poppyland*. The book remained a best seller for many years, and became a usefully picturesque sales tag under which travel agents could advertise the coast. *Poppyland* is little more than mildly agreeable to read today but accurately suggests the combination of smart simplicity on the beach and rural peace and (supposed) innocence in the surrounding countryside, which is what drew late-Victorian visitors to Cromer.

Its development was financed by a mixture of local, Norwich and London money. The Royal Links Hotel, for instance, was a London speculation, as was the earlier and much more modest rebuilding of the Red Lion Hotel in 1887, the latter by 'Mr John Smith of London', who developed a good deal of Cromer. The Grand and Metropole Hotels were built and owned by Norfolk syndicates, in the former of which Benjamin Bond Cabell had an interest; the chairman of both was Sir Kenneth Kemp, a Norwich banker who was also involved in developing the delightful Arts and Crafts Royal

71. The Metropole Hotel, built to the designs of G.J. Skipper in 1893-4.

Arcade in Norwich in 1898-9. The two hotels (Pl. 71), the little town hall and the Norwich Arcade were all designed by the able Norwich architect G.J. Skipper, built and embellished by Norwich craftsmen, and furnished and fitted throughout by the Norwich firm of Trevor Page and Co., who had a financial stake in the ownership. The same team were employed by members of the local Jarvis family who had acquired both the Hotel de Paris and Tucker's Hotel in the course of the nineteenth century, and rebuilt the Hotel de Paris on a much larger scale in 1894-5 (Pl. 72). These three cheerful red brick hotels were in up to date 'Queen Anne' manner, with high roofs, cupolas, balconies, delicate ornamental detail in brick and wrought iron, Japanese wallpapers, stained glass, and Moorish smoking-rooms, all nicely combining to produce exactly the right atmosphere of seaside prettiness and gaiety. It is sad that only the Hotel de Paris has survived: the Grand and the Metropole were demolished in recent decades; the architecturally very different Royal Links Hotel was destroyed by fire before the war.

Cromer in the nineteenth century was run by two bodies, with an overlapping membership but not always on the best of terms: the Cromer Protection Commissioners, established in 1844, were responsible for the sea front, and the Local Board of Health (transformed into the Urban District Council in 1894) looked after the town. The composition of the two bodies gradually changed. The Bond Cabells ceased to be represented after the death of Benjamin Bond Cabell, leaving three small daughters, in 1892. The Gurneys, Buxtons, Hoares and Barclays, by now very much the Cromer aristocracy, remained generous supporters of all local charities and good causes, but had less and less to do with running the town. Ultimately they retired to houses in the surrounding countryside where, in large numbers, they still remain. The field was left open to the Cromer hotel-owners, solicitors, auctioneers, shopkeepers and builders, as

72. Looking along the pier to the new Hotel de Paris, built to Skipper's design in 1894-5.

they grew in confidence and prosperity with the Cromer boom.

It was this group which was largely responsible for the last development of Victorian Cromer, the rebuilding of the esplanade in the 1890s and the building of the pier in 1900-1. A pier had been proposed several times — below the Red Lion Hotel in 1887, and below the Grand Hotel in 1895, but enough money had never been raised. In 1897 a storm obligingly blew away the old jetty, and Alex E. Jarvis, chairman of the Protection Commissioners, presided over the financing and building of the new pier in the same position at the foot of the steps leading to his newly rebuilt Hotel de Paris. The pier was opened in 1901, with much pomp of speeches and lunches, while the Blue Viennese Band played in the new bandstand (Pl. 69). A contemporary camera caught the men who planned it all in prosperous Arnold Bennett attitudes at the entrance to the pier: Alex E. Jarvis, plump and confident, with his curly homburg and big moustache; William Churchyard, owner of the Cliftonville Hotel (about 1899, with nice Arts and Crafts detailing) on the West Cliff; and the inevitable lean, discreet straw-hatted solicitor, E.M. Hansell, clerk to the Commissioners and every other possible local body (Pl. 73).

Although Cromer remained prosperous and select up till the 1914-18 war, its peak was passed and in the 1920s easier transport and warmer beaches gradually drew its fashionable clientele away. Between 1911 and 1931 its population remained almost static, at a little over 4,000. To a visitor today it still seems predominantly a nineteenth-century town, and all the more charming for that, a nostalgic mixture of fishing town and old-fashioned resort, with summer visitors ambling quietly through its narrow streets, and the evening sun lighting up its broad uncrowded beaches.

73. Cromer worthies at the opening of the pier in 1901.
74. (right) Unexecuted design for a terrace in Harrow, Middlesex, by Thomas Harris, 1860.

7 PIPE-DREAMS IN MANCHESTER

William Sharp Ogden has been entirely, and some may think deservedly, forgotten. Little is known about his career, and his few identifiable buildings are completely without interest. If he has any right to fame it must lie in his books. Of these, *Manchester a hundred years ago* (1875), *Sketches of Antique Furniture* (1888) and *Shakespeare's Portraiture* (1912) have little except curiosity value. But the designs in *Christian Gravestones* (1877) are at least original; and in *Mercantile Architecture* (1876; enlarged eds. 1885 and 1892) oddity and originality are carried to lengths which deserve to be called inspired. What, one may wonder as one turns the pages, lay behind these extraordinary designs? What influence, if any, did they exert?

Ogden was born in 1844, practised in Manchester from the 1870s to the 1890s, and died in London in 1926. It is not known where he studied architecture or under what architect or architects he worked before setting up on his own. Unless further evidence comes to light, surmise as to what influenced him must depend on his designs. These suggest that he should be placed as one of a group of Victorian architects, scarcely cohesive or consistent enough to be called a school, but of interest because it experimented with new ways of creating movement in architecture.

Most architecture does not, or at least should not, move. But the technique of giving an illusion of movement to essentially static buildings is one that from time to time has interested architects. It seems to lie behind the very curious and clever design by Thomas Harris for a proposed terrace in Harrow, Middlesex, published in the *Builder* of 20 October 1860 (Pl. 74). The approach behind this had already been foreshadowed by the same architect's much less ambitious design for a shop building in South Audley Street, published in the *Building News* of 18 February 1859 (Pl. 75). The shop, unlike the terrace, was actually built but has been demolished.

The *Builder* linked the Harrow design to a pamphlet published by Harris in the same year, *Victorian Architecture: A few Words to show that a National Architecture adapted to the wants of the Nineteenth Century is obtainable*. In spite of its intriguing title, the pamphlet itself is of little interest; nothing in it would lead one to expect the terrace. Admittedly, the latter can perhaps be related to Harris's statement that 'Brickwork, from the variety of good coloured bricks available, presents a larger scope for originality of design than any other material', and to his suggestion that red brick, as 'implying strength', should be used for constructive bands and relieving arches. But the statement gives no idea either of Harris's peculiar form of originality, or of the use to which he put his brick relieving arches in both terrace and shop.

The shop building was a remodelling of an earlier house, but in spite of the constraints of a limited brief and little money Harris did everything he could to get away from the conventional rectangular grid typical of London terraces and to be found in the houses to either side. The façade was kept on the move by shallow but complex recessions in the brickwork, by differences in the size and rhythm of the windows, and above all by its elaborate variety of shaped window heads and relieving arches — the latter used in excess of any structural need. Brick of three different colours was combined with blocks, courses, and voussoirs of stone to give an impression of continuous but also continuously interrupted movement. In looking at the engraving, the eye jumps from opening to opening and arch to arch. The line of the brick arches is broken by the interposition of windows or of blocks of stone; in one place the arches give the illusion of interlacing, in another, the bricks have jagged heads so that the arches seem to be bursting through the surrounding brickwork.

In his Harrow design, Harris set out, as Sir George Gilbert Scott had done in Broad Sanctuary, Westminster, to reinterpret the conventional early nineteenth-century formula not just for an individual terrace house, but for an entire terrace. Harris's reinterpretation was, by the standards of the time, outrageous, but it was also cleverer and more entertaining than Scott's, and it is sad that it was never built. All the devices of his North Audley Street design were reused and amplified. The main material seems to have been intended to be stone, but pierced by an extraordinary variety of openings and threaded through by an equally extraordinary variety of courses and relieving arches of brick. The lines of the arches are constantly interrupted by voussoirs of

92

75. A shop by Harris in South Audley Street, London, 1859.

stone; the central archway is framed in a counterpoint of reversed arches and arches of different section; as at North Audley Street jagged brick edges proliferate. Three-dimensional modelling is provided by porches, bay and oriel windows, buttresses, balconies, turrets, the central tower, and ten different varieties of dormer windows. The cumulative effect is of a restless and flickering movement that is almost, but not quite, chaotic. In fact, the line of the main balconies and the ridge line of the roofs provide just enough of a framework to prevent the composition from dissolving; and the apparently wild diversity of elements is subtly orchestrated so that it gradually builds up to the central tower.

Stripes, diapers, and arches of different-coloured brick or stone, curves overlaid on or opposed to other curves, and a profusion of faceted and splayed surfaces are to be found in many buildings of the later 1850s and the 1860s. The intention behind them often seems to be to produce strength, variety, or at times just originality, rather than movement. They are commonest in Gothic Revival buildings, but also appear in Classical, or more or less Classical, ones. They are by no means absent from, and indeed often were pioneered by, architects such as William Butterfield, G.E. Street, J.L. Pearson and George F. Bodley — the architects backed by the *Ecclesiologist*. But such architects usually kept them subordinated to strong and relatively simple compositions, and to a much closer approximation to medieval Gothic architecture. It was the architects whom Goodhart-Rendel classified as 'rogues' who used them in the most profusion. The rogues make up a curious and by no means unified group, the best description of which would be a negative one. They were the architects of whom the *Ecclesiologist* disapproved. Besides Thomas Harris, they included E.B. Lamb, S.S. Teulon, Bassett Keeling, Joseph Peacock and, in Scotland, F.B. Pilkington.

In 1864 the *Building News* pilloried Bassett Keeling's Strand Music Hall in an article by J.P. Seddon entitled 'Acrobatic Gothic'. The adjective was applied both to the activities for which the Music Hall was built, and to the 'high jinks and comic capers' of its architecture. This, admittedly, was eccentric rather than interesting; but 'acrobatic' is a suggestive way of describing those varieties of rogue architecture in which the eye is stimulated to move or jump to such an extent that the building becomes the architectural equivalent of a complicated trapeze act.

Harris's two buildings have a strong acrobatic element. The vinegar warehouse by R.L. Roumieu in Eastcheap, of 1868, uses somewhat different means to develop the technique even further (Pl. 76). There are hints of its approach in other buildings by Roumieu, but the Eastcheap warehouse is his masterpiece. The *Builder* commented at the time that 'the design, if a little overdone, may be considered picturesque and

76. Vinegar warehouse, Eastcheap, City of London, by R.L. Roumieu, 1868.

original'. Reactions to it and to his other buildings have always been mixed. Hitchcock calls them 'wild fantasies ... hardly worth considering'. Pevsner describes the Eastcheap warehouse as 'utterly undisciplined and crazy'. Both descriptions seem unfair to a dazzling piece of architectural juggling in which Roumieu, as the juggler, appears to know exactly what he is about.

The design is worked out in terms of diagonals and receding planes. The three main planes are those of the principal building face, the recessed face at the back of the arched openings, and the face of the six projecting canopies. The main diagonals are provided by the gables over the canopies and main entrance and, on the skyline, by the crisscross of the brickwork diapers and by a wide variety of arched openings. The façade reads like a succession of overlays, each cut away to reveal the layer behind it and kept on the move by the main diagonals and by a bewildering series of chamfers, corbels and setbacks. These make the eye slide in and out and to and fro, or leap from point to point as diagonals are interrupted and then taken up again. Yet, as in Harris's Harrow terrace, the composition is strong enough to keep the façade from dissolving into chaos.

94

77-80. Four warehouse designs, from W.S. Ogden's *Studies in Mercantile Architecture* (1876).

William Sharp Ogden almost certainly knew of the Eastcheap warehouse, for it was illustrated in the *Builder* in 1868, when he was twenty-six and must have been well started on his professional career. At any rate, in his *Studies in Mercantile Architecture* (1876) he plays a similar game with unflagging zest through fifty different designs.

Studies in Mercantile Architecture was published jointly in London and Manchester. It contained, as the title-page announced, 'fifty suggestive designs for warehouse, shop and office buildings, suitable for the commercial districts of large cities'. Each design carries a date, running from 1869 to 1875. The plates follow a short introduction. The latter — as tended to be the case with the more outrageous productions of Victorian rogues — gives no hint that the contents are in any way unusual, or other than down-to-earth commercial designs, economically tailored to their function. They are described as 'eclectic in character; the author preferring to select and combine features of beauty or utility from any available source, all picturesqueness of grouping or detail save that springing from evident and natural requirements being avoided'.

The book received a short but appreciative notice in the *British Architect* (which at that period was published in Manchester) and a much longer, but much more critical one, in the *Builder*. In the latter the anonymous reviewer's reactions were mixed but on the whole scathing. The book showed, he wrote, a 'desire for something clever and out of the way, an almost total absence of real taste and refinement in style and detail, combined with a considerable degree of cleverness and originality ... The vulgarity of some of these designs is astounding ... The author seems to have a great fancy for playing clever, or at least odd tricks with string-courses and window labels, especially of making the latter interpenetrate and cross each other, in a manner which is essentially unarchitectural ... No designer possessed of a particle of what may be called architectural morality would perpetrate such a thing ... Entire want of repose is a quality which no cleverness can atone for. There are a good many designs in it for which the author will probably condemn himself before very long [the book was presumed to be written by a young man]. But there is a certain spirit, cleverness and originality about even some of the more objectionable ones, which is, perhaps, more promising than merely dull good taste running in a well known groove.'

This was at least the kind of review calculated to make readers curious to look at the book; and a look at it shows what the reviewer was getting at. 'Clever, or at least odd tricks' and 'entire want of repose' are abundantly in evidence; stylistic consistency and correct use of the grammar of Classicism or even the accepted Victorian conventions of Gothicism are entirely absent.

What is interesting about the designs (Pls. 77-80) is the way in which they experiment with ways of obtaining 'entire want of repose', or to put it in positive terms, the maximum of movement. They do this by numerous variations and combinations of intersection, interruption, opposition, continuation and explosion. Mouldings and arches intersect one another, arches and gables cut through horizontal or vertical mouldings, the line of a roof reappears underneath the cornice in the form of a moulding. Arches start off from their two springing points but change into some other shape and fail to come to a peak; horseshoe arches carry the eye round two-thirds of an interrupted circle; mouldings are unexpectedly discontinued. Curves are broken into by triangles; some are set in opposition to other curves of a different radius; convex curves are opposed by concave ones; large-scale motifs are violently contrasted to similar small-scale ones. A line is carried across or down a façade, changing direction as it goes, so that it sweeps, snakes or seesaws. Voussoirs, glazing bars or incised ornament are treated so as to give the impression of radiating lines exploding from a central point through the surrounding elements.

In nearly all the designs, several of these devices are combined in one façade; any one element can often form part of several different and unexpected sequences. There are almost no closed shapes or conventional rhythms. The eye is constantly surprised or bewildered and kept continuously on the move. It is encouraged to behave in much the same way as it does when watching a tennis match, a fireworks show or a display of acrobatics; in this way an illusion of architectural movement is obtained.

The plates in *Studies in Mercantile Architecture* are all elevations; there are no plans, no perspectives, and only an occasional section, added as a detail on the elevations. These sections show that on occasion the glazing was intended to take the form of curved or polygonal bays, recessed or projecting between the masonry piers, thus adding another element of movement. Otherwise no information is given as to surface modelling, materials or structure. Ogden himself had probably not thought much about these; some of the designs would have been almost impossible to transform into three dimensions, and in others random lines and patterns have apparently been added in order to increase the effect of movement, without relating to any intelligible detail of ornament or construction. They are experimental exercises rather than designs for real buildings; there is no evidence or likelihood that any of them were built.

Clearly, however, many of them were conceived as relying heavily on iron or steel, which, of course, was common practice for mercantile buildings by the 1870s. Without an element of metal construction, the high proportion of window to wall found in some of the designs would have been impossible; so would one of the most distinctive features of the shops and offices — the filling of the ground floor with sheets of plate glass, above which the masonry piers of the upper floor appear to be suspended. The balancing effect produced by this device gives these particular designs an extra degree of surprise and insecurity, which Ogden clearly enjoyed.

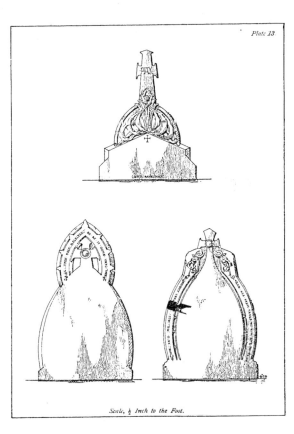

Stylistically, Ogden's claim that his designs were eclectic was all too justified. Like other architects of the time, he seems to have been experimenting with an outrageous eclecticism as a route toward a modern 'Victorian' style. Façades start off and end vaguely Classical but in between are wildly Gothic or Rundbogenstil, Corinthian columns support piers of Gothic section, Flemish gables are combined with Greek anthemions, Georgian arched window-heads merge into Gothic arches, Rococo cartouches are mixed with Lombardic tracery. Even when whole buildings are more or less Classical, the accepted grammar of the orders is disregarded; columns are truncated or distorted, pediments perch on top of voussoirs or arches. Some designs are fairly consistently Gothic; their stylistic treatment is often equally wild, but less distressing than in the Classical designs, because the acrobatic effects that Ogden aimed at relate to an element that is actually to be found in Gothic architecture. Much of the detail derives from contemporary buildings, especially from those by the more offbeat or outrageous architects; apart from the possible influence of Roumieu and Thomas Harris, there are what appear to be echoes of Bassett Keeling's churches, 'Greek' Thomson's warehouses, and E.L. Paraire's public houses. But the character of the final mixture is unique to Ogden.

In 1877 Ogden produced another book of designs, *Christian Gravestones; illustrated by 150 examples* (Pl. 81). In the introduction, he wrote: 'In issuing this little volume the Author has endeavoured to work out certain fixed principles, the observance of which he thinks is of the first importance, viz., simplicity of outline, severity of detail, and a general motive of design in which the Cross or other Christian emblem, monogram, or text are leading features. "Style", as generally understood and as the expression of various systems of thought is intentionally avoided, the object being to obtain an elastic and harmonious combination of workable detail, at once effective, inexpensive and durable.'

81. A page from Ogden's *Christian Gravestones* (1877).

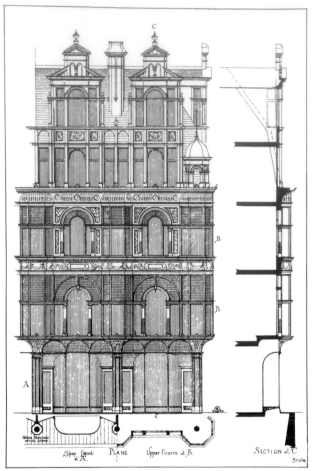

'Some of the best of these designs,' the introduction concludes, 'were prepared as studies for my Father's grave stone and these suggesting the others I dedicate them to his memory. Dear old Father; warmest, truest friend. Peace to thee.'

As in *Studies in Mercantile Architecture*, the unexceptionable sentiments of the introduction give little idea of the nature of the plates that follow — unless, perhaps, there is a forecast in the adjective 'elastic'. The designs, although by no means as stimulating as those in *Studies*, are clearly related to them. They are based on various interactions and contrasts of curved and straight lines, some obtained by the outlines of the stones, others by incision. A few of the monuments are decorated with interleafing foliage made up of distinctively stiff and curling fronds, as though cast in metal. Most of the shapes and motifs relate to conventional gravestones of the period, but they are combined and distorted by Ogden in a way that makes *Christian Gravestones* a curious and rather disturbing little book.

Second and third editions of *Mercantile Architecture* (as the title was now abbreviated) were published in 1885 and 1892. The second edition had five additional designs, and another five followed in the third edition, which also contained an appendix on hydraulic lifts. Stylistically, the additional designs could be described as commercial 'Queen Anne' (Ogden called them 'free classic'), fairly crude in the second edition and rather more restrained in the third. They have little of the wild movement of the 1876 designs; much their most interesting feature is their glazing (Pl. 82). All the buildings appear to be designed to have a metal frame, and as a result are lit by almost continuous glazing; roofs and gables as well as the main wall surfaces are sometimes filled with glass. The space between the piers is invariably given over to bow or bay windows; in one design elaborately profiled glazing on the first and second floors is carried in front and well clear of the iron columns of the main structure, to produce a genuine and very early example of curtain walling.

Ogden was clearly proud of his glazed metal-frame structures. They are referred to both in the subtitle ('specially prepared to combine Lightness with Constructional Design') and in the new introduction of his second edition. The latter draws attention to the combination of piers and glazing in the new designs: 'an arrangement at once satisfactory to the eye and of vast importance as yielding almost uninterrupted light. It will be seen that considerable prominence is with this intention given to the Bay or Bow Window, forms which readily lend themselves to any detail: are picturesque, agreeable and profitable, as giving additional floor space, allowing more glass and facing the light at several angles, are superior to any other kind of window.'

The *Builder*, in its review of the 1876 edition, had already pointed out that bow windows give less rather than more light than ordinary ones. This fact is a common-

82. A design from the second edition of *Mercantile Architecture* (1885).

place to anyone who has experience of lighting calculations, and if Ogden did not know of it, he ought to have. But one suspects that, in spite of his protestations that 'Convenience and Utility must ever be of the first importance', what really attracted him was the aesthetic excitement of devising delicate multi-storied lanterns of curved and faceted glass. The idea almost certainly derived from earlier 'Queen Anne' buildings by better-known architects — such as the New Zealand Chambers by Richard Norman Shaw, of 1871-3, and Belcher and Son's Queen Anne Chambers, Poultry, of 1875. But Ogden carries it considerably further.

The known executed buildings by Ogden, all in Manchester, are Read's Buildings, on the corner of Peter Street and Deansgate (1878); York Street Synagogue, Cheetham (c.1889); Sunday Schools, Broughton Congregational Church (c.1889); and the Talmud Torah School, Best Street, Cheetham (c.1894). Some of these were built in partnership with E.W. Charleston. None is of the slightest interest; the contrast between them and the designs in Ogden's books is almost ludicrous. Although the *Builder*, reviewing *Studies in Mercantile Architecture* in 1876, described the designs in it as 'typical of a certain type of Manchester architecture' and labelled them 'Manchester goods', they appear to bear little resemblance to any known Manchester building by Ogden or any other architect. It would seem that Ogden's taste was so out of step with Manchester's that he made no attempt to sell it to the few clients that came his way.

Ogden's other published works, and what little is known of his life, suggest a character out of gear with his contemporaries and reacting to the situation by slight eccentricity. He was the grandson of that 'revered but ruptured Ogden' (as Canning is said to have described him) who called the famous meeting at Peterloo, and the great-grandson of Peter Ogden, a Manchester antiquarian whose sketches of the city, made in the 1770s, he reproduced or professed to reproduce in *Manchester a Hundred Years Ago* (1875). Although W.S. Ogden declared that the contents were 'not ... mere fancy pictures but genuine representations', the sketches look so much like buildings in the style of Norman Shaw and other contemporary architects as to suggest that they were either substantial redrawings, or complete fabrications.

His *Sketches of Antique Furniture* (1888) is chiefly remarkable for the crudity with which the various examples are drawn. Ogden himself was something of a collector and antiquarian; in his will he distributed his collections of engravings, topographical drawings, prehistoric and classical pottery, and other antiquities to the Manchester Museum, the Whitworth Gallery, and the Society of Antiquaries. He owned a supposed portrait of Shakespeare, which was reproduced in his *Shakespeare's Portraiture* (1912). It seems likely that he had some kind of private income. There is no evidence that he practised as an architect after the 1890s. He died in London in 1926.

In the 1885 edition of *Mercantile Architecture*, Ogden complained of the 'complacent obtuseness' with which the first edition had been reviewed by 'one or two of the professional papers', as opposed to 'that admirable and unprejudiced paper the *British Architect*'. He was presumably referring to the review in the *Builder*. But, apart from an on-the-whole friendly notice in the *British Architect*, the second and third editions were ignored in the professional press. The fact that the book ran to three editions suggests that it enjoyed some popularity; perhaps it had an influence on late nineteenth-century commercial and public-house architecture, but it is hard to point to specific examples. By the time of Ogden's death what little reputation he had enjoyed

99

as an architect had been forgotten; the only (short) obituaries were in the *North Western Naturalist* and the *Manchester City News*.

In 1904, however, his old ally the *British Architect* gave him one last piece of publicity. On 14 October of that year it published a leader entitled 'L'Art Nouveau', together with two pages of illustrations by Raffles Davison, showing new buildings in Brussels. One passage mentions Ogden as providing possible prototypes for the style:

'It is a good many years since there was published in Manchester a book entitled "Mercantile Design", by Mr. Ogden, which contained the germ of a good deal that was inventive and good about the methods of l'art nouveau; and though, when it was published the energy and restlessness of much of it was over the heads of current ideas, it deserves some recognition as an attempt to break loose from the bonds of academic formality and servile tradition ... When we saw the latest erection of l'art nouveau in Brussels the other day, we felt that the whole motif of the design had a most remarkable parallel in more than one of Mr. Ogden's designs published now some twenty years ago.'

These comments have some point. However outrageous as a designer, Ogden was by no means despicable. If he had been one of a group, rather than out on a limb in Manchester, he might have produced some remarkable buildings. Even if his designs lack Art Nouveau's sinuous line, asymmetry and freedom from historicism, in some ways they do point suggestively toward it: in the flickering detail, experiments with movement, and attempts to escape from style of the 1876 designs; in the undulating glass walls and turrets of the later ones. The building in Brussels which struck the *British Architect* (and which was illustrated by Raffles Davison) was a nearly completed office block near the General Post Office, but perhaps the parallels with buildings such as Saintenoy's Old England Store in Brussels, or Guimard's Maison Coilliot in Liège (Pl. 83) are even more suggestive. Was this pure coincidence? Or did copies of *Mercantile Architecture*, by some chance, find their way to Brussels or to Paris?

83.   The Maison Coilliot, Liège, Belgium, by Hector Guimard, 1898-1900.
84. (facing page)   Coming up the Suir to Waterford.

85. (right)   The author, sisters, cousins and governess on the drive at Curraghmore in 1939 or 1940.

A COUNTRY-HOUSE CHILDHOOD

Mr Huston, of Castle Huston, told his cook that if she sent the soup up cold again he would shoot her. She did send it up cold, and he did shoot her. Mr Cooke, of Cookesborough, thought that he was turning into a fox. The Earl of Antrim wanted to be buried upright at the top of the glen, looking down on his castle at Glenarm, but the coffin bearers were so drunk, or so exhausted by the climb, that they buried him upside-down instead. The O'Sheas, of Garden Morris, had a family tree hanging in the gentlemen's lavatory that showed their descent from Adam. Mr FitzGerald, of The Island in County Waterford, kept his first (dead) wife in a box in the hall. Old Miss Morley, of Mayfield, could only sweat through her tongue, like a dog; I used to watch her with fascination for evidence of this peculiarity.

These were the stories and the people who floated around in the background of my boyhood when I went for holidays in Ireland in the 1940s. No doubt the tales were improved in the telling, for no one enjoys creating legends more than the Irish — or, for that matter, the Anglo-Irish. It was to the latter that my mother's family belonged. My grandmother, aunts, uncles and cousins lived in seven country houses of all shapes and sizes, within twenty miles of each other in Counties Waterford, Kilkenny and Tipperary (Pls. 86-91).

They were part of the great nexus of Protestant Anglo-Irish families, descendants of Norman or Elizabethan adventurers, Cromwellian soldiers or Georgian bishops and lawyers, who for centuries had been the ruling class of Ireland. Most of their land had been bought out by the government by the Land Act of 1905, and what power remained to them had gone by the time Ireland became independent in 1921. A selection of their houses had been burnt down in the troubles that preceded and followed independence. A steady trickle were selling up and moving off to England or the colonies, but when I was a boy, large numbers were still living where they had always lived.

They all knew each other, or about each other. They all went up to Dublin in the summer for the Horse Show and stayed in the old-fashioned comfort of the Shelbourne Hotel on Stephen's Green. They met at race meetings or on the hunting field and danced foxtrots and eightsome reels at hunt balls together. They drove indomitably for many miles to go to parties or stay with each other. Their houses could be spotted with ease because the woods, fields and gardens around them, known collectively as the 'demesne', were almost always surrounded by a stone wall eight to ten feet high, often stretching for several miles along the road. It sounds impressive but seldom was, since the walls were inevitably covered in ivy and usually falling down.

The lodge gates, when one finally got to them, could be astonishingly grand, with pillars, coats of arms, towers or castellations. There was usually, in those days, a family living in the lodge, and someone (often a minute child) would come running out to open the gates. Beyond the gates, the drive (always known as the avenue) could run for a mile or more. It was never tarred and was almost invariably pitted with large holes needing careful navigation by the car, pony trap or bicycle in or on which one was progressing. In my boyhood it was seldom by car, for petrol in the war years was hard to come by, except for priests and doctors. I remember the frustration of jogging along the roads to race meetings in a trap and being passed by carloads of jovial priests heading for the same destination.

One could never tell for certain from the entrance what kind of house there would be at the end of the avenue. Ballysaggartmore, for instance, where my great-aunt Clodagh lived for a time, had one of the grandest sets of castellated lodge gates in Ireland, and a castellated bridge on the avenue that was even grander. All this had cost so much in the early nineteenth century that no money was left over with which to build the house, and my aunt and her children had to live in the stables.

Alternatively, very modest gates could lead to houses of apparently limitless size and grandeur. Anglo-Irish families liked making more of a show than their income warranted. One way of doing this was to unite house, stables, outbuildings and farm buildings into one grand composition and either string everything out into a line, as at Russborough in County Wicklow, or wrap it around an enormous entrance court, as at Curraghmore, my mother's old home in County Waterford. At Ballyseedy Castle in Kerry half the front was a sham and had no rooms at all behind it.

Comfort was never a feature of these houses. They were heated by open fires of turf or damply hissing logs. Central heating was either non-existent or did not work. At Mount Congreve in County Waterford (where the flowerbeds in front of the house were planted with carrots) the butler presented each of the dinner guests with a rug as they entered the dining room. Washing in the morning was by means of copper cans of hot water, wrapped in towels and delivered by a housemaid. Running a bath in the vast, cavernous tubs was always a gamble. Would or would not the thin trickle of dark brown water emerging from the hot-water tap — connected to an equally cavernous boiler a hundred yards or so away — ever turn hot? The answer was usually not.

The water may have been cold, but the welcome never was. They were hospitable houses, full of laughter and good stories, and their woods, lakes, rivers, boats, horses, stables, haylofts and barns made them wonderful places for children. Inside the houses were stone-flagged corridors long enough to bicycle along, and endless staircases and hiding places ideal for games of catch and hide-and-seek or midnight feasts.

There was a hidden room above a trapdoor at my Uncle Billy's Woodhouse that Victorian children had obviously enjoyed finding and using too, because its walls were decorated with crude but lively drawings of Victorian ladies and gentlemen in top hats and bustles. An even more exciting secret space at Curraghmore could only be reached by pulling out the books and shelves of a built-in bookcase in the billiard room and crawling through the gap that was revealed. Earlier generations of children had been there too, and left behind a cache of rusting swords and military helmets, wonderful for dressing up.

It was when I was about fourteen that I started to notice things I had not noticed before. The billiard room ceiling at Curraghmore, for instance, was decorated with delicate fronds of rococo plasterwork: baskets of flowers and heads of gods and goddesses. The room in which we played table tennis was lined with oil paintings of eighteenth-century London and a huge Flemish allegory of the Four Evangelists. Soon I began to burrow in the bookcases that lined the billiard room, library and corridors, and to disinter crumbling folios of architectural engravings that no one had looked at for a hundred years or more. I was entering into an exploration of the country house that has occupied much of my life ever since.

In the 1950s and 1960s I spent long happy weeks exploring Ireland and Irish country houses with friends in the Irish Georgian Society. These were times of excitement and discovery. Very little had been written about Irish houses, and we drove along empty roads through wet, beautiful countryside never quite knowing what we were going to find. The house we were looking for could turn out to be a heap of rubble or a burnt-out shell, or be full of nuns or lunatics — or bales of hay piled beneath superb Italian plasterwork, as was the case at Riverstown in County Cork before the Irish Georgian Society acquired it.

But many of the houses we visited were still lived in and filled with the contents that had always been in them. The fact that there was not much money in the Irish country-house world meant that much had decayed but little had been altered. The walls could be streaked with damp, the wallpapers hanging in strips, and the carpet worn into holes, but the colours, wallpapers and carpets were often the original eighteenth-century ones. All over Ireland there was still a wealth of furniture, china, silver

86-91. Six of the houses. (Left, top to bottom) Curragmore, Co. Waterford; Whitfield Court, Co. Waterford; Woodhouse, Co. Waterford. (Right, top to bottom). Newtown Anner, Co. Tipperary; Castletown House, Co. Kilkenny; Ballydavid, Co. Waterford.

and pictures in tall, exquisitely proportioned rooms, with high sash windows through which one looked out over green country to the mountains.

They are happy memories, shadowed now with melancholy. The romanticism, affection and nostalgia that supports country houses in England scarcely exists in Ireland, where many, and perhaps most, people think of them as an alien import. Moreover, Ireland is not a rich country. Except in the North (which is a different story), it has nothing comparable to the National Trust, with its great string of country houses and generous grants of government money that subsidize repairs and renovations to historic buildings of all varieties.

A few Irish houses have reasonably assured futures, like the magnificent Georgian mansions of Russborough and Castletown, which have been set up as charitable trusts, or Malahide Castle, which the Irish government has taken over (but only after most of the contents had been sold); perhaps no more than a few dozen still belong to the families that have always lived in them, and one or two of these are still kept up in some style. But year after year more and more are being sold and their contents dispersed. Of the seven family houses in which I stayed as a child, only Curraghmore and Whitfield are still lived in by my relatives. Little is left from the days that I remember, when huge teas of soda bread, honeycomb, hot scones, cakes and biscuits without end were laid out on white table-cloths before the blazing fireplace, when the blue paraffin flame flickered beneath the silver teakettle, and it seemed to a child that nothing could ever change.

92. The seventh house. Georgestown, Co. Waterford.
93. (right) The view across Lough Ennell from Belvedere.

2 BELVEDERE AND THE WICKED EARL

Of all the inexhaustible wealth of strange stories connected with the Anglo-Irish gentry in the eighteenth and nineteenth centuries, few are better or stranger than that of the 1st Earl of Belvedere and his wife.

On 7 August 1736, Robert Rochfort, as he then was, married as his second wife Mary Molesworth, the daughter of the 3rd Viscount Molesworth. It must have seemed a highly suitable marriage. The husband was young, attractive, intelligent and rich; the wife only sixteen, well-connected and very pretty. Lord Orrery wrote approvingly to the Bishop of Cork a few months later: 'Mrs Rochfort has gathered new Beauties by her Marriage. She charms more as a Wife than she did as a Maid. This, my Lord, is a fine incitement to unmarried Ladies to quit an unprofitable life for the happy Hours of the Nuptial State.' In view of later developments the remark was an unfortunate one.

The Rochfort family had large properties in Westmeath, which they represented in Parliament continuously from 1696 to 1833. The main seat of the family was at the old house of Gaulston, and here Robert Rochfort took his young wife. Next door at Belfield lived his younger brother, Arthur, with his family. A few miles away was the pretty landscape of Lough Ennell, the attractions of which were much appreciated in the mid-eighteenth century, with its new cult for the beauties of nature. About 1740 Robert Rochfort began to build a small house on a hill above the lake and called it Belvedere. Next door a third brother, George, built another house, known then as Rochfort, though the name was changed in the nineteenth century to Tudenham.

The power of the Rochforts obtained recognition in 1738, when Robert Rochfort took his first step up into the peerage and was created Baron Belfield. But in 1743 the family hit the news in a more lurid fashion. On 2 May of that year the Earl of Egmont wrote in his diary: 'Last post several letters from Ireland gave an account of a most unhappy affair that lately passed in Dublin. Robert Rochfort, Baron Belfield of that kingdom, who some years ago married a daughter of Richard Viscount Molesworth for love, she being very handsome though no fortune, and used her in the tenderest manner, was privately informed that she cohabited unlawfully with his younger brother. Upon which he put the question to her, and she with consummate impudence owned the fact, adding that her last child was by him, and that she had no pleasure with any man like that she did with him. My Lord thereupon locked her up in the garret, and in his rage took a charged pistol with him with intention to find out his brother and shoot him, but that very night he went on board a ship and sailed for England, where he now lies concealed, if not fled abroad. My Lord Belfield then went to Lord Molesworth, and telling him his unfortunate case, asked his advice what he should do? My Lord replied he might do what he pleased; that having committed such a crime as incest, and confest it, he should have no concern about, and the rather because she was only his bastard by his wife before he married her. My Lord Belfield resolved to be divorced, is now prosecuting her as an adultress, and we are told that when separated, she will be transported to the West Indies as a vagabond.'

In March of the next year Lord Belfield crossed over to London, where Mrs Delany described in a letter to her friend Mrs Dewes meeting him at dinner: 'They say he has come to England in search of *him*, to kill him wherever he meets him; but I hope his resentment will cool, and not provoke him to so desperate an action, and he does not appear to have any such rash design, but is more cheerful and composed than one could expect him to be; he is very well-bred, and very well in his person and manner; his wife is locked up in one of his houses in Ireland, with a strict guard over her, and they say he is so miserable as to love her even now, she is extremely handsome, and has many personal accomplishments.

> A fairer person lost not heaven; she seem'd
> For dignity compos'd and high exploit;
> But all was false and hollow'.

Lord Belfield waited sixteen years before he had his revenge on his brother. Whether the couple were guilty or not will perhaps always remain disputable. Fashionable opinion at the time seems to have taken it for granted that they were, and her father accepted the wife's guilt; but in the eighteenth century opinion tended to be heavily weighted in favour of the husband. His wife made a confession, but it is said that this was extorted from her by force, and that for the rest of her life she protested that she was innocent. In any case, the punishment inflicted on her and her brother-in-law was out of proportion to any transgression they may have committed, and reveals an extraordinary tenacity and virulence in her husband.

Arthur Rochfort fled the country and settled ultimately at Wakefield in Yorkshire. He does not seem to have returned to Ireland until 1754 when, on a 'Necessity of personally looking into my own affairs', he came over to Dublin 'contrary to the Desire and Advice of every friend I have'. So he says himself, in a curious little pamphlet published by him in Dublin the same year, *Kiss a Patriot's A..se, or Letters between A—r R—f—t, Esq. and E—d P—y, Esq.* In this he accuses Edmund Pery of insinuating that he had been especially brought over by his brother George Rochfort 'in order to distress and hullo me at his Lordship' — that is, at his brother Lord Belfield. Arthur Rochfort challenged Pery to a duel, which would have taken place (as appears from Lord George Sackville's correspondence) if it had not been stopped at the last minute at the instigation of Primate Stone.

The fact that Lord Belfield took no action on this visit apparently encouraged Arthur Rochfort to come to Ireland again in 1759. But this time his brother (recently created Earl of Belvedere) sued him for adultery with his wife sixteen years before, and obtained £20,000 damages. 'Mr Rochfort', wrote Mrs Delany on 12 May, still totally in favour of the husband, 'is imprisoned for life, being charged with damages impossible for him to pay. Before the trial came on Lord Belfield offered him his liberty, and that he would not prosecute him if he would *quit the kingdom* — he *refused the offer* and *well deserves his fate.*' So Arthur Rochfort went to prison and appears to have died there some years before the death of his unrelenting brother.

Meanwhile, ever since 1743 Lady Belvedere had been living shut up in Gaulston, Lord Belvedere himself having removed to his new house at Belvedere. Her children were occasionally permitted to see her, but otherwise she was allowed no visitors; she had, however, plenty of servants, a good wardrobe and the use of a carriage, as long as she did not pass outside the demesne walls. Much of her long hours of solitude she spent in drawing: 'Her pictures were all on gloomy subjects, in character with the depressed state of her mind.'

Lord Belvedere sometimes visited Gaulston, but never to see his wife. He was, however, walking one day in the garden when she managed to surprise him, and fell on her knees in front of him. He was touched, and hesitated for a moment. But when his friend turned to him and said, 'Remember your honour, My Lord', he recollected himself and moved on without speaking. From then on a servant was ordered to attend her wherever she walked in the grounds, ringing a bell to warn people to keep away.

In 1756 or thereabouts, after twelve years of solitude, Lady Belvedere, with the aid of some faithful servants, escaped from Gaulston and fled to the house of her father in Dublin. He refused to admit her. Within twenty-four hours her husband had discovered her and she was back in captivity. Here she spent the next eighteen years, in much stricter custody than formerly; her children were no longer allowed to see her, her movements were more restricted and her comforts curtailed. She used to walk in the gallery at Gaulston and stand gazing at the pictures 'as if conversing with them'.

In November 1774 her husband died, and her son, the new Earl of Belvedere, came to release her. He had not seen her for eighteen years, and the change was appalling. 'She had acquired a wild, scared, unearthly look, whilst the tones of her voice, which hardly exceeded a whisper, were harsh, agitated and uneven.' Her clothes were in the

Belvedere House, Mullingar, Co. Westmeath.

fashion of thirty years back. At first she did not seem to realise what was happening, but at length 'in fearful accents she faltered out: "Is the tyrant dead?"'

Lady Belvedere did not survive her husband many years; she went ultimately to live with her daughter, the Countess of Lanesborough, and on her death-bed reasserted her innocence of the charge that had been made against her.

Such is the story of Lady Belvedere's imprisonment, as told (with much more detail) by John Charles Lyons, first in an article in *Chamber's Edinburgh Journal* of 21 November 1846, and then in a footnote to his account of the Rochfort family in that rare and fascinating book *The Grand Juries of the County of Westmeath* (1853). The Lyons family lived at Ledestown, across the lake from Belvedere, and had been friends and neighbours of the Rochforts since the early eighteenth century. It perhaps ought to be remembered, however, that J.C. Lyons was writing long after the event (though he says that his account was based on an earlier document) and was probably not averse to improving a good story. But the main events — the scandal, the trial and imprisonment of Arthur Rochfort, and the thirty years' confinement of Lady Belvedere — are indisputable.

The old house at Gaulston was sold by the 2nd Earl of Belvedere to Lord Kilmaine, who rebuilt it. This later house has also been demolished, and all that remains at Gaulston are the ruins of the church in its churchyard, the walled gardens and a heap of rubble in an empty field. But Belvedere, where the Earl lived in gaiety and luxury while his wife was shut up six miles away, is still there (Pl. 94). It is a house with a wonderful situation, cunningly designed so that only at the last moment does one realise that this is the case; it is not until the car sweeps round the corner to the front of the house that one suddenly sees the gleaming expanse of Lough Ennell stretching, scattered here and there with islands, to the far horizon (Pl. 93). The name of the house, Belvedere, then becomes easy to understand.

As one stands in front of the house one can see, to the left of the view across the lake, another vista down through thick trees to a large and shattered Gothick ruin, silhouetted crazily against the sky (Pl. 95). This ruin is a sham, and its story is typical of Lord Belvedere. Next door to Belvedere was Rochfort, later known as Tudenham, the

112

94. Belvedere House, Co. Westmeath, from an old postcard.
95. (top right) The ruin.
96. (bottom right) The folly in the park.

house of his younger brother George. It was a fine mid-eighteenth-century building, considerably larger than Belvedere; the distance between the two houses was about a quarter of a mile, and Rochfort figured prominently in the view from the front of Belvedere. At some time, probably about 1760, the two brothers had a quarrel, and Lord Belvedere put up the ruin to close the view to George Rochfort's house. This it still effectively does, though, by the irony of time, Tudenham is today a ruin too. According to Lyons, Lord Belvedere 'went to an enormous expense in getting over from Italy a celebrated Florentine architect of that day, named Barradette, to superintend the erection of the ruin'. No such Italian architect of that name can, however, be traced, and such sham ruins were much more typical of English or Irish than Italian taste.

An endearingly small brother to the big ruin at Belvedere exists at the other end of the park, in the form of a Gothick arch that closes the vista running west from the house (Pl. 96). Lord Belvedere also built an octagonal Gothick summer-house, looking out over the lake on an eminence nearer the house. but this has since fallen into ruin. These garden buildings, their siting, the planting of the park as a whole and the house itself all show that Lord Belvedere had considerable taste, whatever his character may have been.

A glimpse of his activities as a man of taste is given in a letter of Mrs Delany's, dated 15 February 1752. She there describes a subscription ball at Dublin of which he was the 'chief manager and contriver', responsible for decorations that recall the ruin and arch at Belvedere. 'On the right hand, from the portico to the end of the stage is diversified by rocks, trees, and caves, very well represented. On the left hand a jessamine bower, a Gothic temple (which is to be the sideboard), trees interspersed, the

114

97, 98. The hall and staircase, photographed in 1961.

whole terminated with a grotto extremely well expresst; three rustick arches, set off with ivy, moss, icicles, and all the rocky appurtenances; the musicians to be placed in the grotto dressed like shepherds and shepherdesses ... The trees are *real trees* with *artificial leaves*.'

Lord Belvedere's treatment of his wife appears to have done him no harm in the eyes of the world, and he pursued a career of gaiety, extravagance and success. In 1751 he was created Viscount Belfield; in 1756 Earl of Belvedere; in 1764 Muster-Master-General of the Irish Army. There is an intriguing account of Belvedere in the last years of his life in a letter from Sir James Caldwell to his wife written on 11 February 1773. Sir James was staying next door to Belvedere at Rochfort; George Rochfort had died and the property had been inherited by his son, Gustavus Hume Rochfort. It was a religious household: 'We are always at breakfast exactly at eight o'clock, and then read

the Psalms and the Bible.' Life at Belvedere was different. 'I dined there yesterday, no person but me, Lord Belfield, and Lord Newtown, by many degrees the handsomest boy I ever laid my eyes on, much handsomer than his mother. He is quite a show. Only think, for us four, a complete service of plate, covers and all, two soups, two removes, nine and nine, a dessert in the highest taste, all sorts of wine, burgundy and champagne, a load of meat on the side table, four valets-de-chambre in laced clothes, and seven or eight footmen. If the Lord Lieutenant had dined there, there could not have been a more elegant entertainment. He has his hothouses five miles off [at Gaulston] and eighteen fires going. There are no such in the kingdom. Three sets of coach-horses in the stables ... A vast contrast between this house and that. Here all regularity and religion, there all debauchery and dissipation.' Eighteen months later

Lord Belvedere was dead, leaving his heir 'very embarrassed in his circumstances, and from his distress must consequently be dependent upon the Crown'.

According to Lyons, the house had hardly been completed at the time of the scandal in 1743, and its architectural character certainly fits in well enough with that date. It is not at all a large building, and was probably originally designed as an appendage to Gaulston, a kind of large fishing-pavilion where a party could put up for two or three nights. There is a significant difference, in what might be called top-drawer houses of the eighteenth century, between houses built for show and houses built for pleasure. In the former class are the principal seats of peers or powerful commoners, designed to impress, and big enough to accommodate large numbers of guests and servants. The latter class includes houses built for a number of different reasons: by a nobleman as a holiday place in which to escape from the formality of his great house, by a politician or rich merchant as a retreat from Parliament or the office, as a lodge for hunting and fishing, and so on. In England in the mid-eighteenth century such houses tended to be called 'villas'. Whatever their use or designation, they share qualities of moderate size combined with a distinction and richness that reveal that they were built by someone of importance or wealth, and set them apart from humdrum houses on the same scale. Belvedere is one of the comparatively few Irish examples.

In spite of its relatively small size, the solid grey limestone, the curved bows at either end, the Venetian windows on the front and the restrained but handsome doorcase all combine to give it considerable presence. Above the Venetian windows were originally semi-circular windows, but these were altered to their present shape in Victorian times, from which period also date the stone steps and terraces running down towards the lake. At either end of the house are the drawing-room and dining-room, each lit by a Venetian window looking out on to the lake, and a bow window at the side. Between them are two small rooms (now run together), a corridor and the handsomely carved main staircase (Pls. 97, 98). The floor above has a parallel arrangement of two large bedrooms above the dining-room and drawing-room, and two smaller rooms between them. At the west end of the house a short wing projects to the north, making the plan L-shaped; this contains three more rooms and the back staircase and was perhaps built a little later than the rest, the staircase at any rate being of late eighteenth-century type. The kitchen and servants' rooms are in the basement looking out on to an area.

The most remarkable features of Belvedere are the rococo ceilings of the drawing-room, dining-room and hall (Pls. 99, 100). These are quite atypical of most Irish work, which usually tends to richness and overcrowding. The Belvedere ceilings have a lightness of touch, a delicate sense of spacing and a gaiety that put them in a different class. The ceilings of the two small rooms that now form the hall are very simple: on the larger one Jupiter astride an eagle scatters lightning furiously across a sea of clouds; the smaller one has another skyscape, this time sprinkled with stars. In the dining-room and drawing-room the work is more elaborate. That in the drawing-room is rococo work at its most delicate, with scrollwork that flickers and crackles like flames around the edge of the ceiling and stretches out a long tongue into the curved recess of the bow window. Figure work here plays a small part, being confined to medallions of Juno, Minerva and Venus at the centre.

In the dining-room the plasterwork is a little heavier and bolder, with an outer ring

116

99. (right)   A detail of the drawing-room ceiling.

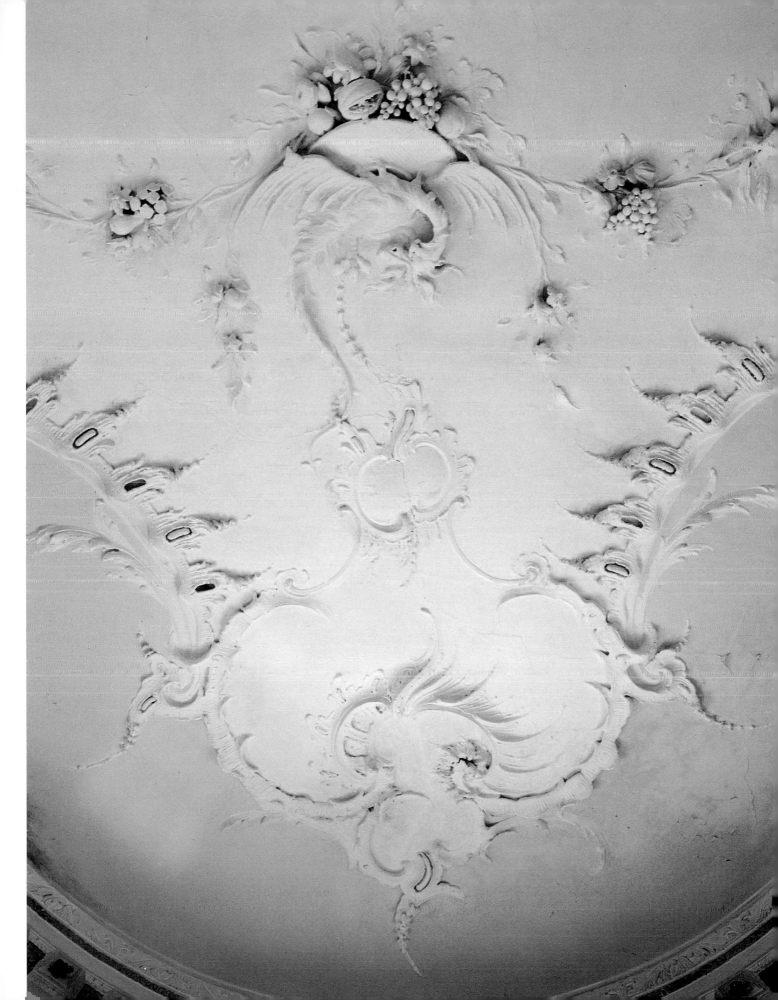

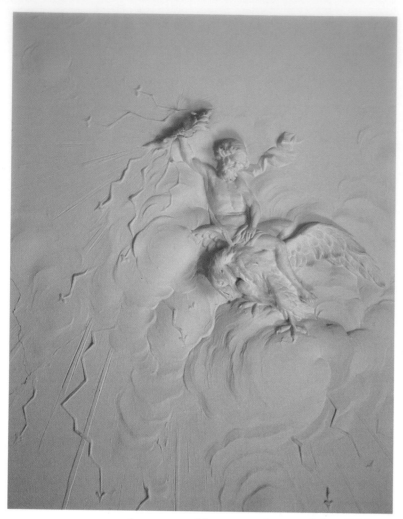

of scrollwork, and an inner ring of clusters of fruit and flowers (one cluster of fruit in a bowl supported on the back of a flying dragon). But the innermost portion of the ceiling is without elaborate ornament, being left as a clear field across which a knot of four furiously puffing cherubs blow knots of scudding clouds.

The only ceilings in Ireland at all close in style to those at Belvedere were the ones formerly at Mespil House, in the suburbs of Dublin. This house (which at the time it was built was still in the country) was started in 1751 by Dr Barry, an eminent Dublin doctor; it has recently been demolished, but the ceilings have been preserved. They are generally recognised as the masterpiece of rococo plasterwork in Ireland, and at the same time quite unlike anything else in Dublin, except, in certain respects, a ceiling formerly in the La Touche bank in Castle Street. The Belvedere ceilings have resemblances to those at Mespil House, which makes it tempting to assign them to the same plasterer: notably the generous use of clouds, certain details of the ornament, the wide spacing, and a light-hearted ease of execution that is very noticeable, although not easy to define. Puffing cherubs are also to be found at Mespil House, and the figure of Jupiter formerly in the drawing-room there is worth comparing with the Jupiter on the hall ceiling at Belvedere. But figures appear much more prominently on the Mespil House ceilings, and this makes Mr C.P. Curran, the great expert on Irish plasterwork, hesitant about ascribing the two lots of ceiling to the same hand. He dates the Belvedere ceilings to about 1754, which would fit in well with the probable date of the house.

In neither case is there any documentary evidence as to the plasterer's name, but there is little doubt that both were the work of a foreigner. The only foreign plasterers working in Ireland at this time whose documented work is known were the Italian Francini brothers and the Frenchman Bartholomew Cramillion. There is a good deal of Francini plasterwork in existence, comparison with which makes it clear that the Belvedere and Mespil House ceilings are by a different hand. The only known work of Cramillion's is the splendid rococo ceiling of the Rotunda Hospital in Dublin, the initial agreement for which was made in 1755. This ceiling is so different in scale and intention from the more intimate and domestic ceilings at Mespil House and Belvedere that comparison is difficult. It is not beyond the bounds of possibility that

100. Jupiter the Thunderer, on the hall ceiling.

Cramillion might have been responsible for the work in all three places; but unless further evidence comes to light, the problem must remain unsolved.

The remainder of the interior fittings at Belvedere are of high quality, and, though without the brilliance of the ceilings, combine to give the effect of intimate luxury at which Lord Belvedere was clearly aiming. The cornices on the ground floor are very rich, and the joinery of doors, wainscoting, staircase and windows admirably solid. There are original fireplaces and overmantels, with some of the rococo brio of the plasterwork, in the dining-room and both parts of the hall. In the drawing-room the present rather heavy overmantel, and probably the chimney-piece, were inserted in Victorian times. All the upstairs rooms have deep cornices and coved ceilings, and in the east bedroom (probably Lord Belvedere's room) there is a fine fireplace.

The story of the 1st Earl of Belvedere and his wife is an especially extraordinary one, but the history of the remainder of the Rochfort family is by no means lacking in interest. In particular the 1st Earl's father and his brother 'Nim' were great friends of Dean Swift; who wrote an entertaining poem, *The Journal*, describing life at Gaulston when he was staying there from June to October 1721:

> At seven the Dean in Nightgown drest
> Goes round the House to wake the rest;
> At nine grave Nim and George facetious,
> Go to the Dean to read Lucretius.
> At ten my Lady comes and hectors
> And hisses George, and ends our lectures
> And when she has him by the neck fast
> Hauls him, and scolds us, down to breakfast ...

The 2nd Earl of Belvedere succeeded to the title in 1774; his father's extravagance left the estate much encumbered, and in 1776 he was given a government pension of £800 per annum. In ten years, however, he had recovered sufficiently to erect Belvedere House in Dublin, a building that demonstrates that he had inherited his father's taste, for its magnificent plasterwork by Michael Stapleton made it the finest private house of its date in Dublin.

On the 2nd Earl's death without heirs in 1814, the earldom and other titles became extinct and the estates were split in two. The Dublin house and the unentailed estates were left outright to his second wife; she married Abraham Boyd, and her descendants by this marriage took the additional surname of Rochfort (though, of course, they had no Rochfort blood). Belvedere and the entailed estates went to his sister, Jane, Countess of Lanesborough, about whose reputation a good deal of racy and probably unreliable information can be found in the more scurrilous publications of the time. Some years after her husband's death in 1779 she married a colourful character, John King, known as Jew King, and sometimes called King of the Jews. His original name was Jacob Rey; he was born in London of poor parents and educated at a Jewish charity school. Later on he became a money-lender and financial agent, specialising, apparently, in raising money for young Irish noblemen on the strength of their prospects. He married Lady Lanesborough in Paris, giving up his religion and abandoning a Jewish wife to do so.

119

They seem to have alternated between England and Italy, and to have lived a somewhat rackety life, veering between poverty and magnificence, depending on how his numerous (and possibly shady) financial transactions were doing. King's profession was not adapted to making friends, and 'the King of the Swindlers' and 'the Fugitive Israelite' were among the more polite epithets applied to him. But in *Records of my Life* (1832), John Taylor, journalist, oculist and an engaging minor figure in the literary life of the times, springs to the defence of both him and his wife. He was certainly no fool, and interesting people were to be met at his table when he had the money with which to entertain them. He dabbled at one time in politics. Tom Paine wrote to him from Paris in January 1793: 'When I first knew you in Ailiffe Street, an obscure part of the City, a child, without fortune or friends, I noticed you; because I thought I saw in you, young as you were, a bluntness of temper, a boldness of opinion, and an originality of thought that portended some future good. I was pleased to discuss with you, under our friend Oliver's lime-tree, those political notions, which I have since given the world in my *Rights of Man*.'

The last Lord Belvedere's death put an end to the financial worries of King and Lady Lanesborough, and brought them into a quiet haven for their old age; she was seventy-seven when she inherited the Belvedere estates. It is to be hoped that her husband came to Westmeath, and can be put in the gallery of characters associated with it: the wicked Lord Belvedere, his unhappy Countess, and Lady Lanesborough his daughter, who was certainly beautiful and perhaps over-susceptible, and of whom Taylor wrote: 'There was an ingenuous simplicity in her manner that seemed almost to approach the innocence of childhood.'

King died in Florence in 1823, and his wife in the same town in 1826, aged ninety. Belvedere passed ultimately to her great-grandson Charles Brinsley Marlay. He was a man of taste and discrimination. During his long life he built up a remarkable collection of pictures, drawings, books and *objets d'art*, specialising in Italian pictures of the fifteenth and early sixteenth centuries and Dutch pictures of the seventeenth century. The bulk of his collection he kept in London, at St Katherine's Lodge, his house in Regent's Park; on his death in 1912 this passed, together with an endowment, to the University of Cambridge, and now forms one of the major portions of the Fitzwilliam Museum. But the residue of his pictures remained at Belvedere. They were left with the house to his cousin Lieutenant-Colonel C.K. Howard-Bury, who lived there until his death in 1963.

Arthur Young, the great agriculturalist, visited Belvedere in 1777, and left a description of it that is hard to better, and may suitably conclude this account. 'Stopped at Lord Belvedere's, with which place I was as much struck as with any I had ever seen. The house is perched on the crown of a very beautiful little hill, half surrounded with others, variegated and melting into one another. It is one of the most singular places that is anywhere to be seen, and spreading to the eye a beautiful lawn of undulating ground margined with wood. Single trees are scattered in some places, and clumps in others; the general effect so pleasing that were there nothing further, the place would be beautiful, but the canvas is admirably filled. Lough Ennell, many miles in length, and two or three broad, flows beneath the windows. It is spotted with islets, a promontary of rocks fringed with trees shoots into it, and the whole is bounded by distant hills. Greater and more magnificent scenes are often met with, but nowhere a more beautiful or singular one.'

101. (right) The entrance front at Newtown Anner.

3 MISS SMITH COMES TO TIPPERARY

In the summer of 1815 Catherine Smith, the daughter of a major in the Royal Marines, went to stay with her uncle at Brighton. She was nineteen or twenty years old, and extremely good-looking. Like most visitors to Brighton at that time, she and her two cousins, Sarah and Margaret Ward, passed the day promenading up and down the Steyne, and savouring the subscription library. On one of her visits she picked up a book and began discussing it with her cousins, oblivious of the interest which her good looks and lively manner were arousing in an elderly gentleman who stood nearby. When they left the library he followed them and got into conversation. After that, her sister later related, 'he joined them every day, to the great annoyance of my cousins, who made it a rule to walk one on each side of my sister as a guard, and greater still was their indignation when he walked into their box at the theatre uninvited'.

Within a week or two a letter arrived, containing a proposal of marriage. The elderly gentleman, it appeared, was Sir Thomas Osborne of Newtown Anner (Pl. 101), an Irish

baronet with estates in Counties Waterford and Tipperary worth £8,000 a year. He was fifty-eight years old, and had not been married before. Miss Smith was not encouraging. 'I am sorry,' she replied, 'that my conduct has been so entirely misconstrued as to lead you to suppose I had any intention of encouraging your addresses.'.

Sir Thomas persevered, and in the end she agreed to marry him. She was an intelligent girl of strong character, but not in the least romantic. Sir Thomas's obvious infatuation, her own lack of fortune, and the prospect of becoming Lady Osborne instead of Miss Smith outweighed the fact that his behaviour was decidedly eccentric, and that he was old enough to be her father, if not her grandfather.

Her own father was recently dead. Although her mother supported her decision, most of her other relatives were horrified. Matters were not improved when the family solicitor in Rochester began to draw up the marriage settlement. Not only was Sir Thomas's manner 'so very outré and singular', but the names of his farms — Garrenmillan, Ballinagigla, Ballinasisla, Vallinvaluna, Carigaready, Inchindrisla and so on — seemed so extraordinary to the Kentish solicitor that he found it hard to believe in their existence. A letter was written to Lord Braybrooke to ask if Sir Thomas was genuine. Lord Braybrooke replied that he was all that he professed to be. Unfortunately, Sir Thomas got to know of the correspondence and was understandably furious.

102. Departure from the front door at Newtown, from a photograph of *c.* 1860, probably by W.D. Hemphill.
103. (right) The entrance hall.

Nevertheless, by April 1816 Mrs Smith was reported by her brother-in-law to be ready 'to run all risks, and to let the sacrifice (for I cannot call it a union) be consummated on Monday next at Rochester'. Catherine Smith herself, he added, was acting 'under a mistaken notion of female vanity and of future grandeur'. Sarah Ward expostulated even while dressing her cousin for the wedding: 'Catherine, it is not too late, break off with Sir Thomas, and I'm sure Mr — will be delighted to marry you.' All to no avail: the marriage took place in St Margaret's, Rochester, on 6 April 1816.

On 8 May the Osborne family carriage drove up the long, straight avenue, wheeled round the gravel sweep, and deposited the unlikely couple at the fanlighted hall door of Newtown Anner (Pl. 102). At once Lady Osborne began to send enthusiastic letters back to her English relatives. She was delighted with the situation of the house. It lay two miles from Clonmel, on the Tipperary side of what is known as the Golden Valley, where the River Suir runs through fertile country between the Comeragh Mountains and the shapely mass of Slieve Namon, the third highest mountain in Ireland.

The house had long views to the mountains and was surrounded by magnificent trees. A little river, the Anner, ran down one side of the estate to the Suir. The Suir salmon, she reported, were delicious, the cream 'so thick you could almost cut it'. The house was 'immensely large; the hall very magnificent, supported in the centre by four pillars [Pl. 103]. Sir Thomas built the whole front of the house, and it does great credit to his taste. You could dance thirty couple in the drawing-room and dining-room, which are of exactly the same size.' At least twenty-six servants sat down to dinner every day in the servants' hall.

But even in the first letters another strain begins to creep in. In the big downstairs rooms 'no sound is to be heard but the cawing of the rooks and the echo of my own footsteps'. Upstairs, on the bedroom floor, 'my maid and I walk along the long corridor, from room to room, without more fear of interruption from a single being than if we were in the deserts of Arabia'. Sir Thomas turned out to be very odd indeed. Moreover, although he remained devoted to his wife, he was aggressively anti-social, and expected her to be the same. For the next five years she seems never to have spent a single night away from Newtown Anner. There was no hope of her inviting thirty couples to dance in the dining-room or drawing-room. She was only allowed to make friends with her husband's cousins, the Christmases of Whitfield, and with Mr Riall, who ran a bank in Clonmel, and his two brothers. Her mother and sister came to stay, but for months at a time no visitors came to the house at all.

She gave birth to a son and a daughter; she looked after her children, made a garden, swam in the Anner, read profusely, played with her pet bullfinch, had the bank manager to tea and watched 'the odious black rain' running down the windows. Nostalgic letters began to arrive in England. 'How I long to see the neat hedgerows of England! Here the fields are divided by earth banks sometimes faced with loose stones — is it not shameful idleness?' Moreover, she had a business-like nature and found one aspect of her husband especially upsetting. 'Sir Thomas was a rale gintleman', she reported the local people as saying, 'if he saw a man driving off his colts along the road he would look the other way.'

In the summer of 1821 Sir Thomas was taken ill. At first, as he mistrusted all doctors, he insisted on calling in the vet; but ultimately he was looked after by an excellent local surgeon, Dr Hemphill. He died on 3 June. Catherine Osborne resisted attempts by her co-executors to put the estate in chancery; she took the case to court, won it, and for the next eighteen years or more ran the property with remarkable efficiency.

The bulk of the Osborne estates were in County Waterford. The ancestor of the family had come to Ireland from England in the time of Queen Elizabeth, and had acquired a substantial portion of the lands of the Magraths. His son or grandson, Richard Osborne, was a successful lawyer in Dublin, sat as M.P. for County Waterford, increased the family estates, was created a baronet in 1629, and lived in two houses and a castle in West Waterford, near Dungarvan. The bigger of the two houses, Ballintaylor, was built in 1619. Nearby, at Ballylemon, according to Charles Smith, the Waterford historian, 'it is said he kept a seraglio of women, from whence this place had its name, Bally signifying a town and loman a kept mistress'.

When his grandsons, Sir John and Sir Richard, both died without children in 1713, the Osborne properties were divided. Ballintaylor went through the female line to the Usshers. The baronetcy was inherited by Thomas Osborne, first cousin of Sir John and Sir Richard. He lived at Tickencor, on the Waterford side of the River Suir, a house which he had probably built in the 1660s. It survives today as an ivy-covered ruin near a bridge of about the same date, half a mile or so from the lodge gates of Newtown Anner. It is a gabled, semi-fortified house, of a type that was built in large numbers in Ireland from the late sixteenth through to the mid-seventeenth century.

In the early eighteenth century this kind of architecture was considered painfully old-fashioned. By 1717 Sir John Osborne, the 7th baronet, was living in a house called Mount Osborne, probably just outside Carrick-on-Suir. In 1739 he made a somewhat surprising move, left his own house and property, and took a lease of Newtown Anner from his friend William Wall of Coolnamuck. The probable reason for this was that the land at Newtown Anner was on the Tipperary side of the Suir, and much better than any of the Osborne lands in County Waterford. The Osbornes continued to make it their residence, although they were still only tenants in 1816, and did not buy the freehold until 1835 or shortly before. There was a small house on the property, probably no more than a farm, which Sir John and his son Sir William enlarged and improved.

Sir William was an M.P. from 1761 until his death in 1783. He was a respected country gentleman, and a member of Henry Flood's Popular Party, which fought to keep the Irish Parliament independent of English influence. Arthur Young, the agriculturalist, visited him at Newtown Anner in October 1776, and commended his scheme of settling tenants on smallholdings on his land in the Comeraghs. His son, Sir Thomas, was also an M.P., but seems to have been remarkable for little except writing eccentric letters to the newspapers, shunning society, and greatly enlarging Newtown Anner between about 1798 and 1802. It is hard to see why he did so. He was not married, did not need a big house, and did not own the land. It was an odd thing to do, but then he was an odd man.

Two pieces of evidence for the new building survive: an unsigned and undated 'Ground plan and elevation of a house built at Newtown for Sir Thomas Osborne, Bart'; and a detailed 'Measurement of carpenter's work finding Workmanship and Labour executed at Newtown for Sir Thomas Osborne, Bart', presented by Adam

Shea on 20 March 1802. The latter details work done amounting to £662 17s. 4d., of which £541 19s. 10d. had already been paid since 5 January 1799.

The plan is puzzling in that it ignores the older building, and shows the new work as a self-contained house. In fact, Sir Thomas butted his big new building against the much lower old one. The combination had a disastrous effect on the way in which the chimneys of the old house drew. To remedy this, the old chimneys had to be extended up the height of the new ones by means of flues resembling flying buttresses, with the oddest effect as seen from the side of the house (Pl. 104).

Nothing is known of Adam Shea. The wording of the surviving bill suggests that he was the surveyor, and possibly the designer, of the new building, rather than just the carpenter. The elevation and plan, which are drawn competently but without much sophistication, may be his. In general, given the secure Classical tradition of the time, there is perhaps nothing about the new work which would be beyond the competence of an intelligent client working with a good builder and craftsman. But the fact that the detail of stonework, joinery and plasterwork all hangs together suggests that there was one controlling mind over all.

As in so many Irish houses of the late eighteenth century, the new front was extremely plain. Its character comes from its proportions, from the way in which the wings are carried up a storey higher than the centre, and from the generous scale of its fan-lighted front door. This leads to a big hall, 50 feet by 20 feet, subdivided by screens of columns, to left and right of the door. At either end are a drawing-room and a dining-room, each 32 feet by 22 feet. Through the hall and on the axis of the front door, a top-lit staircase leads up to a long corridor serving the bedrooms on the first floor.

The entrance door, the doorway from the hall to the staircase, the big arch at the head of the stairs, and the arches along the bedroom corridor are all delicately detailed in low relief, with much fluting and reeding. The wooden staircase balusters are exceedingly thin and elegant. The stone columns at the entrance, the columns in the hall, and what the surviving bill refers to as the 'fancy pilasters' of the joiner's work are variants of the columns of the Tower of the Winds in Athens, as popularised by Robert Adam at the Adelphi in London and elsewhere.

The hall columns are of timber, but the capitals were finished off by the plasterers, on a base supplied by the carpenter. The plasterers were also responsible for the pretty centrepiece of the hall ceiling, with its outer circuit of vine leaves and bunches of grapes, and for the deep frieze in the drawing-room, in which sporting dolphins alternate with garlands and cornucopias of flowers. The present chimney-pieces in the

126

104. The old and new buildings from the garden.
105, 106. (top left and right) Two views on the staircase.
107. (bottom right) The view from the house, from the photograph by W.D. Hemphill, *c.* 1861.

main rooms are all early Victorian. A delicate chimney-piece of coloured marbles in the main upstairs bedroom was perhaps one of the original ones on the ground floor.

Sir Thomas may have been an oddity, but he left his descendants with a very agreeable house. The new entrance front was dignified but friendly, the rooms behind it stylish and spacious, but not in the least overpowering. The rooms of the old house at the back were snugger and more intimate. The combination of old and new building, which led to such eccentric results on the exterior, generated the design of the staircase, which ties the different levels of old and new work together, and is the most distinctive feature of the interior. The stairs rise with a sweeping curve up to a landing which gives access to the first-floor rooms of the old building, and continue in a straight flight up to the new first floor (Pls. 105, 106).

The height, spaciousness and combination of curves that this arrangement produces makes walking up and down the stairs a continuous pleasure. The delicately faded green of its walls was lined until recently with coloured engravings of members of the court of Louis XV, in pretty early-Victorian frames. They were a charming but, for an Irish house, somewhat unexpected adjunct to the staircase, the result of a marriage and line of descent which was ultimately to make Newtown Anner the home of an English duke.

A singularly beautiful photograph of about 1860 shows the view from the dining-room window (Pl. 107). In the foreground Lady Osborne looks down at her daughter. Beyond, a horse stands harnessed to a mower, two women gardeners hold their brooms, the long evening shadows fall across the grass, and a vista through the woods leads the eye to the Comeragh Mountains, hazy in the evening light. The view has changed little today, and sums up much of the character of this secluded and lovable Irish house.

128

108. Celebrations for the coming-of-age of Catherine Isabella Osborne.

The photograph is one of a set taken by W.D. Hemphill, surgeon, grower of orchids, collector of Waterford glass, skilled ivory-turner and one of the most gifted, least known of early photographers. He lived in Clonmel, and was the nephew of the Dr Hemphill who had attended Sir Thomas Osborne in his last illness. He became a close friend of the family, who posed for him in fancy dress for numerous of the set-piece photographs popular at the time. Hemphill took four views of Newtown Anner, and a view of the drawing-room (Pls. 107, 109-12). Prints of all of them were preserved in albums in the house, along with a photograph of the family in a pony chaise and carriage before the front door at Newtown Anner, which is probably also by him (Pl. 102). The external views were reproduced in his *Abbeys, Castles and Scenery of Clonmel* (1861), and in a two-volume memoir of Lady Osborne by her daughter, published in 1872.

Lady Osborne, as a result of the death of her elderly and eccentric husband in 1825, had been left in charge of Newtown Anner, the Osborne estates, and two small children. Her son died within three years, aged only seven. The Osborne baronetcy was inherited by his uncle, but Newtown Anner and the estates, or the great bulk of them, went to his sister, Catherine Isabella. She had become an heiress.

129

109. The lake, photographed by Hemphill.

Lady Osborne, after a brief spell of gaiety, became extremely religious. Her efforts to convert the local population to Protestantism were far from well received by the Catholics of Clonmel. Much of her daughter's memoir of her is filled with letters to and from clergymen, one end of the hall was curtained off as a chapel, and according to her sister 'there never was a week but what some meeting was held in the hall at Newtown, or prayers in the evening with very long addresses'. After breakfast, she would sit at an open window giving money to the beggars who came up the drive to talk to her.

In the intervals she studied Greek, started up three schools in and around Newtown, and ran the estates, which in the 1830s were drawing a sizeable extra income from copper mines at Bonmahon. But she was increasingly occupied in bringing up and bringing out her daughter. In 1833 they went together on tour in France, Italy and Switzerland. In Switzerland, Catherine Isabella took lessons from the gifted Swiss painter Alexandre Calame. He drew a pretty title-page for her sketching book, and later sent a series of Alpine views to Newtown Anner.

On 3 July Catherine Isabella came of age. The event was celebrated in style: dinner for 1,400 tenantry, followed by dancing round a maypole in front of the house,

130

110. Looking down to the temple in the garden, photographed by Hemphill.

tea and buns for 400 schoolchildren, fire-balloons, rockets and bonfires on the Comeragh Mountains. The scene is recorded in a contemporary watercolour (Pl. 108). Miss Osborne and her friends joined in the dancing, and were celebrated by a Captain Chaloner:

The long, long dance in endless files
Was cheer'd by high-born Beauty's smiles
For midst the rustic maze
The graceful Heiress oft was seen
Gliding along the velvet green
To Erin's ancient lays.

Five years later she married Ralph Bernal, who added Osborne to his name in recognition of his wife's property.

Lady Osborne lived on at Newtown, with her daughter and son-in-law, until her death in 1856. As they were often away she seems to have continued to run the house much as she had done for the previous nineteen years. It was she who was responsible for remodelling the garden between 1846 and about 1850. She had been a keen gardener since her marriage. In 1817 Patrick Broderick, of Clonmel, built her an elaborate greenhouse, long since demolished but shown in a drawing by Edward Hayes, dated 1818. In that year she built a grotto, which survives, down by the lake. In 1819 she wrote describing how she was decorating it with shells and reported that 'I have two flower gardens, and in one I have sown every seed myself'.

The partial failure of the potato harvest in 1846 set off the creation of the garden as it survived up to recent years. In this and the succeeding years of the Famine, as Dr Hemphill describes in his book on Clonmel, 'She felt justified in giving the reins to her innate love of beautifying everything around her. She employed a large number of the starving peasantry in cutting down unsightly hills and elevations, filling stagnant ponds or converting them into beautiful canals and sheets of water, making walks and terraces, and succeeding in converting one of the most uninteresting portions of the demesne into as lovely and enjoyable a spot as the eye could rest on.'

The principal feature of the new work was a water garden to the west of the house. It was fed by a stream running into the Anner, and took the form of a square moat of water made up of a lake along the eastern side (Pl. 109) and three canals running out of it, with grass or gravel walks along them. A steep slope on the east side of the lake rose up to a terraced walk and flower garden in front of the house. A straight walk led between flower-beds and trellised roses from the bow window of the boudoir to the

111. The dovecote.

terrace. Its line was continued by a walk on the other side of the lake, which led the eye to a wooden Doric temple, known as 'Lady Osborne's Summer-House', which rose above the western canal (Pl. 110). To the north of the flower garden, and on a lower level approached by flights of stone steps between Irish yews, was a square pleasure ground with walks running round it, one of which originally ended in a conservatory. The dovecote which still stands at one corner of the flower garden may have been part of the original scheme (Pl. 111).

All this was laid out at a time when formal gardens in the Italian manner were enjoying a vogue, as an alternative to the 'gardenesque' style of shrubberies, winding paths and kidney-shaped flower-beds. The Newtown Anner garden must have been influenced by this vogue, and certainly contained Italian elements, perhaps partly inspired by an Italian tour made by Lady Osborne in 1840. But it was much more secret and enclosed, and much gentler, than the formal gardens, bright with bedded-out flowers and elaborately embellished with balustrades and carved stonework, such as Charles Barry and W.A. Nesfield were popularising in England at the time.

It seems to have been designed by Lady Osborne entirely without professional help except from her head gardener, Mr Mulqueen, who, according to her daughter, 'took in and carried out Lady Osborne's masterly designs in landscape gardening with singular facility and felicity'. The result was a creative fusion of Italian formality with the ample water and lush deciduous trees of Ireland. It was perhaps at its most beautiful, as is often the case with formal gardens, when the passage of time and the planting of later generations had softened its original lines. But it suffered an irreversible blow when the level of the Anner was lowered in the 1950s, and most of the water was drained out of the lake and canals.

Lady Osborne's son-in-law, Ralph Bernal Osborne, and his father, Ralph Bernal, were both interesting men. The Bernals belonged to a Spanish Jewish family which

112. Hemphill's view of the drawing-room.

came from Seville to London by way of Amsterdam, and set up in business in the eighteenth century as West India merchants, acquiring plantations in Jamaica in the process. Ralph Bernal inherited a comfortable fortune, which he used partly to fight elections (he was a Whig M.P. continuously from 1818 to 1852), and partly to collect works of art. His collection became one of the most famous of his day. It crammed his house in Eaton Square to bursting, and when he died in 1854 was auctioned in 4,294 lots, in a sale of 'Works of Art from the Byzantine period to that of Louis Seize' (as the Christie's catalogue put it) which lasted for thirty-two days. The collection included portraits, furniture, porcelain, faience, enamels, metalwork, ivory, glass, and arms and armour. It realised nearly £71,000. The sum seems derisory today but was found sensational by contemporaries, judging in terms of the money and art values of the time. It should be compared with the even more famous sale of the entire contents of Stowe, held at the house in 1849, which raised £77,000.

Little except a few family portraits and some good pieces of Irish Georgian furniture at Newtown Anner dated back to earlier Osborne days. Its best contents came from the Bernal marriage and must either have been bought in, or reserved from the sale. They were only the leavings of the Bernal collection, but this was so vast and impressive that even its leavings were of considerable interest. In addition to a sizeable amount of eighteenth-century porcelain, Newtown was especially rich in seventeenth and eighteenth-century portraits, including a good Cuyp, two Allan Ramsays, a Wright of Derby, and a superb Largilliere of an as yet unidentified French Marshal.

These were mostly displayed in the hall, drawing-room and dining-room. The dining-room seems always to have been simply decorated, but the drawing-room was done over by the Bernal Osbornes, perhaps in 1854; a letter from Lady Osborne to her daughter, probably written in that year, refers to her as 'alone in your disconsolate house full of workmen'. The room was repapered, using a diaper design with a scrolled border, and fitted up with an Aubusson carpet, a Venetian chandelier, and pelmets, overmantel, mirror and brass and steel grate with matching furniture, all in the Victorian Rococo style (Pl. 112).

Ralph Bernal Osborne followed his father into politics, but otherwise their careers had little in common. He was a wit, a dashing and handsome man-about-town, an enfant terrible of the dinner table. Indulgent Victorian society allowed him to say pretty well what he liked. In politics his friend Disraeli described him as the 'chartered libertine of debate', and his sparkling and slashing speeches in the House of Commons were famous; the news that 'Osborne is up' could be guaranteed to fill an empty House in a few minutes. But, in terms of political success, all this brought him to was the position of Secretary to the Admiralty and an official residence in Admiralty House, between 1852 and 1858. As his entry in the *Dictionary of National Biography* puts it: 'His failure to reach those positions which his talents justified is due to his want of official industry and to the absence of that sobriety of judgement which is dear to the average Englishman.'

The Bernal Osbornes had two daughters, Edith and Grace. The envelopes which the two sisters and their friend Fanny Currey amused themselves with decorating with visual extravaganzas and scenes of Irish life were one of the agreeable surprises of the library cupboard at Newtown Anner (Pl. 113). Both grew up competent watercolour artists, Edith, who became Lady Blake, being especially talented. But it was her younger sister Grace who inherited Newtown Anner when her mother died in 1880.

In 1874 she had married the 10th Duke of St Albans as his second wife. The Dukes of St Albans were descended from Charles II's favourite mistress, Nell Gwyn. On his deathbed he is supposed to have said: 'Don't let poor Nelly starve.' She did not starve, but she and her descendants did less well than Charles II's other illegitimate offspring. Grace Osborne's husband owned Bestwood Lodge, an aggressively Victorian house near Nottingham, and about 9,000 acres, mainly in Nottinghamshire and Lincolnshire. It was a substantial country gentleman's rather than a ducal estate.

Newtown Anner became his second seat, and was inherited, on his wife's death in 1926, by their son Lord Osborne Beauclerk, a man who excelled his Bernal Osborne grandfather in never hesitating to say what he thought, or do what he liked, throughout his life. On the death of his half-brother in 1934 he became the 12th Duke of St Albans. He sold Bestwood Lodge, and continued to make Newtown Anner his home. His wife, widow of the 6th Marquess of Waterford, predeceased him; when he died in 1964 he left a life interest in Newtown Anner to Juliet, widow of the 7th Marquess, and her second husband, Lieutenant-Colonel John Silcock, who had been sharing the house with him. It was sold, and its contents removed, after her death in 1987.

In this way Newtown Anner left the dwindling number of Irish country houses which retain their original contents and are lived in by the families which built or in-

herited them. Much of its character has inevitably been drained out of it. It was not a great house, but it had great charm, made up of many elements not all of which have been described: the wide-branched cedar and long views to the mountains in front of the house; the spacious white-washed stableyard and friendly kitchen court at the back; the railway line running through the kitchen court, by which wood and turf were carried into the house; the small, dark, book-lined rooms in the old wing, and the albums which their cupboards would disgorge, full of photographs of Victorian house parties, or letters from Dickens, Disraeli and other eminent Victorians; the Spy cartoons which jammed the walls of the gentlemen's lavatory, and the photographs of Silcock racehorses which replaced them; the dinner gong hanging between elephants' tusks at the foot of the stairs; the barrel-topped Irish chests which flanked the hall door, one filled to bursting with family papers; the wisteria and pineapple plant climbing round the fan light; and the doormat inscribed with 'welcome', a welcome which the house and its occupants never failed to give this writer for more than fifty years.

113. Decorated envelope sent to Mrs Osborne by her daughters in 1868.
114. (right) Tullynally Castle, Co. Westmeath, from the air.

4 MODERNISING AN IRISH COUNTRY-HOUSE

When we turn on a tap or a switch, we seldom if ever pause to think how much trouble and discomfort we are saving ourselves. We can camp out for a week or two in a remote cottage with nothing but candles and water from the stream, and think what jolly fun it is; but it would be less fun if it was for a lifetime, winter included, and still less fun, even with innumerable servants thrown in, in a thumping great country house instead of a cottage, and least fun of all if the country house was damp as well as cold, among the bogs and lakes of central Ireland. This essay traces the progress of such a house from near-medieval technology (or lack of it) at the end of the eighteenth century to something approaching twentieth-century standards of comfort. It deals first with its water supply and lighting, and then moves on to the other services.

The house concerned (Pl. 114) has reverted in recent years to its original name of Tullynally Castle, but for more than two centuries it was known as Pakenham Hall, after the family which still lives there. At the end of the eighteenth century it was a square classical block with the remains of something much older concealed behind its late-Georgian façades. It stood 300 feet above sea level, towards the top of a steepish hill running down to Loch Derravaragh, two miles away. It was lit by candlelight and heated, like all the houses big and small around it, by turf fires fuelled from the surrounding bogs. It had no piped water supply and no water-closets; the nearest fresh water

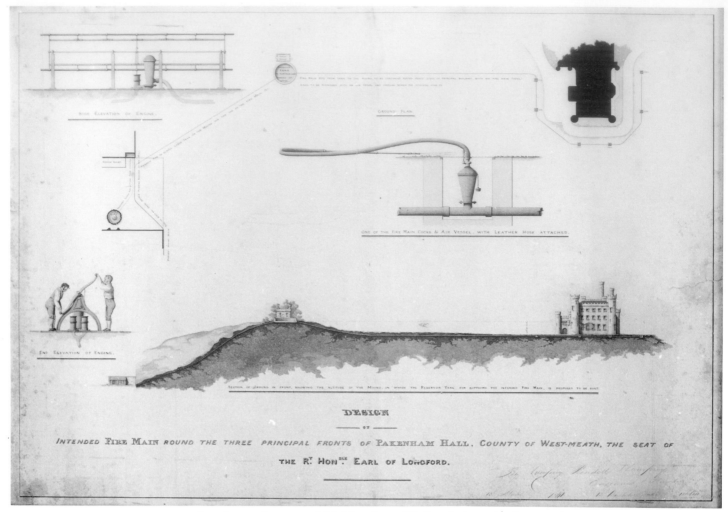

DESIGN
— OF —
INTENDED FIRE MAIN ROUND THE THREE PRINCIPAL FRONTS OF PAKENHAM HALL, COUNTY OF WEST-MEATH, THE SEAT OF

THE R.T HON.BLE EARL OF LONGFORD.

was a spring down the steep hillside about 80 feet below the house. A stream meandered from the spring down towards the lake, supplying on its way the farm buildings and kitchen gardens, which formed a separate cluster of enclosures and buildings about half a mile from the house. Just how the spring water was conveyed to the house, and what use, if any, was made of rainwater, remain uncertain.

Around 1800 Francis Johnston, the best architect of his generation in Ireland, gothicised and castellated the house, for Thomas Pakenham, 2nd Earl of Longford. He supplied it with battlements, round towers at the corners and the extended (and soon disused) name of Pakenham Hall Castle. The technological side of this expenditure was modest but curious. On the kitchen courtyard side of the house, a four-storey tower was built, almost detached from the main building but connected to it by a short umbilical cord of passages. The tower was dedicated to water-closets; there was a luxurious single one on the ground floor and paired ones side by side in little cubicles on the floors above and in the basement. The closets were almost certainly fuelled by a rainwater tank at the top of the tower; the plans do not show where the soilpipe ran to, but it is unlikely to have run very far. The house at this stage contained only one bathroom, possibly supplied from the same tank; this would have been supplemented, as in all nineteenth-century houses, by hand-filled baths set up in the bedrooms.

In 1841 a first attempt was made to pump water up from the stream to the top of the hill. There was already a wooden water-wheel in the farmyard; it worked a pump

115. A design made in 1841 for supplying water to the house in case of fire.

sending water through a rising main a little way up the hill to a cistern which fed a fountain and pool in the garden. Lamprey, Rendell and Lamprey, the Dublin engineers, got out a scheme for extending the system (Pl. 115). Their exquisite drawings hang today in the hall at Tullynally. They show a water reservoir on the highest local point, a little hillock looking across to the entrance front of the house. The reservoir was about 100 feet above the level of the waterwheel. It was to be supplied by extending the rising main to it, and replacing the existing water-wheel by a more efficient one of wrought iron, 21 feet in diameter, to give the extra power. An engine-room next to the reservoir, containing a hand-operated pump, was to be turretted and castellated, so that it would look amusing from the windows of the house.

The little men toiling away at the pump in the drawing were not envisaged as supplying the house with a running water system. The reservoir was only intended to feed a fire main, by snaking round three sides of the house with cocks at regular intervals to which leather hoses could be attached. The purpose of the handpump was to get pressure into the main, so as to produce a jet powerful enough to rise to the upper storeys of the house. In fact, the only part of the system to be installed was the iron water-wheel; perhaps it proved unable to pump the water up the hill, but in any case the reservoir, engine-room and fire main were never built.

This abortive 1841 scheme was the prelude to another outburst of building between 1842 and 1849. The architect was the ubiquitous Sir Richard Morrison, and under his direction the house sprouted two long parallel wings, enclosing separate kitchen and stable yards (Pl. 116). Both wings are elaborately castellated and faced externally with a solid grey limestone that turns black in the rain. A big flagstaff tower was built at the junction of the new and old work. The object of all this was to bring the house up to improved early-Victorian standards of convenience. The new buildings contained larger and more precisely differentiated servants' accommodation, including elaborate laundries. They also provided a private family wing, as was fashionable at that period. The bachelor 3rd Earl of Longford moved into the ground floor of this, and his mother into the floor above. They made themselves comfortable, each with

116. Looking along the stables and past the laundry tower to the main building.

their own bathroom, bringing the total in the castle up to three. The arrangement did not last very long, and the number of bathrooms was not to be equalled again until 1916.

The Morrison addition went one further than Johnston's lavatory tower in attempting to make use of rainwater. All the roof gutters and surface drains around the kitchen courtyard drained into a big underground tank below the surface of the yard. This connected to a hand pump in the laundry which pumped up into a tank feeding the laundry sinks. An existing pump in the basement, originally feeding the sink in the butler's pantry, and the abandoned external pump in the stable yard, were probably part of the same system, though the stable pump may be a later replacement. It is not clear how the new bathrooms were supplied. In any case the system does not seem to have worked, for it was completely overhauled and enlarged when the 3rd Earl died and was succeeded by his brother in 1860.

The 3rd Earl's nickname of 'Fluffy' does not suggest a forceful character. He seldom visited Ireland in his later years; he died at a Charing Cross hotel, aged only forty-three, leaving a doctor's bill of £1,500 and £500 a year to a lady in Oxford Street. His brother, thus translated from the indigence of a younger son, was a middle-aged army officer, precise, kindly, and given to occasional disturbing outbreaks of whimsical humour. He married a Welsh heiress in 1862. His army experience had made him interested in technical matters, and between his succession in 1860 and his death in 1887 he dedicated much of his time to modernising his house and estate. The successive waves of equipment which he installed seem ponderous and inefficient enough today, but must have been thought marvellously up-to-date in mid-Victorian Westmeath. He kept all his letters and accounts neatly docketed, and entered what he did into a little notebook entitled 'Memorandum of Improvements'.

'Spoke to servants in the house and the people at farmyard', he recorded in his

138

117. Looking to kitchen and stable yards across the rainwater tank which fed the water-closets before a pumped water supply was installed.

diary on his first visit to his newly inherited property. 'Did it very well. May God's blessing be upon this house and upon this family.' A few weeks later the comment was sharper: 'Countess's new wing damp ... Doonford willing, but fat and lazy.' He soon got to work to make changes. One of his first achievements was to get rid of Francis Johnston's lavatory tower, which by 1860, if in use at all, must have been a squalid and malodorous object. He replaced it by a smaller projection containing three w.c.'s instead of seven; this more modest supply was more in line with the water available, which came as before, from a rainwater tank, still in existence at the top of the projection (Pl. 117). The replacement of the tower initiated the remodelling of the whole water system under the direction of J. Rawson Carroll, a Dublin architect. It was still dependent on rainwater; all that was achieved was to make the most sophisticated possible use of an unreliable source. Tanks were scattered at strategic points all over the roof, with the maximum possible area draining into them. The courtyard tank was retained, but took only surface drainage and the overflow of the tanks. The system of soil and waste-pipes was extended and improved, with inspection manholes at regular intervals (the effluent was drained away and used to fertilise the park at the bottom of the hill). These new improvements maintained ten widely dispersed w.c.'s and a number of sinks. But the number of bathrooms went back from three to one, for the Earl and his wife never used the private wing and dismantled the baths there. Perhaps this represented a more realistic assessment of what a rainwater system could be expected to do. On the other hand the mid-Victorians in general were keener on w.c.'s than on baths; unlike the previous generation they put sanitation before comfort.

The great technological breakthrough came at last in 1875, when for the first time in its history the house was properly connected to a reliable water supply. On 26 May Lord Longford wrote to his wife: 'Mr Carroll and the Pumpman measured and calculated all yesterday and all this morning. We agreed that there is no other course than to horsepump from the spring to a new tank in the Flagstaff Tower, and so it is to be.' The breakthrough must have been due to an improvement in the quality of available pumps rather than available power; if the family had been prepared to run to the expense of a steam-operated pump water could have been pumped up to the house decades earlier. The horse, in fact, is unlikely to have had to pump beyond the 1880s, when the water-wheel in the farmyard was replaced by a turbine. An oil-driven water pump was supplied by Hornsby and Sons of Grantham in 1906. The new water supply had its disadvantages; the spring emerged out of a limestone soil, so that the house, instead of an unreliable soft-water supply, now got a reliable but extremely hard one.

As the letter quoted above indicates, the new water tank was (and still is) at the top of the flagstaff tower (Pl. 118). At Tullynally, as elsewhere, later generations discovered that towers and turrets erected by their grandparents for romantic reasons had

139

118. The flagstaff tower, built in 1842-9, came in useful for containing a water tank in 1875.

their practical uses. These included the housing not only of water tanks but also of bathrooms, which inevitably began to increase as soon as the water to supply them was available. At Tullynally a second bathroom was installed further down the flagstaff tower, probably before 1900. Running water in the house still only penetrated into the northern fringe of the main building until 1916, when two further bathrooms were put into the south-east tower. A ponderous new hot-water boiler was installed in the basement cellars at the same time; previously hot, or rather tepid, water had been inadequately supplied by a boiler working off the still-room range, probably one of the 4th Earl's improvements of the 1860s.

The chunky new porcelain baths with their massive taps still exist, side by side with more modern wash-basins. They were installed by Richard Mullally, of Mullingar. The 5th Earl had been killed at Gallipoli, waving his walking stick as he led his brigade into battle. Mullally had been given the commission by the agent, G.R. Stewart, who had been impressed by his modest estimate and had not realised that the system also needed an expensive water-softener, for which Mullally had not estimated. There was a nasty scene, leading to a long and indignant letter from Mullally. 'The unwarranted attack which you publicly made upon me in your office on Wednesday,' he wrote, 'was so foreign to me that I was stunned for the time. Since I started business thirty years ago, I have had to deal with Gentlemen no matter how humble their position. I may state, Sir, I am happy in the unblemished reputation which myself and my family hold in the country, and I expect from you the refutation due to my honour.' Stewart replied disclaiming any intention to insult; the episode assumes a symbolic character, the new technology sticking up for its dignity against the arrogance of the landed class.

Lighting at Tullynally pursued a roughly parallel advance with water supply, but a considerably less complicated one. The first sign of any improvement on candles appears in the 1842 drawings. These show alcoves along the corridors containing figures of classical ladies holding up colza lamps. Similar colza-lamp holders were modelled in the early nineteenth century by Humphrey Hopper, and can still be found, though none survive at Tullynally. They were replaced in 1860, when one of the 4th Earl's first improvements, along with the new lavatory tower, was to supply the house with gas. A gasometer and gas-house were erected by the farmyard; the whole operation

119. Abandoned technology in the stable yard.
120. (right) The Hall. Hot-air heating installed in 1807 enabled one of the two fireplaces to be replaced by an organ.

costing £600, about twice the estimate. The gas lit only the hall, staircases and corridors. The living-rooms were lit by paraffin lamps, and the bedrooms still by candles. In 1906 an estimate for £1,350 for replacing gas by electricity seems to have alarmed the 5th Earl, for electricity was not put in until the 1920s. Little enough remains of Tullynally's gas; gas-house and gasometer have been demolished, but a farmyard gate has posts made of converted gas pipes, and in the stable yard a broken gas-standard above an abandoned water pump bears silent witness to two redundant aspects of Victorian technology (Pl. 119).

Heating Tullynally was, and still is, an all-but-insurmountable problem. The cold there in an eighteenth-century winter must have been appalling. The dominating room in the house is the enormous hall (Pl. 120); it is approximately 40 feet square and 30 feet high, and probably represents the roofing over a former internal courtyard. In any case it was beyond the capabilities of the eighteenth century to warm it, even though it had two fireplaces. The other rooms, though not nearly as large, are large enough. The fires were fuelled almost entirely with turf from the surrounding bogs. Coal was a luxury which had to be imported from England. The gradual extension of the Royal Canal in the first years of the nineteenth century made it possible to bring it by water as far as Mullingar, thirteen miles from Tullynally. But it played little part in the economy of the house until the railway came to Float Station, five miles away, in the late 1850s. The Morrison plan of 1842 shows great boxes for turf scattered at strategic points all over the house, but no storage space for coal or even wood.

The first breakthrough in heating came in 1807. The Pakenhams had as their neighbours the remarkable Edgeworth family of Edgeworthstown. Maria Edgeworth, the novelist, is the best-remembered member of the family today, but she always thought of herself as inferior to her father, Richard Lovell Edgeworth, who was a follower of Rousseau, an educational pioneer, an inventor, sometimes a crank and a bore, but all in all a remarkable man. He fitted up a semaphore telegraphic system between Edgeworthstown and Tullynally (the first in Ireland) and earned the undying gratitude of the Pakenham family by warming their hall for them. Maria Edgeworth describes, in a letter written in December 1807, 'the immense hall so well-warmed by hot air that the children play in it from morning to night. Lord L. seems to take great pleasure in repeating twenty times that he was to thank Mr Edgeworth for this.'

Nothing remains of the system today and there is no evidence to show exactly how it worked or how it was fuelled. But it worked well enough for one of the fireplaces to be taken out and replaced by the Gothic organ which is still there. The other fireplace was refitted about 1820 with a six-foot-high Gothic chimney-piece made of cast iron (Pl. 121). This superbly massive object used to be surrounded by an almost equally massive fender (over which a minute housemaid newly arrived from England was discovered one morning vainly trying to climb in in order to light the fire).

Maria Edgeworth's reference to the children playing in the hall from morning to night suggests that her father's Rousseauesque ideas about education may have penetrated to Tullynally along with his scientific expertise. But perhaps it was only typical of the relative informality of Irish country-house life, which used to delight visitors accustomed to the more rigid conventions of England. The Tullynally hall has remained to this day the warmest room in the house, a venue for meetings of all sorts and games for

all ages; over the years it has attracted into its hospitable maw a wonderful miscellany of objects, of sofas, books, organs, harps, celtic cooking pots, bronze deer, stuffed fish, rockinghorses, swords, family portraits and other oddments, presided over by an Irish elk's head dug up out of the bogs, the inevitable status symbol in all big Irish country houses.

The female figures holding colza lamps, which are shown in the designs for the house drawn up by Sir Richard Morrison in 1842, stand on what appear to be stoves. This elegant method of combining heat and light, and extending some of the warmth of the hall to the corridors did not last very long, if indeed it was ever installed. In 1860 the 4th Earl of Longford succeeded his brother, and began his long reign of improvements, which extended to heating as well as lighting and water supply. In 1861 he introduced central heating into the staircase and hall, and the Edgeworth system, if it was still functioning, was replaced. In 1866-7 he extended the pipes to the corridor of the main building, and in 1874-5 to the corridors of the west wing; this, which had been built as a private family wing for his brother and mother, had stood empty since his brother died but was now converted to schoolrooms and nurseries.

The 4th Earl's elephantine boiler has been replaced, but his massive radiators still lurk behind the cast-iron grilles with which he concealed them on the staircase, and hot water still trickles through the ponderous pipes exposed in the corridors and under gratings in the hall. The central heating never reached the servants' quarters or any of the living-rooms or bedrooms; in 1874-5 the Earl installed a gas stove in the turret room off the library, presumably the room in which he worked himself. Otherwise the

121. The cast-iron chimney-piece in the hall.

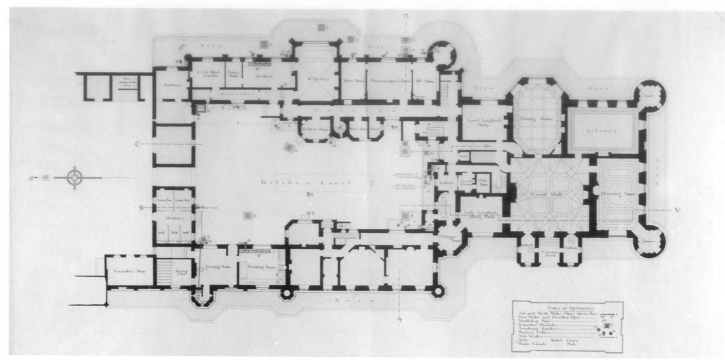

rooms were heated by fires burning a mixture of wood and coal; turf was banished to the outer extremities, as the fuel of the peasantry. The change is noticeable in the plans of Tullynally drawn up by J. Rawson Carroll in the early 1860s (Pl. 122); the turf boxes shown on the Morrison plans have all disappeared, to be replaced by wood or coal stores.

Tullynally as the 4th Earl left it could never have been described as a warm house, except in one or two places; but it was warmer than it had ever been before. There would have been few houses in Ireland or England that were much warmer, and a great many that were colder. Central heating and gas lighting in the hall and corridors, running water in two or three bathrooms, paraffin lamps and open fires in the living-rooms, candles, open fires and water-jugs in the bedrooms, was the Victorian half-way house between manual labour and piped services. It meant a certain increase in comfort, but no very noticeable saving of labour, and whatever this was was more than swallowed up as a result of higher Victorian standards; there were still innumerable fires to be laid, lamps to be cleaned, and cans of hot water to be carried to the bedrooms each morning and evening.

Technologically the house lived off the 4th Earl until electricity was introduced in the 1920s. His son, the 5th Earl, like many of his generation, was not technically minded; his ruling passion was for land and hunting, and his main contribution to the amenities at Tullynally was to consider and reject the possibility of introducing electricity in 1906. It was not till after the 1914-18 war, as rising taxation and wages began to make inroads into the size of country-house staffs, that labour-saving devices became increasingly important for survival.

Unfortunately there are no precise records of how many servants there were at Tullynally in the nineteenth century. Just before 1914 the indoor staff, including nursery and laundrymaids, amounted to about twenty, which by the standards of the time was not especially large. It still occupied, with modifications, the wing with which Sir Richard Morrison had greatly extended the house in the 1840s. But here, as everywhere, the 4th

144

122. Plan of the ground floor in about 1865.

Earl made his mark, most noticeably in the equipment of the kitchen and laundry.

The kitchen at Tullynally is a splendid room (Pl. 123), but has the disadvantage from the point of view of the country-house archaeologist that it was in regular use until a few years ago; as a result the gigantic cast-iron range installed by the 4th Earl in 1875 was replaced by an Aga in about 1940. But the great ovens (made by L.A. Bryan, of Bride Street, Dublin) with their funereally clanging iron doors are still there, and the dresser is still gleaming with brassware probably bought for the kitchen when it was built in the 1840s. Most interesting of all is the survival of the cooking apparatus made redundant by the 1875 range. 'Mrs Sims,' wrote the 4th Earl in that year, 'consents to a one-fire range in place of the kitchen furnace, and so it is to be.' What the replaced furnace consisted of was no fewer than five separate fires each in its own brick-arched pigeon-hole under the ledge beneath the huge triple window, with hot

123. The kitchen.

plates of different shapes and sizes above them. These separate fire recesses are linked horizontally and have flues to either side. They would have beeen supplemented, for roasts in particular, by a fire in the great arched recess later filled by the 1875 range.

But it is the laundries which remain the least altered part of the servants' wing at Tullynally, for they have been little used since the 1920s. Morrison, when he designed his addition in 1842, paid more attention to them than to any other part of the servants' wing, and detailed drawings survive. They were entered from the kitchen courtyard, and consisted of a wash-house (Pl. 124), an ironing-room and a drying-room. The wash-house was fitted with two long rows of wooden washtrays, one of which survives, supplied with water from a high-level boiler; water was pumped up into this by hand from the big rainwater tank beneath the courtyard. In the ironing-room next door the plans show long tables and an ironing stove; the latter is still there, a Ridge Laundry Stove No. 4, made by Smith and Wellstoods Ltd, with a sloping top and a ledge half-way up on which to heat the irons (Pl. 125). The drying-room was up a flight of stairs off the ironing-room with a serpent of iron pipes coiled to form a flat square in the middle of the floor. The boiler which heated the pipes also served the

124. The wash-house in the laundry.

stable harness-room, which was underneath.

The drying-room was clearly not expected to do all the drying, for there was an open-air walled drying-yard beyond the stables. A turret staircase leading down from the ironing-room, opened into a railed area, as in a London house. This formed a sunken passage which ran along the front of the stables, through a tunnel under the stable archway, and round to the back, where a flight of steps led up to the drying-yard. This route enabled the laundrymaids to carry the washing to the drying-yard without meeting any of the grooms; and although the drying-room and harness-room were adjacent and linked by hot-water pipes, their entrances were in separate courtyards. There is little doubt that the object of all this was sexual, or rather anti-sexual.

In 1863-4 the 4th Earl recorded in his notebook 'sundry fittings in laundry'. These included new mangles and a new drying-room, the latter reducing still further the chance of any sexual misadventures. The two iron-fitted

mangles in the laundry today date from this period, while the wooden one at the end of the washtrays is possibly an 1840s survival. The bigger of the new mangles was used for sheets. It resembles some terrifying instrument of torture, with a heavy roller designed to grind inexorably along iron rails across the sheets laid out on a flat surface below. Both mangles were made by Thomas Bradford and Co. of Manchester. The washing thus more efficiently squeezed, was carried to the new drying-room (Pl. 126) which replaced the former harness-room. Its eight ponderous wooden racks could be trundled out on rails, loaded up, and pushed back into a heated chamber. This method was obviously more efficient than the old one and as a result the drying-yard was disused; the turret staircase to the sunken walk was taken out and a w.c. put in its place. The drying-yard, overgrown and abandoned behind its locked door and high walls, became a place of mystery to the children of the next generation.

The laundrymaids, however much curtailed (and they are remembered as 'apt to be pretty'), remained a semi-independent group. For the Tullynally household, like Victorian country-house communities everywhere, underwent the polarisation into little interlocking groups which makes them such fascinating study for the anthropologist.

125. A stove for heating irons, installed in the ironing-room in the 1840s.

This essay can conveniently leave the house at tea-time just before the 1914-18 war, as remembered by Miss Reason who came to the family as a lady's maid in 1911. Tea — not just a cup of tea, but a meal — is being served in eleven different places. The gentry are in the drawing-room, the younger children, nannies and nurserymaids in the nursery and the elder children with their governess in the schoolroom. The upper servants, including the ladies' maids, are in the housekeeper's room, the laundrymaids in the laundry, the kitchen maids in the kitchen, the housemaids in the little house-maids' sitting-room, the charwomen in the still-room, the footmen in the servants' hall and the grooms in the harness-room. A riding master who comes weekly from Dublin for the children, being too grand for the grooms and servants but not grand enough for the gentry, is having tea off a tray on his own.

148

126. Racks in the drying-room, fitted up in 1863-4.
127. (right) Looking across the River Suir at Waterford to Reginald's Tower and the cathedral spire.

5

THE NOBLEST QUAY IN EUROPE

The mellifluous stanzas of the *Faerie Queene* turn away momentarily from fictitious landscapes to praise the rivers of Ireland, among them:

> The gentle Shure, which passing sweet Clonmel
> Adorns rich Waterford.[1]

At Waterford the Suir is gentle, certainly, but a gentle giant, who has brought to the city the greater part of its wealth, its history, its importance and its beauty. It is the views of Waterford from or across the Suir that remain most vividly in the memory — above all as one used to see it coming up from the sea on the old ferry-boat, when one rounded the last bend of the peacefully winding river and saw the long low line of multicoloured houses stretching along the quay, still half asleep in the early morning sunshine, with the spire of the cathedral rising above them (Pl. 127). Kings and armies have sailed up the Suir to Waterford, and moulded the history of Ireland in doing so; cattle, corn and cloth have been floated down it from the inland counties to Waterford warehouses and out again in Waterford ships to England and America; prosperous

Waterford merchants have dotted its banks with their pleasant country houses, and its broad expanses give the city a feeling of spaciousness and scale not to be found in many larger and more important places.

There is no ford at Waterford: the river is far too wide and deep, and remained unbridged up to the late eighteenth century. The name is a Danish one, and the 'ford' in it comes from the same root as 'fiord': Waterford is either 'Weather Haven' (Vedra-fiord) or Vader-fiord, a haven dedicated to a Norse deity. The Danes came up the Suir in or around 853,[2] and founded the city, probably on the site of a Celtic settlement. They had sailed down from the north to Ireland first to plunder and afterwards to colonise: at much the same time as Waterford they founded the cities of Dublin, Cork, Limerick and Wexford, also on broad inland waterways, and introduced the concept of the town to Ireland, for the Irish Celts were not a town-dwelling people. They walled their towns to defend themselves against the native inhabitants; and their memory is preserved in the best known of Waterford's ancient buildings, Reginald's Tower, which looms bulkily on the waterfront at the junction of the Mall and the Quay. The tower marks the north-east corner of the city walls, and is named after Reginald the Dane, who ruled at Waterford around the year 1000. But the present tower is probably a later medieval rebuilding of the original Danish one. It originally rose straight out of the water; to the east (to the left, as one looks from the Suir) where many of Waterford's best eighteenth-century houses were later to be built, a protective belt of marshy ground stretched to the stream known as John's River or John's Pill ('pill' being local dialect for a small tidal river); to the west the ground rose gently to the cathedral, and the Danish walls went along the river front until they turned inland where the Victorian Gothic clock tower now stands. Later, probably under the personal direction of King John, the walls were extended, and a further chunk enclosed to the south and west. The riverside wall has disappeared completely, but much of the inland wall survives, though often hidden behind later houses.

150

128, 129. Looking across the Suir at Waterford to Reginald's Tower, the spire of the Protestant cathedral and the medieval tower of the Franciscan church.

Discussion of the walls has carried the story out of the Danish into the Norman period. Strongbow came to Ireland by way of Waterford, landing in the harbour and assaulting and taking the town in August 1170. He was immediately married, in the Danish cathedral of Waterford, to Eva, daughter of Dermot McMurrough, who had invited the Normans to Ireland to help him recover his kingdom of Leinster. Henry II became alarmed at his subject's increasingly independent kingdom-carving, came over in person in 1171, landed at Waterford on 18 October, and made a triumphal march up to Dublin. For the next 400 years Waterford remained notably loyal to the English Crown. King John, when still Earl of Morton, landed there in 1185 and then or a little later gave a charter to the Priory of St John — hence John's River, John's Hill and John's Street in Waterford today. He returned in 1210, lodged, according to tradition, in a palace opposite the west end of the cathedral (where the Widows' Apartments now are), enlarged the city walls, minted coins, presented the city with a sword and mace which are still preserved among the city regalia now on show in Reginald's Tower, and granted it a charter in 1215.

Henry III, Edwards I, II and III, Henry VI, Edward IV, Henry VII and Elizabeth each gave the city one or more charters. Richard II visited it in 1394 and 1399. In 1487, when Lambert Simnel was crowned in Dublin as Edward VI, Waterford refused to recognise him, and in 1497 it repulsed Perkin Warbeck after an eleven-day siege, and drove him over to Cornwall. It was in gratitude to the city for its loyalty on this occasion that Henry VII conferred on it what still remains its motto: *Urbis Intacta Manet Waterford*. In 1536 Henry VIII sent over a cap of maintenance by the hands of William Wyse, of a leading Waterford family, who was a member of his household and served in his entourage at the Field of the Cloth of Gold.

The links that bound Waterford to the Crown were ones of mutual self-interest. It was essential for the Crown to keep it loyal, for Waterford (by way of Milford Haven or Bristol) was then the main port of communication between England and Ireland.

151

And the citizens of Waterford had no reason for being friendly towards the inhabitants of the country around them, who from the time the city was founded regarded its increasing wealth as their natural prey.

The Reformation put a strain on the city's loyalty to the English Crown, for Waterford remained almost entirely Catholic. But up till the end of the sixteenth century the change made less difference than might have been expected. There was little religious persecution in the city under the Tudors, and it was still governed by an exclusively Catholic corporation. The main change was that the religious houses were dissolved, and the churches handed over to the Protestants. As, up till Cromwellian times, these were only a tiny handful, the natural and unfortunate result was that Waterford's many medieval churches fell into decay, and most of them have disappeared, apart from an occasional mouldering fragment.

The buildings of the Priory of St John were granted to Henry VIII's favourite, Sir William Wyse, and gradually reduced to a fragment. The only important medieval remains in Waterford today, apart from the city walls, are the shells of the Dominican and Franciscan churches. The former (founded in 1226) is an inconspicuous ruin, complete with tower, tucked away in a back street in the centre of the town. The Franciscan Friary of the Holy Ghost, founded in 1240 by Sir Hugh Purcell, is larger and more impressive; its tower, with characteristic Irish crenellation, figures prominently with the cathedral spire and the tower of the modern Franciscan church in the views of the town from across the river (Pls. 128, 129). In plan, it is typical of all Irish Franciscan churches; it has a central tower, no transepts, and aisles, nave and chancel, the latter ending in three elegantly slim lancets. In 1541 the abbey buildings were granted to Patrick Walsh, of an old and prominent Waterford family. He adapted and endowed the nave and side chapel of the church as the Holy Ghost Hospital, an almshouse for poor men and women.[3] Many later Walshes emigrated to Spain or the Canaries, but the family continued to nominate the Master up till at least 1818.[4] The hospital is the oldest and most historic of Waterford's many charitable institutions and still a considerable landowner in the city. In the nineteenth century it moved to new buildings on the edge of the town, taking some interesting large medieval wood carvings with it.

In 1693 the choir of the church was handed over to a congregation of French Huguenot linenweavers, who had been encouraged to settle there as a result of the revocation of the Edict of Nantes. Hence it is still commonly called the French Church. But as the Huguenots gradually got absorbed into the rest of the population, the congregation dwindled. The roof fell in about 1810, and since then the church has been a ruin.

In the first half of the seventeenth century there was an efflorescence of talent among Waterford men. The old merchant families of the city, by now established, rich, and often considerable landowners outside the city bounds, produced a series of eminent Counter-Reformation churchmen — Waddings, Whites, Lombards, Walshes and Sherlocks — who gained the city an international reputation. Their forcing-house was the school in Kilkenny run by the Waterford-born Dr Peter White, whom Anthony Wood called 'the happy schoolmaster of Munster'. 'In the realm of Ireland', wrote Stanyhurst, the Irish historian, 'was no grammar school so good, in England, I am well assured none better than the school of Dr Peter White, from which as from a Trojan horse issued men of distinguished literary ability and learning.'[5] Peter Lombard became

Archbishop of Armagh, Thomas Walsh Archbishop of Cashel. Three Wadding brothers were prominent Jesuits — Luke an eminent theologian in Spain, Michael active in the Mexican mission, and Peter at one time Chancellor of the Jesuit University of Bohemia. Their cousin Ambrose was a Jesuit professor in Germany. Peter White's brother Thomas founded the Irish College in Salamanca. Stephen White, of Clonmel, probably a connection (some say a brother) of Peter and Thomas, was one of the greatest scholars of his age, and the first man to make serious study of the great wealth of Irish Celtic manuscripts in European monasteries.

But the Franciscan Luke Wadding, brother of Ambrose and cousin of the Jesuit brothers, was the most renowned of Waterford churchmen. This many-sided man founded the College of St Isidore in Rome, and was a formidable scholar and copious writer, best remembered today for his great history of the Franciscan order and his edition of the works of Duns Scotus. But he was also an ardent and active Irish patriot. When the Irish rebelled against England in 1641 and formed the Catholic Confederacy, he used all his considerable influence to support his countrymen. In 1645 he succeeded in getting Cardinal Rinuccini sent out from Rome as the Papal Nuncio to the Confederacy, equipped with money, arms and ammunition, including 36,000 dollars which he had raised himself.

It was inevitable that in this period Waterford's loyalty to the King should come under increasing strain. There were violent clashes between the city council and James I; although Charles I patched up the relationship and in 1626 gave the city the Great Charter under which it operated until 1841, Waterford joined the Catholic Confederacy in 1642. Rinuccini disapproved of the peace signed between Charles I and the Confederacy (as a result of the Civil War in England), and left Ireland in February 1649. In August, Oliver Cromwell landed at Dublin. For eight days in November he assaulted the city walls of Waterford but failed to take the city. However, in June 1650 the Cromwellian troops, commanded by General Ireton, laid siege to it again, and it was surrendered on 10 August.

The proud, ancient and prosperous city of Waterford emerged from the next eight years reduced to the lowest depths of humiliation, its monuments pillaged, its citizens scattered and its wealth gone. In March 1651 the leading families of Waterford were given three months to be clear of the city bounds. Waddings, Wyses, Aylwards, Sherlocks, Walshes, Lombards, Whites, Dobbyns and other old and wealthy Waterford families vanished from the city annals, in which they had long held the dominant position. Some of them retired into the country, and gradually sank to the level of the peasantry. Many went abroad and never returned. Some filtered back after the Restoration, but the majority even of these left Ireland after the Battle of the Boyne in 1690. In 1658, according to the 1659 census, the population of Waterford was reduced to 950. 'Of these,' says Edmund Downey in his *Story of Waterford*, 'no less than 538 were foreign adventurers — mostly English — the rest being natives who because they were labourers and menials — and therefore could not be dispensed with — had been permitted to remain in the conquered, plundered, and degraded city.'[6]

The terrible hammer-blow of the Cromwellian occupation was repeated throughout Ireland. And Waterford, like the rest of Ireland, gradually recovered from it. In the course of the seventeenth and eighteenth centuries it became once more a prosperous city. A new oligarchy arose, composed, like the old one, of a few heavily intermarried

153

families. Few of these new families had been in Waterford before 1650, and inevitably they were all members of the Protestant Church of Ireland. Catholics and Nonconformists were excluded from the city government; Catholic chapels were only allowed on sufferance; the Protestants, though in a minority, ruled the town and drank King William's health on the anniversary of the Battle of the Boyne. It was not a just situation. But within their limitations the city councillors worked hard and conscientiously for the improvement of the town. They found it decaying, insanitary and ruinous; they left it with buildings both public and private of which it could justifiably be proud, and with the noblest quay in Europe.

Up till the eighteenth century the quay at Waterford extended from Reginald's Tower to where the clock-tower now stands opposite the end of Baron's Strand Street. Behind it the city walls ran between it and the town. The quay was extended to the west in 1700, and in 1705, during the mayoralty of David Lewis, the northern stretch of the walls was taken down, and the town thrown open to the river.[7] At various times in the eighteenth century there were further extensions to the quay, and it was paved for its whole length of about a mile in 1776. The proposal was extolled in a Waterford newspaper of the time as likely to make 'the finest Parade in Europe'.[8]

On 29 June 1736 the Corporation paid £20 to the Flemish painter William van der Hagen for the view of Waterford which still hangs in the town hall (Pl. 131).[9] This shows clearly how by then the opened-up quay was already lined with the houses and warehouses of Waterford merchants. Prominent in the middle of the waterfront is the new Exchange, built in 1715, on the site where the Post Office is today. The houses on the extreme right are part of a new extension to the town laid out outside the walls in 1725 around new streets called (almost inevitably at that date) King Street, George Streets Great and Little, and Hanover Street. A good deal of rebuilding inside the line

130. Central area of Waterford. Detail from the plan published by Richards and Scale in 1764. The 'New Chappel' is now St Patrick's Church; the 'Great Chappel' was to be enlarged as the Catholic cathedral.

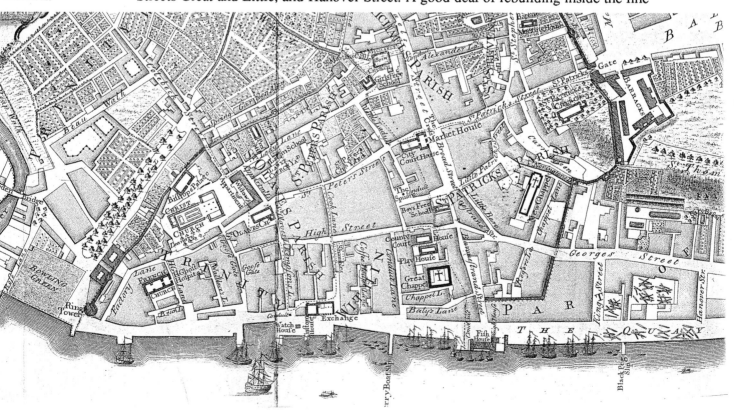

of the walls was also going on in the mid-eighteenth century. Many of the houses of this date
have disappeared because, as tends to happen in
all towns, the smart residential area moved
steadily out (eastwards in Waterford) and much
of the centre became slummy. The least-touched
area is that around the Protestant cathedral, where
Lady Lane is the best surviving example of an old
Waterford street, medieval in narrowness and
name (the vanished Lady Church was in it) but
lined with substantial Georgian houses (Pl. 132).

At the end of Lady Lane and adjoining the
cathedral is one of the architectural highlights of
Waterford, the superb Bishop's Palace. This was
started in 1741 by Bishop Charles Este on the
line of the city wall, which was broken down to
make way for its east front. The marshy ground
below this front had been drained around 1735
and planted with a double row of elms, known as
the Mall, leading to a bowling green adjoining
Reginald's Tower by the river.

The front of the bishop's palace which enjoyed this agreeable prospect is built of beautifully cut limestone ashlar and has the handsome

155

131. (top) View of Waterford in 1736, by William Van der
Hagen.
132. (right) Looking along Lady Lane to Mason's School.

133. The Bishop's Palace, with the spire of the cathedral beyond it, designed by Richard Castle, *c.* 1740.

reticence of the best Irish Georgian architecture (Pl. 133). The researches of the Knight of Glin have established that the palace was designed by Richard Castle — architect, amongst much else, of Powerscourt, Russborough, Westport and Carton, and in Dublin of Leinster House and the Rotunda Hospital. The Doric centrepiece on the Mall front, with the circular niche above it, is typical of Castle's style. The entrance front is similar to designs made for Bishop Milles in 1739 by the English architect William Halfpenny, and Castle probably adapted these for his successor. Inside, the palace is a disappointment. Bishop Este was, one suspects, in the best tradition of worldly eighteenth-century prelates. His Waterford palace would have been big enough for an archbishop; and at Kilkenny, where he was bishop before, he built a palace almost as large. But he died in 1745, leaving the Waterford palace unfinished and somewhat of an embarrassment to his successors. In more recent years it became the home of Bishop Foy's school, founded in 1704 by Nathaniel Foy.

Between Bishops Foy and Este came Bishop Thomas Milles, who, though a learned man, was regarded with suspicion by his ultra-Protestant flock — Dean Swift reported that he was suspected of wearing a crucifix. His monument at Waterford is the little church of St Olave's, a Danish foundation adjoining the cathedral, which he rebuilt in 1734. Apart from a Victorian east window it remains exactly as described in Smith's *Waterford* in 1746, complete with canopied bishop's throne, three-decker pulpit, black and white marble paving and pedimented reredos (Pl. 134).

St Patrick's church at the opposite end of the town is the Catholic counterpart to St Olave's. It is that great rarity in Ireland, an eighteenth-century Catholic chapel. It had been built by 1764, when it was described as the 'New Chappel' on Scale and Richards' plan of Waterford (Pl. 130). Like St Olave's, it is a building of few architectural pretensions but it has considerable charm and is vividly evocative of the period in which it was built, when the penal laws against Catholics were still in force (Pl. 135). But religious bitterness in Waterford was, fortunately, rapidly decreasing. The end of the century saw the remarkable phenomenon of a Catholic and a Protestant cathedral both being designed by the same architect, John Roberts. It is time to look at Roberts, and at the mainly Protestant families who were his clients.

In August 1650, when the Cromwellian troops had stormed into Waterford, and Ireton, their general, had turned out the bishop and lodged himself in his palace, a little boy called Mason wandered into the cathedral and found the soldiers in occupation and dinner being cooked in one of the aisles. He used to relate to his children how he

134. (top right) Inside St Olave's Church, built in 1734.
135. (bottom right)   St Patrick's, a rare surviving example of an eighteenth-century Catholic church in Ireland.

'got a roast chicken from one of the cooks, whilst Captain Bolton, a fanatic, was preaching in the pulpit, attired in jackboots'. One hundred and twenty-three years later, his great-grandson Henry Alcock, and the jackbooted captain's descendant Alderman Cornelius Bolton, sat together on the committee that organised and financed the rebuilding of the cathedral.[10] Also on the committee was Bolton's cousin or nephew Simon Newport, great-grandson of a Dutch merchant who came to Ireland with William of Orange, and founder of the Waterford bank celebrated in the phrase 'as good as Newport's notes'. Another member was Alderman William Morris, whose family first turn up in Waterford records in 1655, when Captain John Morris was licensed to ship 'Irish vagrants' as slave labour to Barbados, in his two ships at Passage (near Waterford) and Limerick.

From such diverse origins came the small group of Protestant families who ruled Waterford in the eighteenth century, and supplied the members of its

highly interrelated and self-perpetuating council of forty. In 1777 the council included three Boltons, two Newports, two Morrises, and no fewer than seven Alcocks, including the mayor. Among other prominent City of Waterford families were Barkers, Congreves, Carews, Christmases, Lloyds and Pauls. They all had big houses in the city itself, and acquired comfortable country houses and increasingly large estates within convenient distance — the Carews at Woodstown and Ballynamona, the Congreves at Mount Congreve, the Christmases at Whitfield, and so on. The Boltons lived at the noble demesne of Faithlegg, down the Suir from Waterford, where Captain Bolton had stormed and captured the castle of the Aylwards in 1649.

Across the river was New Park, home of Sir John Newport, M.P. for the city, with its fine picture collection including 'two paintings which are among the best works of Carlo Dolce and Salvator Rosa'.[11]

But the members of this Waterford oligarchy were as proud of their city as they were of their own homes, and enriched it with fine public buildings and spacious streets. Their monopoly of public life became harmful only in the nineteenth century, when they had developed from city counsellors into country gentlemen for whom the corporation's main function was to provide comfortable berths for their younger sons. By then they probably deserved their uncomplimentary local nickname of the 'Forty Thieves'. The old Catholic oligarchy, the Waddings, Wyses, Sherlocks, Whites and their fellows had been smashed by the Cromwellian irruption in 1650. Their Protestant successors were dislodged as effectively, if more gently, by the Municipal Reform Act of 1841.

The son of the little boy who adventured into the cathedral was Sir John Mason, prominent in the municipal and charitable life of the town around 1700. As executor to Bishop Gore, he was responsible for the tall but self-effacing block of almshouses known as the Widows' Apartments, built in 1702 opposite the west end of the cathedral, where King John's palace is said once to have stood. Two of his daughters married Alcocks; another, Elizabeth, supplied money for a new reredos in the cathedral,

136. Inside the Protestant cathedral designed by John Roberts and built in 1774-92, with plasterwork installed after a fire in 1815.

and a fourth, Mary, endowed a free school for Protestant girls. The school was in Lady Lane, and is still standing, though no longer used as such; it is a pretty little building with 'Pietas Masoniana MDCCXI' inscribed in the pediment. The reredos vanished when the cathedral was rebuilt in the 1770s.

The old cathedral was a building of considerable historical and architectural interest, and incorporated a good deal of the structure of the original Danish building of the late eleventh century.[12] But in the 1770s Gothic was not admired in Ireland, and to the Waterford Protestants, consumed with a fervour for modernising and rebuilding the town, the old building must have seemed unsightly and out of date, besides being in a bad state of repair. Plans for rebuilding both cathedral and palace were produced in 1739, in the time of Bishop Milles, by William Halfpenny, an architect with Bristol connections. There was a strong trading link between Waterford and Bristol, which is perhaps how Halfpenny came to be involved; but the plans were never carried out.

In 1773 Thomas Ivory, the Dublin architect, was asked to report on the condition of the cathedral, and recommended that it be rebuilt.[13] The commission for the rebuilding went, however, not to Ivory but to a Waterford man, John Roberts.[14] He was the grandson of Thomas Roberts, described as 'a Welshman of property and beauty', who settled in Waterford about 1680. John's father, also Thomas, was a carpenter and builder who built the new gaol for the Corporation in 1727, and brought a water supply to the quay in 1742. John (1714-96) is said to have studied as a young man in London, though under which architect is unfortunately not recorded. He was back in Waterford by 1750, when he was paid for supplying new windows to the courthouse and cathedral. At the age of about seventeen he had made a runaway match with Mary Susannah Sautelle, of a Waterford Huguenot family. The marriage worked out well in the long run, for Richard Chenevix, Bishop of Waterford, was also of Huguenot stock and a friend of the Sautelles. He employed John Roberts to finish off the new palace, and gave him and his wife a lease of the old one. In January 1774 the cathedral committee selected his plan for the new cathedral;[15] no doubt the bishop's support helped to sway their decision.

John Roberts was the builder as well as the architect of the cathedral. It took some years to build; subscriptions for the steeple, which does not seem to have been part of the original design, were being raised in 1783,[16] and the whole building was not finished until at least 1792. The result was the finest eighteenth century ecclesiastical building in Ireland, and one of a piece with its surroundings, which are all of the same period. The spire in particular is unfailingly satisfying; it is built of the same cool grey limestone as the bishop's palace, and soars up from its square base to its octagonal steeple in a series of delicately modulated stages. St Martin-in-the-Fields and other spires by James Gibbs are an obvious source of inspiration; but the Waterford spire is not a copy but an original creation.

Inside, the plan is a somewhat unusual one with an open antechapel (probably originally intended as a baptistry) at the west end as though in an Oxford or Cambridge college chapel. A number of monuments from the old cathedral were re-erected in this antechapel, and from it one looks down the airy enfilade of columns of the main nave to the pedimented reredos at the east end (Pl. 136). The plasterwork of the vault dates from a restoration after a bad fire in 1815; there was another

restoration in 1891, when the galleries were taken out and the bases of the columns given their present marble casing.

A hundred yards or so from the cathedral is the town hall, the next in date of John Roberts's Waterford buildings. Its history is a curious one. In 1781 the corporation decided to promote development on the bowling green (where the Tower Hotel and adjacent buildings now are).[17] The green was divided into lots, which were put up for auction, except for two, which were leased for thirty-five years at a nominal rent to (almost inevitably) Cornelius Bolton, Robert Shapland Carew, Henry Alcock Jnr and Simon John Newport, for the purpose of erecting on them a playhouse and assembly rooms.[18] In 1783 it was decided to move the site across the Mall to one under the city wall. The same lessees were given a new 999-year lease at one shilling a year, and it was agreed that when the assembly rooms were built the mayor was to have 'full use of the intire Ground floor for Publick Entertainments'.[19]

In 1787 Prince William Henry (afterwards William IV) was given an 'elegant breakfast' by the corporation in the New Rooms (as they were called), and the local newspaper announced the completion of the 'Grand Banqueting Room' there in 1788.[20] In 1813 the corporation bought out the remainder of the lease for £3,000, and moved the city offices there from the Exchange on the Quay.[21] In this way the New Rooms became the town hall, though the 'playhouse' continues to this day to occupy one end of the building. Its façade lines up alongside that of the bishop's palace, which is set back from the road immediately beyond it. With its sequence of arched windows set in arched recesses (Pl. 137), it has the same kind of delicate grace as the cathedral spire — perhaps too much delicacy, for the centre is a little weak for a building of its size. In its design it is reminiscent of Thomas Ivory's small public library at Armagh, which was built in 1771 and probably influenced it. Inside are a series of huge rooms, admirably suited for entertainments if far from convenient for public offices. Their decoration is very simple: the most notable feature is the enormous Waterford glass chandelier in the council chamber. According to contemporary newspaper accounts this was installed in 1802.[22]

In 1792 the corporation granted a plot of land in Baron's Strand Street to the Catholics for a new church, 'it being the earnest wish and desire of this board to accommodate every description of their fellow citizens with every advantage which can tend (by facilitating the publick Worship of the Deity) to promote Religion and Virtue'.[23] The plot adjoined that of the 'Great Chapel' shown on the old plans, and on the enlarged site thus obtained the new Catholic cathedral was built. The architect was once again John Roberts. He achieved the remarkable feat not only of designing two cathedrals in one town but of giving the two buildings absolutely different characters,

137. The Town Hall, built to Roberts's designs in 1783-8.

each suited to its own religion. The Protestant cathedral is cool and northern, redolent of lawn sleeves and the communion service; the Catholic cathedral, with its forest of huge Corinthian columns, is warm, luscious and Mediterranean (Pl. 138).[24]

Roberts was over eighty when he designed the Catholic cathedral, but still mentally and physically active. He was accustomed to get up at six in the morning to superintend the workmen at the cathedral. One morning he rose by mistake at three, found the unfinished building deserted, sat down in it, fell asleep, and caught a chill

161

138. The Catholic cathedral, designed by John Roberts and commenced in 1792.

that killed him. This remarkable man was then eighty-two. He had had twenty-one children; his youngest surviving son was Thomas Sautelle Roberts, a well-known Irish landscape painter; his great-grandson was Field Marshal Earl Roberts of Waterford and Kandahar, V.C., the minute and great-hearted 'Bobs' so beloved in the British army.

John Roberts was buried in the French church, where his monument announces that 'he was the person who designed and built the Catholic Church, the Catholic Chapel, the Leper Hospital, the public rooms etc. in this city'. The Leper Hospital (later known as the Infirmary) was built in 1785 as an amplification for more general purposes of the leper hospital founded by King John in the thirteenth century, and endowed with lands near Waterford still known as Leperstown. Its large but very plain façade is in a commanding position on St John's Hill, at the edge of the town. Roberts's monument does not mention an architecturally much more interesting building, that has been convincingly attributed to him. This is the present Chamber of Commerce, in O'Connell Street (formerly Great George Street), looking down Gladstone Street (formerly Little George Street) to the river. It was built as a private house by William Morris. Downey, the Waterford historian, dates it 'about 1795', which would put it right at the end of John Roberts's life, like the Catholic cathedral. But on stylistic grounds one would be tempted to put it ten years or more earlier.

William Morris's family had been prominent in Waterford since the John Morris who shipped vagrants to Barbados in 1655.[25] His grandfather Benjamin (d.1741) owned a big tan-yard in Waterford and was buried in the cathedral. His father married a Kilkenny heiress and in 1775 had landed property in Kilkenny and County Waterford valued at £3,000 a year.[26] Inevitably he was married to a Carew, his daughter to an Alcock, and his sister-in-law to a Newport. His family was one of the richest in Waterford, but even so one would like to know why he built a house splendid enough for an earl in Dublin. The sheer size of its façade, dominating Gladstone Street, is extremely impressive. The windows, as elsewhere in Waterford, have been given Victorian surrounds, but the beautiful doorway at the head of its double flight of steps is original, and leads to a series of rooms that still retain all their exquisite eighteenth-century plasterwork. The finest feature is the oval staircase, one of the most elegant in Ireland (Pl. 139). It remains a never-failing delight to walk towards this staircase, follow up the delicate curve of the balusters, and suddenly see the walls blossom out into eagles, swags and garlands high up above one's head.

The house did not remain a private one for long. In 1815, shortly after William Morris's death, it was sold to the Chamber of Commerce, who still occupy it.[27] Other big Waterford houses have had, on the whole, a less fortunate history. The two most fashionable residential streets in the late eighteenth century were New Street, on the south, and the Mall, on the east. The New Street houses sank to slum tenements and have all been destroyed except one. The Mall remained respectable but gradually ceased to be residential. The best houses in it were those built in the 1780s on the bowling-green site, and most of these have been a good deal mutilated. But on the far side of the site, away from the Mall and on the corner of Rose Lane and Adelphi Terrace, the fine house now occupied by the police, and formerly by the County Club, has been little altered externally. This house was probably built by Simon Newport, the founder of Newport's bank, who died in December 1817 'in his house on Adelphi Terrace', according to contemporary newspapers.

139. (right)   The staircase of the Chamber of Commerce.

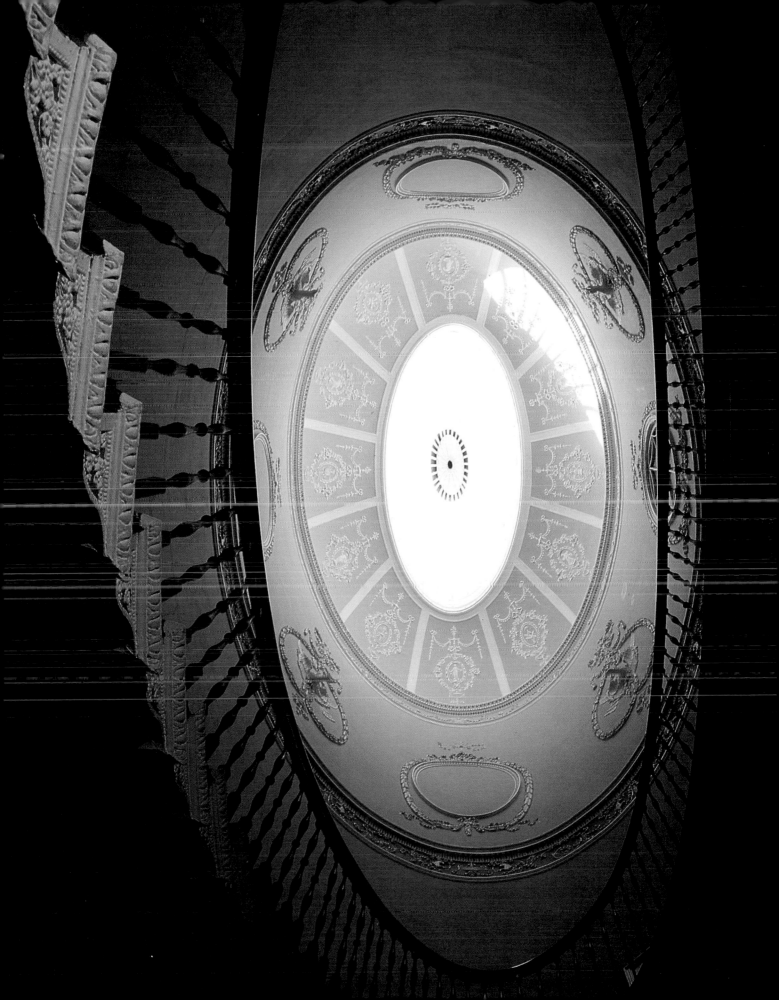

Newport's bank must have seemed the most solid and respectable institution in Waterford, and the Newports, along with the Alcocks, came to dominate city affairs and actually made a pact with each other to take turns in nominating officials for vacant jobs. One day in 1815 a boat crossed to the city from across the river, where the Newports had their elegant country houses. Shortly afterwards the bank closed its doors. The boat had brought the news that the bank had failed, and that William Newport had committed suicide. The failure ruined many, and dealt the commercial life of Waterford a blow from which it took years to recover.[28] Although the Waterford oligarchy retained its monopoly of the city government until the municipal reforms of 1841, its self-confidence had gone, and there was little public building for another twenty-five years. What, with all its faults, remains the great age of Waterford architecture was over.

The quay at Waterford has always been busy. In Elizabethan times Sir George Carew wrote that 'there is more shipping in that harbour than in any part of Ireland'.[29] In the same passage he comments that 'the people of Munster are Spanish at heart'. Waterford's Spanish connections at that time were very strong. The town exported fish, hides, salt meat and corn to Spain and the south of France, and in return supplied French and Spanish wines to the whole of Ireland. Of its own products the best known were aqua-vitae and a particularly shaggy kind of rug. An Irishman wearing a Waterford rug in Elizabethan London was attacked by dogs, who mistook him for a bear.

In the seventeenth and eighteenth centuries the wine trade diminished, but the corn trade continued to flourish and the town acquired a new speciality: provisioning ships sailing (mostly from Bristol) to America. Cattle swarmed into the huge market square outside the town at Ballybricken; corn was milled along the Suir and floated down the river to the warehouses on the quay. The ships also picked up young Irish labourers in large quantities and took them out to Newfoundland for a season's work. Some of these seasonal workers stayed on, and formed the basis of a substantial Irish colony.

The eighteenth-century produce for which Waterford has acquired the greatest fame was glass. The Waterford glass factory[30] was started by an uncle and nephew,

164

140. Adelphi Terrace at the east end of the quay, built by two Quaker brothers in about 1785.

George and William Penrose, in 1783. They had their works at the west end of the quay. In 1799 the Penroses handed the business over to one of their partners, Jonathan Gatchell, and the Gatchells ran it until 1851, when it closed. In 1802 the works had moved to a new site inland from the quay, off Anne Street, though a quayside warehouse and shop were retained. The reputation of Waterford glass was high (particularly in America), but the factory was never a large one. It certainly never produced more than a fraction of what has been attributed to it since, mostly in the widespread and erroneous belief that all Georgian glass with a blue tinge came from Waterford. There are, in fact, few pieces that can be documented with absolute certainty. Among them are the chandelier in the town hall, installed in 1802, and the two very grand chandeliers originally in the Irish House of Lords in Dublin, and recently bought back by the Bank of Ireland, which now occupies the old Parliament building. These, as the newspapers reported at the time, were seen and admired in the Penrose works by Prince William Henry (later William IV) when he visited Waterford in 1787.[31]

The Penroses and Gatchells were Quakers. The Quaker community has been prominent in the commercial life of Waterford from the eighteenth century up to the present day. Quakers were particularly active in the milling and baking business, and built a string of corn mills all the way up the Suir valley from Waterford to Clonmel and Cahir (the Jacobses, of the biscuits, are a branch of the well-known Waterford Quaker family). Their Waterford meeting-house is entered off O'Connell (formerly King) Street, near the Chamber of Commerce. The inconspicuous entrance archway gives no idea of the considerable size of the late eighteenth-century building it leads to. This contains a gigantic meeting hall, now disused, and a series of smaller rooms, grouped round an entrance hall with an elegantly curved staircase. Although, as was suitable for the Quakers, the detail is simple, the scale of the building is impressive evidence of the prosperity of Waterford Quakers in the eighteenth century.

An architecturally more conspicuous Quaker contribution to Waterford is the grand block of three terrace houses where the ferry-boat used to berth, known as Adelphi Terrace (Pl. 140). The houses are situated at the extreme east edge of the quay, and their high, mellowed brick façades form an elegant introduction to Waterford as one comes up the river — but one wonders for how long, since unfortunately two of the three houses have been allowed to become derelict. They were built by two Penrose brothers, Samuel and William (nephews of George, and first cousins of William, of the glassworks). This branch of the Penroses seems to have had a timber, and later a shipbuilding, business here since about 1782, when there are references in the corporation

165

141. A staircase ceiling in Adelphi Terrace.

minutes to 'Mr Penrose's new quay'.[32] The houses were probably built shortly afterwards,[33] and called Adelphi Terrace in imitation of the Adelphi in London, built by the brothers Adam. Indeed, not only were Samuel and William Penrose brothers, they were married to two sisters, Mary and Margaret Randall, of Cork. The middle one of the three houses, where William's son Jacob was living in 1839, has what, though on a much more modest scale, is probably the best eighteenth-century staircase in Waterford after the Chamber of Commerce (Pl. 141). Its neighbour became, in the mid-nineteenth century, the home and Waterford offices of another Quaker family, the Malcomsons. The Malcomsons remain something of a legend in Waterford. They were originally Clonmel corn millers, but branched out into cotton and shipping, made great fortunes, minted their own coinage, built mills, shipworks, villages and a series of large houses, and then went dramatically and finally bankrupt in 1874.

In 1797 the Quakers acquired the Georgian house of Newtown, on the outskirts of Waterford, where they started the school which continues to this day (it is now non-denominational) and has a fine reputation in Ireland. The house had previously belonged to the leading Catholic family in Waterford, the Wyses.[34] From the Middle Ages until the time of Cromwell the Wyses thickly stud the pages of Waterford history; they frequently served as mayors, and were granted the building and lands of the abbey of St John by Henry VIII. They lost much of their property under Cromwell and William, and, like all Catholics and Nonconformists, were barred from taking any part in public life. As a result, they moved into commerce and industry, and became millers, manufacturers and mining entrepreneurs, not always with success.[35]

The house at Newtown (Pl. 142) was built by John Wyse, who went bankrupt in 1796 — hence the sale of his house to the Quakers. His grandson Sir Thomas Wyse must share with the colourful and romantic revolutionary Thomas Meagher (whose father was at one time mayor of Waterford) the claim to be the most distinguished Waterford citizen of the nineteenth century. Sir Thomas Wyse became a notable politician, fighter for Catholic emancipation, educational reformer, and finally British

166

142. (top left) Newtown School, built as a private house by John Wyse, c. 1780, and sold to the Quakers in 1792.
143. (top right) The Presentation Convent, designed by A.W. Pugin and begun in 1842.

Minister to the new kingdom of Greece, which for a short time he virtually ruled, and where he died in 1862. He was a man of wide culture and many friends, who brought a breath of internationalism to Waterford — not least by his marriage (albeit a brief and unhappy one) to Letitia Bonaparte, the niece of Napoleon.

Wyse had been one of the commissioners for rebuilding the Houses of Parliament. In this connection he must have met Augustus Welby Pugin, whom he employed to design an unassuming Gothic front for his house on the edge of Waterford, the Manor of St John. One suspects that he also had something to do with the choice of Pugin as architect for the Presentation Convent, which adjoins the Manor (Pl. 143). Pugin's architecture tends to be feebler than his personality, but the convent, which was started in 1842, is one of his most convincing buildings. It is convincing in its complete lack of pretention; it relies for effect not on elaborate ornament but on good proportion, solid construction, and a telling contrast between the rich brown stone of the main walls and the cool grey of the dressings.

But the classical tradition remained strong in nineteenth-century Waterford. In the same few years as the Pugin convent the new city and county court-house was built by St John's River, on the site of the medieval St Catherine's Abbey (Pl. 144). It was opened in 1849 and was one of the first achievements of the reformed corporation which was brought in in 1841, breaking the power of the old oligarchy and allowing Catholics and Nonconformists to play their part in local government. The previous court-house had been on a different site, on the hilltop at the other end of the town, where the Victorian city gaol later stood, until it was destroyed in its turn a few years ago. The old court-house was built in 1784 and was a little-known work of James Gandon, the greatest eighteenth-century architect in Ireland. A watercolour and a rare unissued engraving show the cool, neoclassical interior which was replaced by the Victorian building.[36] According to Edmund Downey, the Waterford historian, the builder of the latter was a Waterford man, Terence O'Reilly. Was he also its architect? He is described as 'architect' in a Waterford directory of 1839, when he was living in Hardy's Road. One wonders whether he designed both the court-house[37] and the Franciscan church in Lady Lane, opened in 1834 and, like the court-house, of an impressive classical simplicity based on a monumental Ionic order (Pl. 145).

There is no mystery about the architect of the Waterford Savings Bank, in O'Connell Street. This was built as the result of a competition held early in 1841. The winning design was by a Belfast architect, Thomas Jackson. Its grand granite façade

144. The court-house, opened in 1849.

was originally surmounted by a large domed clock-tower — taken down many years ago. Inside, the banking hall has been little altered and above it is a gigantic and opulently classical boardroom which suggests a certain folie-de-grandeur in the original directors, for it would not disgrace the Bank of England.[38]

In the nineteenth century the east side of the town became the fashionable residential area. There are pleasant terraces of about 1820-30 by the court-house, and more on the adjacent St John's Hill. A little row by the General Hospital are among the smallest, but also the prettiest. But there is no space to say more than a few words about Waterford's expansion in the nineteenth century. Catholic emancipation in 1829 led, as one might expect, to a great age of ecclesiastical building. Among the many religious orders and institutions that flourished and built in this period, the one most intimately connected with Waterford was the Christian Brothers, started by Ignatius Rice, who, in the face of great discouragements, kept a school for poor children in Waterford in the early years of the nineteenth century. From these small beginnings there grew the great organisation that has played a leading part in education in Ireland and throughout the world.

In spite of the vicissitudes of its history, Waterford has survived into the mid-twentieth century with a wealth of interesting buildings of all periods, and a highly individual character and charm. The remarkable revival of the glass industry in recent years may herald an economic boom for the town. Intelligently directed, this could preserve and enrich its character. Or will Waterford go the way that Galway has gone, and let uncontrolled redevelopment reduce the city to a visual shambles?[39]

145. The Franciscan church, opened in 1834.
146. (right) Looking across the parapet at Wollaton Hall, Nottinghamshire.

III Country-House Excursions

147 (right)   Ox-skull on the sarcophagus of the monument to Sir Robert Dormer (d.1552) at Wing, Buckinghamshire.

1 THE HAYNES GRANGE ROOM

The Haynes Grange Room stood until a few years ago marooned and to a large extent unnoticed in the Costume Court of the Victoria and Albert Museum (Pl. 148). Its position was a relic of a previous museum arrangement, changes in which had left it stranded; in January 1980 it was dismantled, not, however, to be re-erected in some more logical situation, but to go into storage, with no plans for its re-erection. Even when it was still in position, comparatively few visitors to the Costume Court took a rest from corsets and crinolines to gaze into it through the two windows that were the only means by which they could see it. Those who did so were in for a rare treat, for the Haynes Grange room is — or perhaps one should say was — one of the strangest and most beautiful in England.

The room was entirely lined with unpainted pine. It was unusually high but not especially large: 17' 6" high, 27' 9" long, and 16' 3" wide. A Corinthian order, articulated by pilasters, rose the full height. This large-scale order of

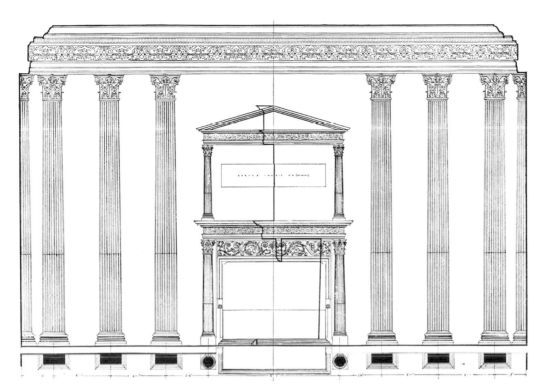

Corinthian pilasters was combined with a much smaller one of Corinthian columns. Two Corinthian aedicules framed two window openings on one of the long walls; opposite the windows another, much wider, aedicule framed an overmantel supported on a lower stage of Corinthian columns, to either side of the fireplace opening (Pl. 149); and two similar but smaller aedicules framed nothing at all on the two short walls (Pl. 150). The fireplace was of stone, with a stone panel of running foliage and scrollwork above it. Carved in raised Roman capitals on the overmantel was a set of Latin elegiacs (Pl. 166). No frame or border enclosed them; the starkness of their presentation corresponded with their message. They exhorted the viewer to live for others and be dead to his material self and the things of this world if he wished to attain to eternal life. The mood of gravity and detachment induced by these verses, by the simplicity of the unpainted pine, the rich sobriety of the Corinthian order and the small size of the windows was accentuated by two more features. The ceiling was decorated with rows of flying pigeons, modelled in plaster in low relief, and originally picked out in blue and red on a black ground.[1] The room had no apparent door; although externally it was entered through a Doric doorcase, the internal door was concealed in the panelling.

The room departed in two particulars from normal classical usage. In the first place the proportions of the Corinthian orders (around nine modules high on the fireplace and twelve elsewhere) were stumpier or more attenuated than usual. Secondly, all the friezes and the underside of all the cornices and entablatures were carved with low-relief strapwork ornament, to a variety of different patterns. In spite of these features, the room could only have been designed and created by people who had considerable knowledge of, and feeling for, the language of the orders.

The room was illustrated in a short and uninformative article published in *Country Life* on 12 November 1904. It was then in Haynes Grange in Bedfordshire, a modest sixteenth or seventeenth-century house which had belonged to the Osbornes of nearby Chicksands Priory since the sixteenth century. The room appeared to have been installed

173

148. (left) The Haynes Grange room, from a photograph taken before it was dismantled.
149.   The side wall of the Haynes Grange room, from the measured drawing by H.J. Harding.

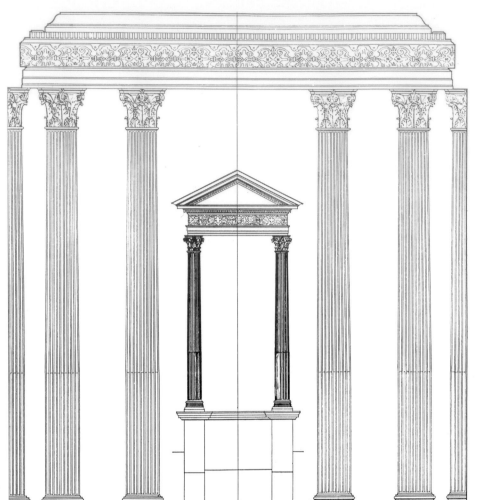

in Haynes Grange at some comparatively recent date. In 1908 Sir Algernon Osborn sold it to a firm of London dealers. It was put on sale as a room attributed to Inigo Jones, offered to the Victoria and Albert Museum, but in the end sold to Sir Edmund Davis and installed in his house in Lansdowne Road, Notting Hill. The museum finally acquired it in 1928, when it was bought by public subscription.[2]

The acquisition was largely due to the efforts of two people, W. Clifford Smith, Deputy Keeper of the Department of Woodwork at the museum, and Professor, later Sir, Albert Richardson. It was probably Richardson who was responsible for a new theory about the room. He accepted that it was designed by Inigo Jones, but suggested that it had been brought to Haynes Grange from Houghton House, at Houghton Conquest near Ampthill, when the house was dismantled in 1794. Richardson lived at Ampthill and had bought the ruins of Houghton in 1923, to save them from destruction. Houghton had been built in or soon after 1615, when the property was acquired by Philip Sidney's sister, Mary, Countess of Pembroke. Externally the house was a conventional Jacobean one except for two remarkable features. On its north and west fronts were (and, in fragmentary form, still are) two three-storey centrepieces or porticoes, each adorned with a Doric, Ionic and Corinthian order, the classical sobriety of which was in marked contrast to the shaped gables and large windows of the rest of the house. Although all documentary evidence was lacking, these features had long been attributed to Inigo Jones.

What could be more suggestive than the existence, three miles or so apart, of a farmhouse containing a room attributed to Inigo Jones and a dismantled country house with features also attributed to Jones? For Richardson, who had a personal interest in Houghton, and whose enthusiasms perhaps tended to run away with him, it was irresistible to make the connection. His theory was repeated and elaborated in a booklet on the room written by Clifford Smith and published by the Victoria and Albert Museum in 1935. This included a convincing suggestion, put forward by H.J. Harding of the Royal College of Art, that the design of the room derived from an illustration of one bay of the Pantheon, in the third book of Serlio's *Architecture* (Pls. 150, 151).[3]

Richardson's theory was widely accepted. Doubts have been expressed since about

150. The end wall of the room.

the attribution to Inigo Jones, but the date and the connection with Houghton have not been at any rate publicly questioned. Many people take his theories as facts. But there are two serious objections to them. In the first place there is no way of relating the Haynes Grange room to the plan or elevation of Houghton. In the second place, it bears no close relationship to any known design by Inigo Jones.

Measured drawings of the south, north and west fronts of Houghton House were made in 1785.[4] T.L. Donaldson measured up its plan in 1867, when much more survived than is there today, and only the east wing was partially missing.[5] Neither plan, window sizes nor ceiling heights relate to the Haynes Grange room. Even Richardson and Clifford Smith (who knew of the 1785 drawings, and probably also of the Donaldson plan) acknowledged this, and were forced to conclude that the room was from the first floor of the largely vanished east front. But since they wrote, eighteenth century plans of all three floors of the house have come to light, and prove conclusively that the room could not have come from Houghton.[6]

Jones's classicism after his Italian visit in 1613-15 was more complex and sophisticated than that of the

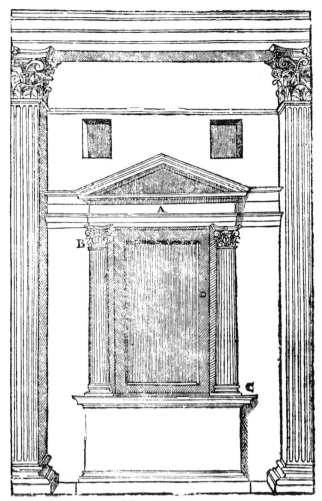

Haynes Grange room; before that it was imbued with a considerable degree of Jacobean fantasy.[7] The gravity and simple grammar of the room seem to come from a different world, and relate to neither period. The aedicules which form such a prominent feature in it were almost never used by Jones, except (and then only occasionally) as doorcases; perhaps the only exception is his unexecuted design for the west front of St Paul's, attributed by John Harris to about 1620.[8] Here they are used externally to frame alcoves for statues, and play a subordinate role in a complex composition; the relationship to Haynes Grange is only marginal.

The purpose of this essay is to put forward an alternative hypothesis. This is that the Haynes Grange room dates from *c.* 1575-80 rather than *c.* 1615-20; and that it was originally commissioned by Peter Osborne, the founder of the Osborne fortunes, and installed by him in Chicksands Priory.

This hypothesis pushes the date of the room back into what I once described as the 'false dawn of Renaissance Architecture in England'.[9] The description is perhaps an over-picturesque one, but it does refer to something which happened; John Aubrey expressed the same idea in different words when he wrote, in the 1660s, that 'under Elizabeth architecture made no progress, but rather went backwards'.[10] In the years around 1550 a small group of powerful patrons commissioned new buildings, or embellishments to old ones, in which a determined effort was made to use the language of the orders correctly. The circle revolved about the court of Edward VI, but the dominant figures in it were not the boy-king but the Dukes of Somerset and Northumberland, who acted successively as Lord Protector. The majority, although by no means all, of the

175

151. Elevation of a bay of the Pantheon, Rome, from Serlio's *Architecture*.

L'Altitude
ou haulteur
lxxiij.piedz.
Largeur
lviij.piedz.

relevant patrons were active Protestants, and many of them were also patrons of the new classical learning. Although work of interest continued to be produced in the reign of Mary, most of the relevant Protestant patrons were in exile or disgrace. Under Elizabeth they came back into power and favour, and inaugurated a new period of classicism in which the important patrons included William Cecil, Thomas Smith, Thomas Gresham and John Thynne. This work of the 1560s and 1570s tended to be more monumental and larger in scale than the work of the earlier period. From about 1580, however, classicism increasingly succumbed to the influx of northern Mannerism, brought to England by various means of which the most important were Flemish pattern-books and immigrant Flemish craftsmen.

If the outlines seem reasonably clear, much within them is not. There are two main reasons for this. In the first place, much of the important architecture of the period has disappeared. Basing House, Somerset House, Theobalds, Holdenby and Elizabethan Chatsworth have all gone, and only fragmentary records of their exteriors and little or nothing of their interiors survive. Moreton Corbet, Gorhambury and the Elizabethan wing of Kenilworth are ruins, Osterley and Hill Hall have been substantially remodelled; in no case is there any visual record of their interior decoration, although a few fragments remain at Kenilworth and Hill Hall. Longleat and Burghley have been comparatively little altered externally, but only a modest proportion of their original interior decoration remains. Dozens of elaborate great chambers survive in fact or record from the period 1580-1620; the only one of any importance left from the period 1550-80 is the great chamber at Loseley and this, although an interesting room, does not belong to the inner ring of patronage. In the second place, the period is still in need of research. The Victorian age attracts researchers like bees to a honeycomb; architects, however dim, and buildings, however dreary, are lovingly resurrected, while Elizabethan art and architecture remains resolutely out of fashion.

However, it is worth working on the basis of what comparatively little is known about this period, and seeing how the Haynes Grange room fits into it. How does its pure but simple classical vocabulary, its aedicules, its reliance on Serlio, its reticent strapwork and the Roman lettering of its inscription compare with documented English work of the mid-sixteenth century?

This has perhaps two dominant characteristics, purity of conception and unevenness of execution. The bulging entablatures, bracket metopes, distorted or embellished columns, gay colours and overall abundance of grotesques, strapwork and ornament

176

152. The triumphal arch put up by the English merchants in Antwerp to celebrate the entry of Charles V in 1550.

of all kinds, typical of late Elizabethan and even more of Jacobean work, are noticeably absent. The stylistic language is that of the High Renaissance, with a French accent. The grammar of the Orders is explored with the relish of those discovering it for the first time, and often expressed with the simplicity of a five-finger exercise. Not always, however; there was so much variety in the knowledgeability of the patrons and the capability of the craftsmen that the results ranged from clumsy naivety to impressive competence and even splendour.

The well-known Strand façade of Old Somerset House came somewhere between the two limits. As an exercise in classical composition it was amateurish, but it had competent elements; even so, the central gatehouse was clumsy compared to the triumphal arch put up by English merchants in Antwerp (probably under the aegis of Sir Thomas Gresham) to celebrate the visit of Charles V in 1550 (Pl. 152).[11] The most remarkable features of the Somerset House gatehouse were two inset panels of sculpture,[12] which, to judge from an eighteenth-century record, were close to those on Goujon's Fontaine des Innocents in Paris.

In the surviving work of the period it is, in fact, occasional individual elements, rather than buildings as a whole, which can be especially impressive. The chimney-piece in the Star Chamber at Broughton Castle, Oxfordshire (which probably dates from about 1554), the internal decoration of one wall of Bishop Gardiner's chantry in Winchester Cathedral (c. 1556-58) and Sir Robert Dormer's tomb at Wing in Buckinghamshire bear comparison with the best contemporary work of the period in France, and were almost certainly by French craftsmen. The architectural framework of the Broughton chimney-piece is admittedly a little clumsy, if quite without mannerist distortion; but the relief panel and the figures are as good — or almost as good — as anything at Fontainebleau, from where they clearly derive (Pl. 153).[13] The frieze is decorated with the wave-like 'Vitruvian scroll' motif that was especially favoured in advanced English work of this period, and that reappears in the Gardiner chantry.

But, handsome though both these works are, the Roman gravity of the Dormer tomb at Wing is even more impressive (Pls. 147, 154, 155). No doubt the spacing of the columns is too wide for a purist; but even so the accomplishment of the carving and detail, and the simple splendour of the sarcophagus under its canopy make it one of the most remarkable products of sixteenth-century art in England. The date 1552, carved on the sarcophagus, needs to be treated with caution; it is the date of Sir

177

153. Chimney-piece in the Star Chamber, Broughton Castle, Oxfordshire.

Robert Dormer's death, and the inscription on one of the brasses let into the wall behind the tomb refers to an event that happened in 1567.[14] Sir Robert's son William married the sister of the Duke of Northumberland's son-in-law, Sir Henry Sidney; his daughter was one of Queen Mary's ladies-in-waiting and became Duchess of Feria in Spain; one would like to know more about the vanished Dormer house at Wing.

Such remarkable isolated works make one wonder how much of the same quality has been lost.[15] But even the surviving examples — apart from the equally remarkable corpus of work centred at Longleat, which will be discussed later — include a good deal that must surprise those who think of Elizabethan architecture in terms of strapwork and mannerist extravagance. Some of it derives, probably or certainly, from engravings. The wall paintings installed in Sir Thomas Smith's Hill Hall in the 1570s are based on engravings from Raphael.[16] Of the four panels of inlay, one dated 1576, which were removed to Hardwick from Elizabethan Chatsworth, at least one derived from an early pre-Mannerist engraving by Vredeman de Vries. In general there is still a great deal of work to be done on the engraved sources of Elizabethan design.[17] Other examples of handsome mid-Elizabethan classicism include the barrel-vaulted stone staircase at Burghley, which probably dates from the 1570s; the noble sarcophagus in St Helen's, Bishopsgate, erected as a monument to Sir Thomas Gresham some time before his death in 1579; the Doric screen of *c.* 1580, originally in the chapel at Holdenby

178

154. (top)   The sarcophagus of Sir Robert Dormer's monument at Wing, Buckinghamshire.
155. (bottom)   The monument.

House, and now in the parish church; the splendid fireplace originally at Heath Old Hall in Yorkshire, which dates from as late as 1585; and two Doric chimneystacks at Lacock, now re-erected in the garden.[18]

The latter are clearly later than the other, and better known, Renaissance work at Lacock, and probably date from the 1570s.[19] They may well be a product of the group of craftsmen based on Longleat. The work of this Longleat group is unique in the period both for its size and for the amount that is known about it.[20] The Longleat archives lavishly document their work at Longleat itself, and give leads to work done by Longleat craftsmen elsewhere; not only are the names of the craftsmen known but a small but invaluable corpus survives of drawings by the two most important — Robert Smythson and the French mason Allan Maynard, who first appears at Longleat in 1563. On the basis of these and of documented work it is possible to attribute a group of related works in the neighbourhood to Longleat craftsmen.

Their achievements were impressive in the sphere both of whole façades and of detail. The culmination of the former was the great series of bay windows that march round the exterior of Longleat, the genesis of which can be traced step by step back to the bay windows of Somerset House. The latter includes a superb chimney-piece almost certainly carved by Allan Maynard, perhaps about 1570; here, uniquely in England, one can sense not only the influence but something of the quality of Goujon. Another Maynard chimney-piece (Pl. 156), though not up to this level, is a remarkably handsome classical design marred only, as so often in England at this period, by the clumsy modelling of the two terms. Maynard's training in France, as is made abundantly clear here and elsewhere, had not extended to figurative carving.

Clumsily drawn grotesque figures are the least attractive feature of a drawing by Maynard preserved in the Longleat archives (Pl. 157). This shows part of the elevation of an unidentified building; the small size of the windows suggests that it dates from the 1560s, before the evolution of the great many-lighted windows that dominate the façades of Longleat as they were remodelled from 1572 onwards. Previous examples cited have been chosen to show the level of competence to which mid-sixteenth century classicism could, on occasion, reach in England. This Maynard drawing has a more immediate relevance to the Haynes Grange room. Its use of aedicules to frame window openings, its combination of a large and a small Corinthian order and the simple, slightly naive but none the less impressive nature of its classicism all suggest that the Haynes Grange room could come out of, if not the same, at least an adjoining drawer.

The Corinthian order shown in the drawing has the distinctive feature of capitals the proportions of which are noticeably squatter than usual. A similar order is used to

156. Chimney-piece at Longleat House, Wiltshire, probably carved by Allan Maynard in the 1570s.

provide aedicule surrounds to a door at the head of the staircase at Wolfeton Manor in Dorset and to the first-floor windows on the entrance front of Chalcot House, two miles from Longleat. Chalcot contains two, and perhaps originally three, stories of aedicules, linked horizontally and vertically. It was altered and perhaps rebuilt in the late eighteenth century, but most of the stonework detail is clearly earlier.[21]

Aedicules feature in much work of the mid sixteenth-century. The Somerset House windows include double aedicules, with a central column rather clumsily placed under the apex of the pediment. A similar motif on the re-erected porch of Grafton Manor in Worcestershire (Pl. 158) is documented as dating from 1567-9;[22] the patron was Sir John Talbot, son-in-law of Sir William Petre, who was Secretary of State under Henry VIII, Edward, Mary and Elizabeth.

Three fanciful aedicules combine with a Corinthian temple front to make the upper stage of the Gate of Honour at Caius College, Cambridge (Pl. 159), one of the highlights of Elizabethan classicism, in spite of occasional solecisms; as so often in this period, one suspects derivation from an as yet unidentified engraving. The gate was the last and indeed posthumous embellishment provided by Dr Caius for the college which he refounded.[23] Caius had studied medicine in Italy from 1539 to 1544, returned to England to become doctor to Edward VI and Mary and President of the College of Physicians, and was Master of Caius from 1559 until his death in 1573.

Edward Harman, another former court doctor and Master of the Barber-

180

157. (top) Design by Maynard for an unidentified project. 158. (bottom) The porch at Grafton Manor, Worcestershire (1567-9).

Surgeons' Company, commissioned a much less sophisticated, but still very handsome, aedicular treatment for the monument which he created in 1565 in the church at Burford (Pl. 160).[24] Other straightforward aedicules include the doorcase at Newark Park in Gloucestershire, which perhaps relates to the Longleat school, and may date from the late 1550s; the chimney-piece in the hall at Hill Hall, Essex, one of the few internal survivals of the work there of Sir Thomas Smith, Secretary of State and classical scholar; and the monument at Stanford in Northamptonshire to Sir Ambrose Cave, Privy Councillor and Chancellor to the Duchy of Lancaster, who died in 1568 (Pl. 161).

The monument to his brother, Sir Anthony Cave, at Chicheley in Buckinghamshire, takes the form of a variation on the aedicule in which the entablature and pediment are supported by female figures (Pl. 162). It was

erected by his wife in 1576. It clearly relates to similar tombs at Turvey in Bedfordshire (Pl. 163), erected to the 1st Lord Mordaunt (d. 1562), and at Hillesden in Buckinghamshire, to Alexander Denton, erected between 1574 and 1576. The unidentified sculptor must have known the works of Goujon, whether from engravings or personal experience, for the relationship of the Chicheley ladies to Goujon's caryatids in the Louvre, and of the Turvey tomb to the monument to Louis de Brézé in Rouen Cathedral, is too close to be a coincidence.[25]

In view of this mid-sixteenth-century fondness for aedicules it seems possible enough that an Elizabethan patron or craftsman could have leafed through his Serlio, had his eye caught by the detail of the Pantheon and reduplicated it to form the panelling of a room. That Serlio was in circulation in England in the 1560s and 1570s there can be no doubt. Smythson and Maynard must have owned, or had access to, a copy; the flaming balls characteristic of Serlio's designs appear in a prototype design

181

159. The upper stage of the Gate of Honour at Gonville and Caius College, Cambridge (c. 1573-5).

by Smythson for the bay windows at Longleat, and Smythson used one of Serlio's Doric chimney-pieces as the basis for the chimney-piece installed in the hall at Wollaton in the 1580s.[26] Whoever carved the hall chimney-piece at Burghley (Pl. 164) must have known Serlio, for it derives from an amalgamation of Serlio's Doric and Composite chimney-pieces with various other Serlian bits and pieces. In general, the Elizabethan use of sources could be described as creative; the reduplication of the isolated Pantheon motif in an entirely different context at Haynes Grange is just the kind of adaptation that one would expect at this period.[27]

To anyone trying to date the Haynes Grange room, neither the ornamental motif carved in stone over the fireplace opening nor the opening itself offers much help. The former could date from almost any time between 1530 and 1650; the latter is of a type which appeared a few decades later, but continued to be used deep into the seventeenth century. Two other features deserve consideration: the strapwork and the lettering.

Bands, friezes and panels of low-relief strapwork (as opposed to strapwork cartouches carved in high relief) can be carried back as a motif to Vredeman de Vries's

160. (top left) Monument to Edward Harman, Burford, Oxfordshire, dated 1565.
161. (top right) Monument to Sir Ambrose Cave (d. 1568) at Stanford, Northamptonshire.

Variae Architecturae Formae, published in Antwerp in 1560. In England their appearance before the outbreak of Vredeman-de-Vriesery at Wollaton in the 1580s seems to be rare, although the use of strapwork is one of the aspects of Elizabethan art and architecture that needs research. A useful example, in that it is securely dateable to 1579 and stylistically is not dissimilar to the Haynes Grange room, is Richard Covert's monument at Slaugham in Sussex (Pl. 165). The sculptor of this is known to have been called Flynte, and was probably also responsible for the fine classical loggia which survives in the ruins of the house at Slaugham, and for a delicately carved chimney-piece at nearby Cuckfield, dated 1574; on this, low-relief strapwork cartouches alternate with other motifs.[28] On the evidence of the strapwork it seems unlikely that the Haynes Grange room dates from before 1570, although a date as early as the late 1560s is not impossible. In the 1590s and early 1600s low-relief strapwork appears in abundance.

The lettering of the inscription (Pl. 166) needs to be treated with caution as an indication of date; there are always cases of client and craftsmen deliberately choosing

162, 163. (top left and right)   Monuments to Sir Anthony Cave (erected 1576) at Chicheley, Buckinghamshire, and to the 1st Lord Mordaunt (d.1562) at Turvey, Bedfordshire, probably by the same unidentified sculptor.

an old-fashioned type. But it suggests a date earlier rather than later in the sixteenth century. The Ms have no upper serif, for instance; and the inscription shows no sign of the influence of Sixtus V's brief but, as far as lettering was concerned, highly influential reign as pope from 1586 to 1587.[29]

In conclusion, since the classical detail suggests a date before 1580, and the strapwork one after 1570, the 1570s seems the most likely decade in which to place the Haynes Grange room. But the room is sufficiently unlike anything else to make the business of dating it a tricky one. It is perhaps not impossible that an independent country gentleman with Serlio in his library could have commissioned it in the 1620s, or even that Inigo Jones could, in special circumstances, have designed it before his Italian visit in 1613. But it is not at all likely. It is much more probable that it dates from the 1570s; that its strapwork is used as a fashionable new motif, rather than a conventional old one; and that the client who commissioned it had contact with court, government or humanist circles.

If one then starts looking for the right context and the right client one does not have to go far — no further than the Peter Osborne who bought Haynes Grange and the adjacent Chicksands Priory in the 1570s. Osborne was born in 1521.[30] From 1551 to 1552 he was Keeper of the Privy Purse to Edward VI. By then he had already married Anne Blythe, the daughter of the first Regius Professor of Medicine at Cambridge, the niece of Sir John Cheke, the great humanist, and the niece by marriage of William Cecil. It was in Osborne's house in London that Cheke died in 1557. Cecil was married to Cheke's sister, who died a few years after the marriage; but, as R.C. Barnett puts it, he 'never allowed himself to forget Mary Cheke', and 'during the rest of his life employed and promoted members of her family'.[31] Osborne's brother-in-law George Blythe was appointed deputy Regius Professor of Greek at Cambridge in 1562, but in the 1570s became Burghley's own secretary, and later secretary to the Council of the North. Osborne himself became Lord Treasurer's Remembrancer in 1553, and kept the office until his death, first under Lord Winchester and then under Cecil — or, as he became in 1571, Lord Burghley. He was M.P. for various boroughs and in general an influential and respected Treasury official. He was a convinced but apparently not an extreme Protestant; in 1566 he became an ecclesiastical commissioner; in 1575 he was one of the executors of the will of Archbishop Parker. His status and the mixture of his interests is shown by the number and nature of the books dedicated to him: John Bernard's *Oratio pia, religiosa, et solatii plena de vera animi tranquillitate* in 1568;

184

164. Chimney-piece of *c*. 1575 in the hall at Burghley House, Northamptonshire.

William Clever's *Paradise for the Soule* in 1574; Abraham Fleming's translation of Virgil's *Bucolics* in 1575; and Timothy Bright's *A Treatise of Melancholie* in 1586.[32] Apart from his documented links with Chckc and Cecil, he must have known Dr Caius, through his medical father-in-law, his many connections with Cambridge, and Caius's own court connections and friendship with Archbishop Parker.[33]

According to family tradition, Osborne bought Chicksands Priory in 1576.[34] In 1578 he was sued by Edward Snowe, brother of Daniel Snowe, the former owner. Snowe claimed the estate as next of kin, and demanded production of the will which he asserted that Daniel had left in Osborne's keeping before he went to Jerusalem. In 1587 Edward Snowe conveyed Chicksands and Haynes Grange to Peter Osborne by fine, but it seems likely that this marked a final buying-off of his claims to the property, rather than that Osborne had been forced to give it up between 1578 and 1587.[35]

Chicksands had been a Gilbertine priory. The Osbornes (or possibly their predecessors the Snowes) pulled down the church and made a house in the monastic buildings round the cloister garth to the south of it.[36] Substantial alterations were made, to the designs of Isaac Ware in the mid-eighteenth century, and of James Wyatt in the early nineteenth.[37] According to I.D. Parry's *Select Illustrations Historical and Topographical of Bedfordshire* (1827), 'in the upper part of the north side is a long apartment called the Pigeon Gallery, having pigeons painted on the ceiling, the cause of which we do not exactly know'.[38] This room is situated over what used to be the north cloister walk at Chicksands, and is now entirely featureless.

This, one might think, takes one home and dry. The pigeon motif appears to be unique to the Haynes Grange

room.[39] Peter Osborne had the necessary court, humanist and religious connections. The serious nature of the Haynes Grange inscription is suitable to a gallery, which was a room intended for exercise and contemplation. To fit it into Haynes Grange the room would have had to be reduced in size, which would explain the absence of a doorway; irregularities in the junctions of the strapwork suggests that the room had, in fact, been reduced. In the larger format the small aedicules could have enclosed windows; if so, the difference between the aedicules could have expressed differences between windows on the north and south sides of the gallery, both of which had an outlook, the south into the former cloister garth, the north on to the site of the demolished church. The curious proliferation of pilasters in the corners of the room to either side of

165. Monument to Richard Covert at Slaugham, Sussex (1579).

VIVE ALIIS IPSIQVE TAMEN TIBI MORTVVS ESTO
QVICQVID VITALE EST SPIRITVS INTVS ALAT
CORPVS PRATA DOMOS VIVI CENSETO SEPVLCRA
NE VIS PECCATIS VLLA SIT INDE TVIS
ASSIDVE MORIENS ÆTERNVM VIVERE PERGE
TETRA DIES MVLTIS SIC ERIT ALMA TIBI

the fireplace could be due to the room having been compressed from a larger one, and there being an excess of pilasters available. There would have been no problem about reducing down a large room, due to the fact that strictly speaking the room is wood-lined rather than wood-panelled, and there is no panel module to be accommodated. The aedicules and pilasters are divided or backed by pine planks of varying width and, with a little cutting of the planks, could have been rearranged to fit a room of any size, as long as it was smaller than the original one.[40]

But, alas, problems of this kind seldom turn out to have simple solutions, and the Haynes Grange room is no exception. One major obstacle remains, and at the moment there is not enough information available to remove it. The Pigeon Gallery as it exists today is too low to take the Haynes Grange room. The present height of the latter is 17' 6"; the height of the Pigeon Gallery, between the floor and the plasterwork below the roof joists, is approximately 15' 4". For various reasons it seems unlikely that the Chicksands ceiling has been lowered; on the other hand it is by no means impossible that the floor has at some stage been raised. Underneath it, is a featureless corridor on the site of the north cloister walk, about 15' 6" high. Like the Pigeon Gallery itself, it has what appears to be nineteenth-century windows, and is rendered on the outside of the window-wall and plastered internally, so that any evidence of changes in window arrangement or floor or ceiling levels is concealed. A floor level a little over two feet lower would have left a viable height for the original cloister walk. A room built above would have been at a lower lever to the first-floor rooms at either end, but such changes of level are in fact found in similar circumstances at Lacock Abbey. Since such a change in level would have been inconvenient, it could well have been evened out during the extensive eighteenth or nineteenth-century alterations of the house. But the building history of Chicksands has never been more than superficially researched, and its fabric has never been thoroughly examined; until more work has been done it is impossible to give a final answer as to whether, dimensionally, the Haynes Grange room could or could not have been at Chicksands.[41]

So one is left with a question mark. However, two conclusions can be stated with some confidence. First, it seems almost impossible that the 'pigeons painted on the ceil-ing' can have been at Chicksands by coincidence. There must be some connection between the Haynes Grange room and the Osbornes. Second, the stylistic evidence makes a date in the 1570s more probable than one in the early seventeenth century; in which case one missing section, and that a little masterpiece, is added to the fragmentary but fascinating mosaic of the English Renaissance of the mid-sixteenth century.[42]

186

166. The inscription over the chimney-piece in the Haynes Grange room.
167. (right) Detail from the painting by Siberechts of Wollaton Hall, Nottinghamshire.

2 SOLOMON'S TEMPLE IN NOTTINGHAMSHIRE

There is nothing else like Wollaton Hall in England — or anywhere else for that matter. Most people would consider this no great disaster, for Wollaton is an extraordinary house, but not a lovable one. But for an architectural historian it presents a fascinating enigma. This does not lie in the main façades. One knows where one is with them. Two main personalities were involved in the house's creation between 1580 and 1588 — Sir Francis Willoughby, the patron, and Robert Smythson, described as its 'architecter and surveyor' on his monument in the parish church. Wollaton's façades are clearly related to those of Longleat in Wiltshire, where Smythson had worked before coming up to Nottinghamshire. There is one significant change, however: Smythson, whether independently or through Willoughby, had got hold of the engravings of Vredeman de Vries, the Antwerp architect, and as a result Longleat's French

classicism has been transmuted by a powerful, not to say overpowering, injection of Antwerp mannerism, in the shape of Flemish gables and an abundance of strapwork ornament.

The puzzle at Wollaton lies in the great turreted block that rises up from the centre of the building to haunt the landscape for miles around (Pls. 167, 168). Admittedly, to a certain extent one knows where one is with this, too. Its effect has been created by inserting a clerestory-lit hall into what would normally have been the internal courtyard of a conventional sixteenth-century house. This was an ingenious development, but it had been anticipated as early as the 1540s at Mount Edgcumbe in Cornwall, a house which was almost certainly known to Willoughby and Smythson.

But the central feature at Wollaton differs sharply from that at Mount Edgcumbe in two respects. The addition of a room of the same floor area above the hall makes it rise far higher and become far more dominant than the central feature at Mount Edgcumbe, which contained only a hall. And its decoration is much more assertive. Massively projecting buttresses support corbelled-out turrets at the angles. The windows are large and all filled with tracery. The general effect is of a combination of church and castle, but none of the detail is actually Gothic. The tracery, for instance, is made up of round-arched lights and circles, and is similar to that in the windows of French churches built from the mid-sixteenth up to the early seventeenth century, in which the desire to continue tradition merged with the desire to be up-to-date. The end result at Wollaton is a sense of overpowering and uncomfortable contrast between the central block and the façades beneath it.

The huge room above the hall is virtually useless. There was, it is true, an English tradition of rooms at the top of towers, or turrets on the roof, specifically designed as spaces from which to admire the view; in reference to the tradition the Wollaton room has been called the Prospect Room in recent years. But other prospect rooms were never very large. Its size makes the room at Wollaton absurdly wasteful for a prospect room, but it is in the wrong place for a room of state. It is cut off from the rest of the house, accessible only by means of a long climb up two cramped newel staircases; moreover, it has no fireplace.

188

168. Wollaton Hall, Nottingham, from the north-west.

An enormous, unusable room, an over-powering central mass, a striking contrast between the centre and the rest of the house. What is going on? What was in Willoughby's or Smythson's mind? These are questions which have never been adequately answered. A hypothesis can be put forward which does go some way to answering them. It is unprovable, because sufficient evidence is lacking, but it is intriguing. Could Wollaton have been inspired by Solomon's Temple in Jerusalem?

To those who believed in ideal, god-given standards of perfection, as most people did in the sixteenth century, Solomon's Temple had an irresistible attraction. For it was certainly god-certified, and probably god-designed. After Solomon had completed it, 'the fire came down from heaven, and the glory of the Lord filled the house'; the Lord appeared to Solomon to tell him 'I have hallowed this house which thou hast built'. Moreover, Ezekiel's scheme for an ideal temple, which was thought to follow the same model, had come to him in a divinely inspired vision. For the Elizabethans, to whom arguments that form follows function had little or no meaning, such a prototype would have had a gilt-edged value, in whatever circumstances it was used.

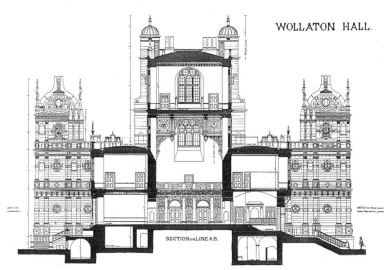

WOLLATON HALL.

SECTION on LINE A.B.

There was a problem, however. What did the Temple look like? A number of written descriptions were available, but they were confusing and conflicting. There had, anyway, been three temples. Solomon's Temple had been sacked or destroyed by Nebuchadnezzar, rebuilt by Zerubabbel, rebuilt or restored again by Herod, and was finally demolished by the Romans. There were accounts of the building of the original Temple in the 1st Book of *Kings*, and the 2nd Book of *Chronicles*. There was Ezekiel's divine vision. All three temples were described, with rather more clarity than in the Bible, by the Jewish historian Josephus, writing in Greek, but translated into Latin by at least the fifteenth century.

But Josephus described Herod's Temple as having been 'built by King Solomon'. Many, though by no means all, scholars assumed that the later temples had been rebuilt or restored upon the same lines as the original, following the same immutable divine model. They tended to draw on all the various descriptions when attempting a reconstruction. Interpreting and reconciling these was fraught with problems. There

189

169. Section of Solomon's Temple in Jerusalem, from the reconstruction by Bernard Lamy, published in 1720. 170. (bottom) The section of Wollaton published in the *Builder* on 13 April 1889.

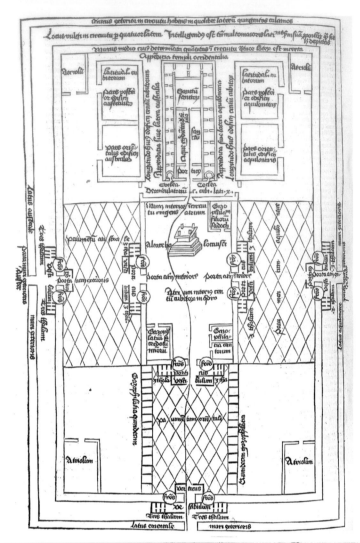

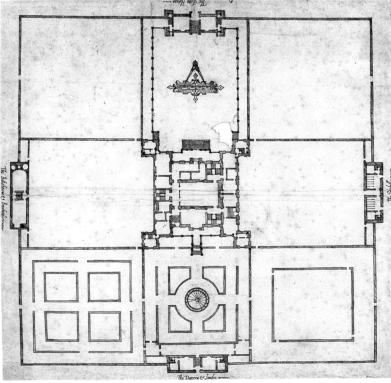

was widespread agreement as to the main lines: the central sanctuary, containing the tabernacle and Holy of Holies, rose in a high compact mass above the subsidiary buildings which enclosed it. But this sanctuary tower could be interpreted as having contained one, two or three stories. Nikolaus de Lyra, the fourteenth-century biblical scholar, gave it three, while Franciscus Vatablus, the sixteenth-century Parisian, gave it one. Both ignored Josephus, who unambiguously described a two-storey sanctuary. J.B. Villalpando, in the early seventeenth century, and Bernard Lamy, ninety years or so later, followed Josephus, although, in an effort to reconcile him with the biblical accounts, Villalpando combined a two-storey sanctuary with a three-storey tower.

The hypothesis put forward in this article rests on the assumption that Willoughby and Smythson had access to both Nikolaus de Lyra's reconstructions and Josephus's text, and tried to reconcile them; Villalpando and Lamy were still, of course, in the future, although it is interesting to see how Lamy, basing his reconstruction on Josephus a hundred years later, produced something strikingly reminiscent of Wollaton (Pl. 169). Josephus features in the earliest surviving catalogue of the Wollaton library, which dates from about 1690. Engraved versions of Nikolaus de Lyra's reconstruction, along with all his biblical commentaries, were incorporated into the multi-volume Latin Bible printed by Anton Koberger of Nuremberg in 1481, reprinted in numerous large editions, at Nuremberg, Frankfurt and Basel, and sold throughout Northern Europe. Koberger's publication may shelter under the several undifferentiated 'Bibles' in the Wollaton catalogue;

but even if it was not in the library there, it was such a widely distributed work that Willoughby is likely to have had access to it. At any rate, it is interesting to take the original biblical texts, Josephus's descriptions, and the Koberger–Nikolaus De Lyra reconstruction, and to consider similarities between them and Wollaton.

The distinctive feature of most reconstructions of the Temple, that of a high tower-like central block (containing the sanctuary) rising out of a skirt of lower buildings, is also the distinctive feature of Wollaton. This arrangement can be derived from the Bible, but is even more explicit in Josephus; he describes how the lower part of the sanctuary in Solomon's Temple was enclosed but 'the upper part had no buildings about it', and how, in Herod's Temple, 'the whole structure ... was on each side much lower, but the middle was much higher, so that it was visible to those that dwelt in the country for a great many furlongs'.

Wollaton resembles the Temple in being built on a hill-top, a position still exceptional in England for a non-fortified domestic building. Its setting, at least as designed, was also exceptional. A Smythson drawing, which may have been carried out, shows an impressively symmetrical array of eight courts around the house, and minor buildings symmetrically arranged around the perimeter (Pl. 172).

There were no close parallels to this at the time elsewhere in England or on the Continent, but it has an intriguing resemblance to the plan of the Temple complex, as engraved by Koberger following Nikolaus de Lyra (Pl. 171). Koberger, admittedly, put the main building to one side of the complex, not at its centre; but on the other hand Josephus described the sanctuary as 'placed in the midst' of the rest. Josephus also described the series of flights of steps which started in the gateway to the main courtyard and finished at the level of the sanctuary. The Smythson plan shows a similar series, and the change of levels in the house as built are a prominent feature of its section (Pl. 170).

The central block resembles the sanctuary as described by Josephus, in consisting of two storeys rather than one or three. The cramped access to the upper room is almost

171. (opp. top) The temple layout, as engraved by Anton Koberger in 1481, after the reconstruction by Nikolaus de Lyra.
172. (opp. bottom) Robert Smythson's plan of Wollaton and its surroundings.
173. Koberger's plan and elevation of the Temple sanctuary.

exactly as in Josephus: 'the king devised access to the upper part of the temple by inserting a winding staircase [*coclea*; literally a snail] for this purpose in the thickness of the wall. For this part did not have a grand portal on the east, as did the lower part, but was entered from small doors on the sides.' Nikolaus de Lyra showed two of these 'cocleae', but put them in circular turrets rather than within the wall thickness (Pl. 173).

Stylistically, Wollaton's traceried windows are reminiscent of Koberger (Pls. 174, 175) and Nikolaus de Lyra. So are its turrets, although here the resemblance is not to Koberger's engraving of the sanctuary but to that of the gateway to the court (Pl. 176). For Koberger, traceried windows were the natural stylistic language of his time for buildings of all types, but for Willoughby and Smythson, they would have had another significance. Disused in a domestic context, they were still the norm all over Northern Europe for churches. If one accepts a Temple prototype for Wollaton, it at once makes sense of a feature which is otherwise an oddity.

In contrast, the perimeter façades of Wollaton are lavishly decorated with Doric, Ionic and Corinthian orders. This contrast could also derive from the Temple prototype. The central sanctuary was the sacred building of the Temple; the rest was given over to ancillary uses, such as storage or accommodation for priests, and therefore a contrast in treatment was

193

174. (left) Looking up to the hall roof at Wollaton.
175. A bay of the Temple sanctuary, after Koberger.

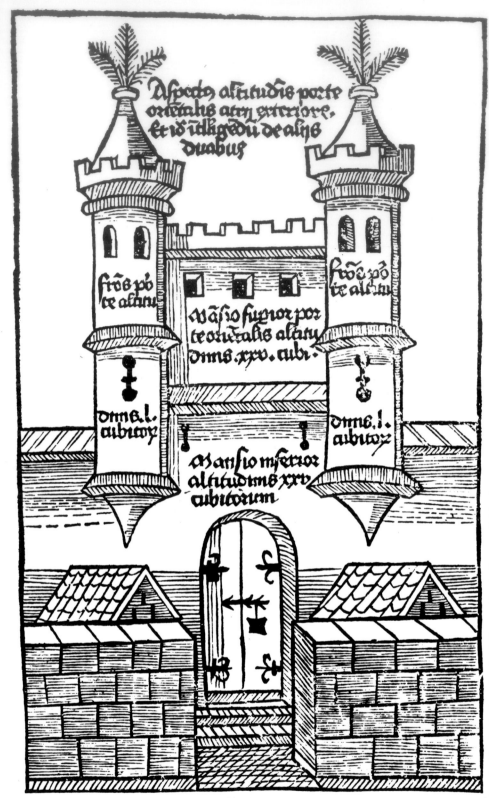

appropriate. And once the authority of the Orders had been accepted, it was tempting to go beyond Vitruvius and look for a divine origin for them. Villalpando, who was Willoughby's contemporary although his researches were not to be published until the end of the century, saw Solomon's Temple as providing the prototype for the Corinthian order; Balthazar Gerbier, in the mid-seventeenth, and John Wood, in the eighteenth century, went further still and saw the origin of all the orders in the Temple.

A similar combination of semi-Gothic traceried windows in the centre and rectilinear windows combined with columns in the perimeter, appears in a design for a Protestant Temple published by Jacques Perret in 1601 (Pl. 177). Here the traceried windows light the central chapel, the square-headed ones the rooms around the periphery. 'Temple' was of course the standard description for a Huguenot place of worship; but Perret's temple seems to be deliberately related to Solomon's, and, most curiously, has so many similarities to Wollaton as to suggest that Perret must have known of it.

Whatever the resemblances, one also has to admit the differences. Neither the dimensions of Wollaton nor its orientation correlate with the dimensions of the Temple. It has no element that can be convincingly related to a Holy of Holies. Although Josephus states quite clearly that the two floors of the sanctuary were of equal height, the upper room at Wollaton is much

176. Koberger's reconstruction of the Temple gateway.

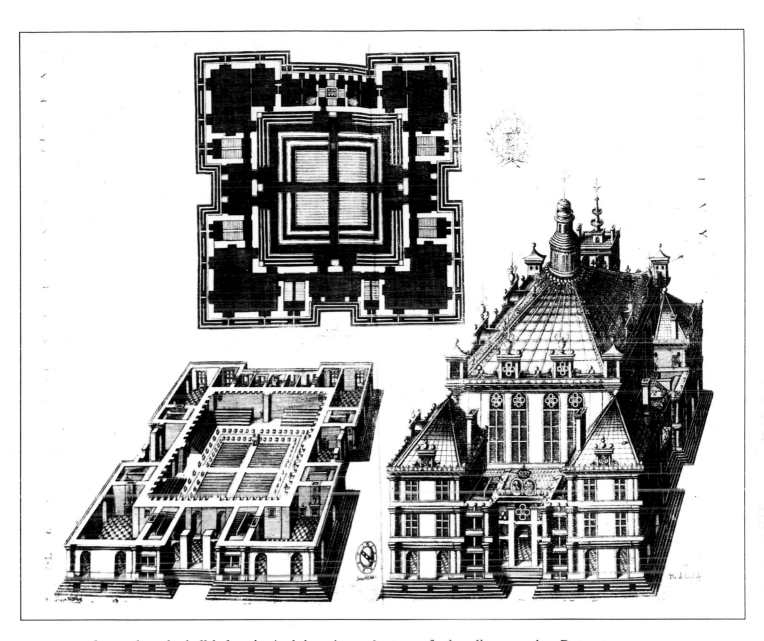

lower than the hall below it. And there is no shortage of other discrepancies. But, set against the similarities, they are not enough to destroy the hypothesis. The Elizabethans treated their sources in a creative rather than a scholarly spirit. Given a learned amateur, like Willoughby, and a gifted but relatively uneducated designer, like Smythson, the need to produce something moderately workable as a country house and the decision to imitate the Temple, Wollaton could have been the result.

But why the decision in the first place? Apart from the general Elizabethan taste for ingenious inner meanings, two other considerations may be relevant: Elizabethan belief in the macrocosm and microcosm as expressions of the chain of being, and the character and background of Francis Willoughby himself. Elizabethans saw repeating patterns stretching from highest to lowest as part of the structure of the Universe. Not only did God's relation to his creation, that of a king's to his kingdom, of a master's to his household, of a parent's to his children, and of the soul to the body, follow similar patterns, but the pattern was essential rather than accidental or metaphorical. It was

195

177. Design for a Protestant Temple, by Jacques Perret, 1601.

therefore appropriate that a king's palace should follow the model of the house of God; for this reason, according to a contemporary witness, Herrera used the Temple as a prototype for the Escorial, and John Webb almost certainly used Villalpando's reconstruction of the Holy of Holies as the basis for his design for Charles II's bedchamber at Greenwich Palace. To extend imitation to the house of a great landowner and local magnate was only to move one step further down the chain.

Willoughby was one of the most highly educated of Elizabethan patrons. He had been born a younger son, brought up in the Humanist circle of the Duke of Suffolk, and sent to Cambridge, not to swagger through the University as a rich young man but to fit himself for a career. It was reported of him that, having 'been bred a great scholar', he later expressed a wish that 'he had been left one hundred pounds by the year and his books'. But, having unexpectedly inherited great estates, he at least had the wealth to express his learning in his house.

According to his descendant Cassandra Willoughby, who wrote a history of the family based on papers most of which have been destroyed, he was also a religious man. She calls him 'a man of great piety and learning', and describes how at Wollaton there were still 'a great many very pious discourses writ by him, and several sermons which he made for his own chaplain to preach, and a collection of the most learned books of his time'. Finally, though he took no part in politics at a national level, surviving papers show how seriously he took his position as a Justice of the Peace, who served as Sheriff of both Nottinghamshire and Warwickshire.

Two surviving documents in the Willoughby papers may be relevant. One is an 'exercise' written by a clergyman, Martin Hill, probably in or shortly after 1580, when he moved from Oxford to a Leicestershire living. The other is a sermon preached at the assizes in 1586 by 'Stanton', perhaps Laurence Stanton, Vicar of Newark and later Dean of Lincoln.

Hill discoursed on how the Jews had ignored Jesus's warning about the destruction of the Temple. 'If', he wrote, 'we become incredulous as those stiff-necked Jews, then doubtless our old enemy Satan ... will not only make entry into the city but he will ransack every parcel thereof, yea, and he will not spare the very temple itself, which is the body of every Christian, but he will pluck the lime from our walls (I mean the flesh) and so separate the stones of the building that he will not leave one bone cleaving to another.' Stanton, preaching to the J.P.s of the county, Willoughby presumably among them, explained how Justice and Peace need to go together: 'where these two lights do shine there is a happy and blessed commonwealth. Read ... of the glory of Jerusalem and Judah in Solomon's time by the presence of Justice and Peace ... he had peace round about him on every side and Judah and Israel dwelt without fear, every man under his vine and under his figs.'

Hill's theme could have been chosen to exhort a patron who had just embarked on a reconstruction of the Temple. Stanton's text showed why Solomon was an especially apposite model for a magistrate. Of course, these passages are not proof; like everything else in this article, they do no more than lend support to a hypothesis. And yet — anyone who has seen that fabulous building, transmuted to gold in the evening sun as it rears up on its hill-top, must wonder whether there is more to it than the desire of a rich man to show off his wealth and indulge in the latest architectural fashions.

178. (right)   A drawing of the hall porch at Holdenby, Nottinghamshire, probably by Sir James Thornhill.

3 RECONSTRUCTING HOLDENBY

Modern historians have worked hard to show that Sir Christopher Hatton could do more than dance well. Admittedly he owed his initial success with Queen Elizabeth to his good looks, skill at dancing the galliard, and ability to write love letters. But although he continued to write love letters to the Queen into middle age, he also became a hard working and capable public servant. He was the Queen's mouthpiece and manager in the House of Commons; he was active on the Privy Council; although he had little legal experience he proved a competent Lord Chancellor. He was one of the main sponsors of Drake's voyage round the world; in gratitude Drake renamed his flagship the Golden Hind after Hatton's crest.

Yet in spite of his achievements and accomplishments Hatton, like other powerful Elizabethans, remains a shadowy figure. The great house which he built at Holdenby, in Northamptonshire, seems equally shadowy. Hatton's contemporary Sir Robert Naunton called him 'a mere vegetable of the court that sprung up at night and sank again at his noon'. Holdenby was as much a 'vegetable of the court' as Hatton; it sprang up in six or seven years, a huge growth bigger than any other private house in England; it sank,

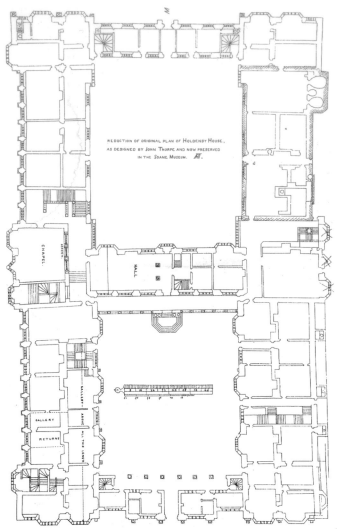

REDUCTION OF ORIGINAL PLAN OF HOLDENBY HOUSE,
AS DESIGNED BY JOHN THORPE AND NOW PRESERVED
IN THE SOANE MUSEUM.

CHAPEL.

SCREEN.

HALL

GALLERY ABOVE ALL THE LENGTH.

GALLERY

RETURN

without adequate record, seventy years after it was completed. By 1662 Thomas Fuller was lamenting its 'beauty and brittleness, short flourishing and soon fading', and seeing it as an 'emblem of human happiness'.

But need it remain a shadow? Its ground plan is in the famous book of plans drawn by John Thorpe (Pl. 179); he probably drew it when he was sent to survey Holdenby in 1606 and 1607. Its general layout is shown in surveys made in 1580 and 1587. It is true that (apart from tiny bird's-eye views in the surveys, which are not meant to be accurate) the first pictorial representations of it date from the early eighteenth century. By then only fragments were left; and by the middle of the century virtually all that remained were archways to either side of the forecourt, and a portion of the kitchen wing, which is now the core of the existing house. But its main façades were symmetrical and based on the repetition of comparatively few basic elements. Enough of these are shown in the early eighteenth-century drawings to enable one to combine them with Thorpe's plan and attempt a reconstruction. This cannot be entirely accurate, because plan and drawings are not always consistent, and no evidence survives for many details. But it can be accurate enough to give a reasonable idea of what Holdenby must have looked like.

The main lines of the house and its surroundings are well established. It was built round two courtyards; there were prominent towers or pavilions at each angle, and further pavilions at either end of the range between the courts. East of the main block was a forecourt, entered by a long-vanished gatehouse and flanked by the two archways that still survive. East of the forecourt was another much larger enclosure known as the Green; to the north of this were the stables and the village.

So much is clear, but plenty of room is left for conjecture. The accompanying aerial view (Pl. 182) is mainly based on Thorpe and on five drawings of the ruins: a crude view by Stukeley, made in 1709; a view by Thomas Eayre, made in about 1720 (Pl. 180); a view by Samuel and Nathaniel Buck, drawn and engraved in 1729 (Pl. 181); and two drawings attributed to Thornhill (Pl. 178). These sometimes contradict each other. On the east (and entrance) front, for instance, although Eayre and Buck agree in showing the corner pavilions articulated by Doric, Ionic and Corinthian orders, Thorpe depicts them lit by pairs of windows of six lights, and Stukeley by pairs of windows of four lights. Since Eayre and Stukeley agree in showing ordinary windows, and Thorpe had a tendency to add embellishments of his own to the plans in his reconstructions, we can dispense with Thorpe's bays; but as a compromise between Eayre and Stukeley, windows of six and four lights are shown in each pavilion, an arrangement which fits the room sizes as shown by Thorpe. The bay windows drawn by Thorpe in the main courtyard have been rejected, but have been kept on the south front to the garden because Eayre clearly shows a bay window on the garden side of the south-east pavilion.

Buck and Eayre, backed by the 1580 survey, make it clear that there were little corner turrets on the east face of the pavilions on the entrance front. The reconstruction gives all four pavilions turrets on their outside corners and a larger tower at the inside corners abutting on to the courtyard. This arrangement is suggested by the plan; the same disposition is found at Audley End, a house almost certainly influenced by Holdenby.

For the entrance front between the pavilions there is nothing to go on except Thorpe; by the early eighteenth century it had entirely disappeared. In restoring the corresponding façade in the courtyard behind it one is on much firmer ground. Its main feature was a central tower, which acted as a porch to the hall; to either side was an open arcade.

Considerable remains of the tower figure prominently in Buck's engraving, in paintings by Wootton at Althorp and Blenheim, and in the two sketches possibly by Thornhill. These charming sketches may be connected with two paintings of Holdenby which, according to Vertue, used to be in the hall at Easton Neston. They show all three stages of the tower, and the beginning of the arcades. For the cupola which surmounted the tower one is back to conjecture; it is roughly shown in the surveys of 1580 and 1587, but there is no evidence for its detail.

The ground at Holdenby drops steadily to the south; as a result the garden front was an extra storey in height. Some at least of this basement storey contained cellars. Buck was the only artist to draw the south front, and by his time it had vanished except for a

179. (opp. top) Ground plan of Holdenby House, Northamptonshire, re-drawn from the plan made by John Thorpe in about 1607.

180. (opp. bottom) The remains of the east front with the hall porch beyond, drawn by Thomas Eayre, c. 1720.

181. (below) The ruins of Holdenby from the south-east, drawn by S. and N. Buck and engraved by them in 1729.

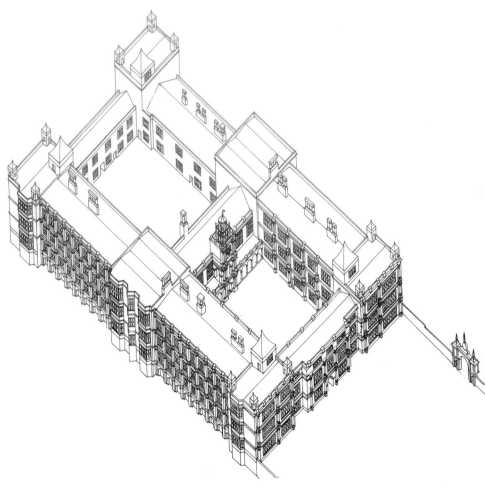

portion of the blind arcade which fronted the basement. At ground-floor level Thorpe shows the front as made up of a continuous window-wall between the central and end pavilions. Instead of being articulated by pilasters or columns, this was apparently subdivided by rectangular piers or buttresses. That this arrangement was the actual one, rather than an embellishment by Thorpe, is suggested by Buck's drawing; it shows piers of this type dividing the arches of the basement arcade, and the butt-end of their continuation up into the ground floor. A similar arrangement survives in miniature on the two forecourt arches.

Perhaps the most controversial feature of the restoration is that it makes the entire south façade (and not just the pavilions) three storeys high above the basement arcade. The main evidence for this comes from Thorpe's plan. His annotations show that the room in the centre pavilion was the chapel; there was a cellar below it, and above was the great chamber. The almost invariable arrangement in houses of the importance of Holdenby was for the chapel to be two storeys high; the household was accommodated at ground-floor level, and the family (or the monarch, if on a visit) in a first-floor gallery. If Holdenby's chapel was of this type, the great chamber must of necessity have been on the second floor. But great chambers could not exist in a vacuum. They were the main ceremonial rooms in big Elizabethan houses and invariably formed part of a suite which included, on the same floor, a withdrawing chamber and best bedchamber, and often a gallery. Thorpe's plan interpreted in terms of normal Elizabethan usage suggests that the main rooms at Holdenby were on the second floor. This arrangement was by no means a rarity at the time; it is found, for instance, at Hardwick and Elizabethan Chatsworth.

All building accounts, or other papers to do with the building of the house, have disappeared. There is no evidence for the exact date at which Hatton started to build. The manor of Holdenby was his own inherited property — probably his only inherited property. His great-grandfather had married the daughter of the manor, and when the

182. An isometric reconstruction of Holdenby from the air.
183. (right) The arches, which originally flanked the forecourt before the east front.

male line died out the Hattons inherited and became small Northamptonshire squires. The old manor house was further down the hill, close to where the parish church still stands, long ago separated from its village. When Hatton became rich and famous, and decided to rebuild, he moved to a more commanding site.

Work was under way in August 1578 when John Stanhope wrote to Hatton that 'on my journey from London I had a little sight afar off of your fair house'. By August 1579 the main structure seems to have been completed; in that month the house was visited by Lord Treasurer Burghley, who expressed himself delighted, although Hatton apologised for its unfinished condition. In 1581, when Barnaby Riche praised the house in *Riche his farewell to the Military Profession*, it was still 'not yet fully finished'. The two surviving archways are dated 1583 (Pl. 183); in 1716 Sir Justinian Isham saw the same date on one of the obelisks, carved with coats of arms, which then still stood in the hall.

Burghley visited Holdenby in Hatton's absence, and stayed the night there. The letter of appreciation which he wrote to Hatton while still in the house is the best surviving contemporary description, and has been much quoted. 'Approaching to the house,' he wrote, 'being led by a large, long, straight fairway, I found a great magnificence in the front or front pieces of the house, and so every part answerable to other, to allure liking. I found no other thing of greater grace than your stately ascent from your hall to your great chamber; and your chambers answerable with largeness and lightsomeness, that truly a Momus could find no fault. I visited all your rooms, high and low, and only the contention of mine eyes made me forget the infirmity of my legs.'

The 'stately ascent' is perhaps further evidence that the great chamber was on the second floor. But Burghley's other comments are even more interesting. He is given to understand that the house is 'consecrated to her Majesty'. It is 'a monument of Her Majesty's bountifulness to a thankful servant'. Hatton had told him that it was modelled on Burghley's own house, Theobalds, but although he is partial to Theobalds 'as my own' it is 'not otherwise worthy in any comparison than a foil'. Finally, 'God send us both long to enjoy Her, for whom we both meant to exceed our purses in these.'

All this gives one food for thought. Hatton had certainly written to Burghley that Holdenby (which he called 'this rude building') was modelled on Theobalds. Later he referred to it as 'my poor house of Holdenby'. But the humble cross-talk of these two politicians should not blind one to the reality. Theobalds was probably the largest and most magnificent private house in England until Hatton built Holdenby, which was just as magnificent and appreciably larger. It was, for instance, considerably larger than Chatsworth — not just seventeenth-century Chatsworth, but Chatsworth as extended to its present size by Wyatville.

Thanks to Elizabeth, Hatton was very rich. He owned large properties in at least five English counties and 10,000 acres in Ireland. He was keeper of the royal park of Eltham and the royal forest at Rockingham. He had been given extremely profitable farms on imported wines, and on first fruits and tenths. In addition to Holdenby his houses included Corfe Castle in Dorset; Ely Place, the huge London palace of the Bishop of Ely, which Elizabeth had forced the unwilling bishop to give up to Hatton; and Kirby Hall, a few miles from Holdenby, which Hatton bought newly built from the executors of Sir Humphrey Stafford in 1575. But, in spite of these resources, his building activities and his life-style exceeded his income; he died heavily in debt.

Burghley said that Holdenby was 'consecrated to her Majesty'. In 1580 Hatton announced that he would leave it 'unseen, until that lady saint may sit in it to whom it is dedicated'. Thornhill's drawing shows the royal arms, not Hatton's, over the porch. The garden range was clearly planned to accommodate the Queen and her court on an extended visit; for himself Hatton provided a second great chamber, on the other side of the hall. When Holdenby later became a royal palace, this and adjacent rooms became the queen's lodgings, and the garden range the king's lodgings.

Was Holdenby just an immensely inflated love letter or loyal emblem in stone, or was it something more? The vast size of Theobalds had a point to it; as Burghley himself put it, it 'started with a mean measure but increased by occasion of her Majesty's coming often'. He was the Queen's chief minister, and she visited him so often that it became in effect an unofficial palace, and had to be enlarged accordingly.

Holdenby had no such point. The Queen never came there once, let alone regularly; Hatton, however influential, was not nearly as important as Burghley. But did he have hopes? As early as 1572 (according to E. St J. Brooks's biography), his uncle, William Saunders, and others were said to 'in all their deeds prefer Mr Hatton above the Lord Treasurer, saying that one day they looked to see wherein Mr Hatton should have one step before him'.

There is something provocative about the comparative measurements of Holdenby and Theobalds. The main block of Theobalds measured 304 by 188 feet, Holdenby 352 by 216 feet. In fact there is no evidence that Hatton himself ever planned to supplant Burghley, but he may have hoped to succeed him. He was, after all, twenty years younger. In such an eventuality Holdenby was ready and waiting to take over from Theobalds.

In spite of much surface cordiality there seems to have been little real warmth in the relations between Burghley and Hatton; the former's visit to Holdenby may not have been entirely friendly. But in the event Elizabeth continued to visit Theobalds rather than Holdenby, and it was Hatton who died first, not Burghley. He succumbed to a sudden attack of cystitis in 1591 at the age of fifty-one, or thereabouts; Burghley survived him by seven years and died in 1598, aged seventy-seven.

Apart from its historical interest, Holdenby is of some architectural importance. To judge from the evidence, the entrance front, and the first and main courtyard behind it, must have made a handsome show. But the entrance front was certainly not as delicate or sophisticated as the contemporary front at Longleat, which still survives; and the courtyard, although larger, must have been not unlike the surviving courtyard at Burghley. It is sad that they have gone, but English architecture may not be all that much the poorer for their loss. The south front is a different matter (Pl. 184). It was one of the showpieces of the Elizabethan age. One would dearly love still to be able to look up from the valley below, up past the deer park, the terraces and the surmounting arcade, to the 350-foot wall of glass that flashed its thousands of diamond panes on the summit of the hill.

Holdenby was the Northamptonshire Hardwick; the local saying 'Hardwick Hall, more glass than wall' had its Northamptonshire counterpart, 'as bright as Holdenby'.

But the south front of Holdenby was nearly twice as long as the main fronts of Hardwick. It was also built some fifteen years earlier. At Holdenby Elizabethan architecture was at an interesting moment of transition; and although it was certainly not a revolutionary house, it contained ideas that were to be pushed much further in the last decades of the century. In it one can see the classical house turning into the lantern house, and the courtyard house beginning to develop into the solid block.

There is a group of great houses built by the inner ring of Elizabethan society in the 1560s and 1570s which can reasonably be described as classical, even if with many qualifications. As far as their planning went, these houses were still in the medieval (or at least the late medieval) tradition. Although they were perhaps more insistently symmetrical than their prototypes they were still built round one or more courtyards, usually entered through a gatehouse; across the courtyard from the gatehouse a porch led into the screens passage of a great hall. Where they were innovative was in their detail. They were full of the excitement of people realising, for the first time in England, that the five classical orders provided a consistent grammar of ornament, and using this grammar with seriousness and enjoyment, though with varying degrees of skill. From the stumpy but sober tiers of columns at Hill Hall in Essex, to the refined delicacy of the bay windows at Longleat, the source of the grammar was Italy by way of France. The bizarre and extravagant shapes soon to be popularised by Flemish workmen and Flemish pattern-books were little in evidence before the 1580s.

But the 1570s also saw another development. Windows started to grow bigger and the area of wall proportionately smaller. This was in direct opposition to the classical tradition and suggested a new and exciting concept. Houses could become lanterns. In 1575 George Laneham described the new wing at Kenilworth as 'a day time, on every side so glittering by glass; at nights, by continual brightness of candle, fire and torchlight, transparent through the lightsome windows'. As the century drew to its close houses increasingly relied for effect on huge areas of glass and bow or bay windows of striking size or form. The orders became correspondingly less dominant; many great houses did without their use as a comprehensive system of articulation, or reduced their

184.   A reconstruction of the south front.

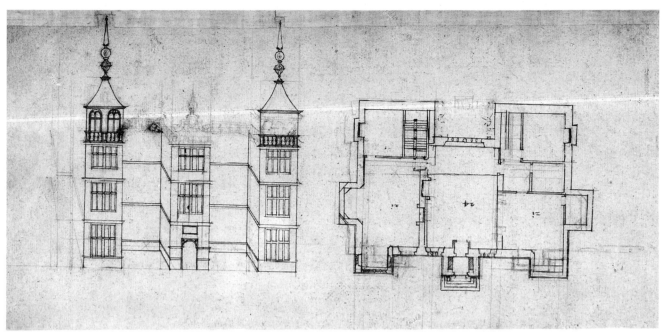

presence to bands of entablatures, marking each storey without intervening columns or pilasters.

The entrance front and main courtyard of Holdenby were richly articulated with Doric, Ionic and Corinthian orders; there were arcaded loggias at both ends of the courtyard. To judge from surviving evidence, this work was influenced by Burghley House, and possibly Theobalds. But the south front used glass more daringly than any other house of its date in England, and probably in Europe. Longleat, as remodelled in 1572-9, had provided perhaps the first foretaste of the effect of a lantern-house. The new wing at Kenilworth, which was completed by 1575, was impressively windowed, as Laneham's account underlines. But neither of them had anything to equal the great wall of glass at Holdenby.

Holdenby was also interesting because of its planning. Hatton admitted that it owed a debt to Theobalds. Its six great towers or pavilions were inspired by the similar ones round the Conduit Court at Theobalds, which Burghley started to build in 1572. But Hatton put his pavilions round two courts instead of one. As a result, Holdenby was more of a single coherent mass than Theobalds, where the Conduit Court adjoined the earlier Middle Court, of different proportions and design. Moreover, the fact that the north and south ranges at Holdenby were two rooms thick increased the effect of the house as a single great block.

This double thickness of rooms was something new in English architecture. It had appeared in one range of the Conduit Court at Theobalds, but with nothing like the scale and boldness of its use at Holdenby. To those with less overpoweringly expansive ideas than Hatton, the arrangement may have suggested the possibility of a great house that was a compact mass, two rooms thick, without courtyards, and heavily windowed all round.

Interestingly enough, such a building seems to have existed at Holdenby, in miniature. Thorpe, in addition to his plan of the great house, also drew a plan and elevation of what he described as 'Holdenby banquet h[ouse]' (Pl. 185). This was almost certainly what came to be known as the Dairy House. It stood at the south-east corner of

205

185. A drawing by John Thorpe, probably of the Dairy House at Holdenby.

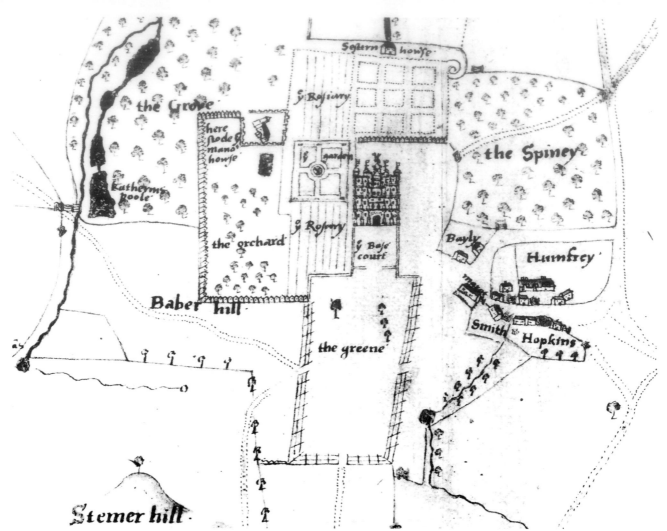

the gardens, was not in existence at the time of the 1580 survey (Pl. 186), but is shown in the survey of 1587 (Pl. 187). In the survey made by the Parliamentary Commissioners in 1650 it was described as 'a goodly fabrick built of hewn stone ... consisting of many fair large rooms'. It was less a banqueting house than what the Elizabethans called a lodge — a smaller self-contained house, which could be used as a retreat from the great house, or for short visits for hunting or other purposes. The building of the Dairy House must, in fact, have taken place at much the same time as the enclosure of a deer park at Holdenby, for this also took place between the 1580 and 1587 surveys. With its square towers, compact double-pile plan and axial hall the house is suggestively reminiscent in miniature of Hardwick, which was not started until 1590. No evidence has come to light as to who provided plans or designs for either the Dairy House or the main buildings at Holdenby, or what artificers worked there. Hatton, in the letter he sent to Lord Burghley in 1579, made one tantalizing reference: 'I humbly beseech you', he writes, 'for your opinion to the surveyor of such lacks and faults as shall appear to you in this rude building.' But he mentions no name. On the other hand, it is known who designed the gardens at Holdenby. In 1597 Sir Thomas Tresham, Hatton's Catholic neighbour, wrote to his steward about a gardener working for his sister, Lady Vaux of Harrowden, and mentioned that he had been trained at Holdenby by a priest who excelled in gardening work. In *Sir Christopher Hatton*

206

186, 187. (above and right) Details from surveys of Holdenby made by Ralph Trewell in 1580 and 1587.

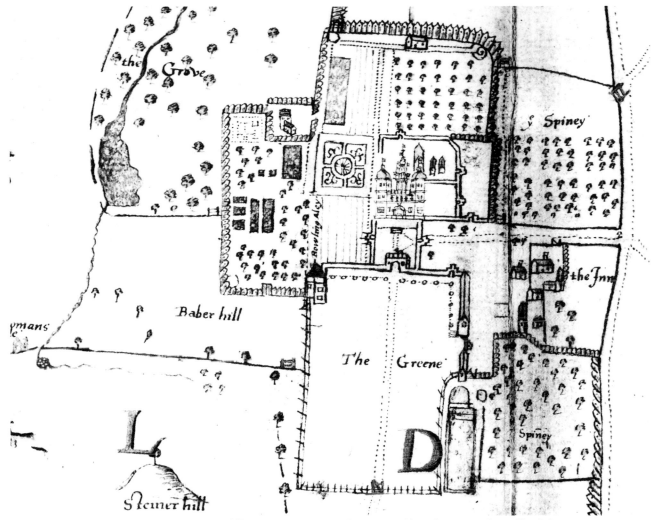

(1946) E. St J. Brooks identifies this priest as Hugh Hall, who was described in *Leycester's Commonwealth* (1584) as 'Hatton's priest' and in 1568-9 was helping with the gardens at Grafton Manor in Worcestershire. He later became involved in a plot to kill Elizabeth, and probably died in prison. Hatton was widely believed to have Catholic sympathies.

The gardens at Holdenby were very ambitious. Many traces of them remain. Their main feature was an intricate knot-garden, on a great platform running the full length of the south front. This platform was artificially raised from the sloping hillside south of the house; it must have entailed a massive operation of moving and piling earth (and must have considerably interfered with the views of the house from the park). To either side of it, terraces dropped down the hillside, those on the west to a rectangular pool by the church, those on the east to a bowling green which led up to the Dairy House. In the 1580 survey each set is described as 'ye rosery'. The platform and pool survive intact, and the shape of the terraces is clearly visible.

John Norden enthusiastically described the results in his *Delineation of Northamptonshire* (1595). 'The situation of the same house is very pleasantlie contrived, mountinge on a hill, environed with most ample and lardge Fields and goodly pasture, many yonge Groves newly planted, both pleasant and profitable, Fishe ponds well replenished, a Parke adjoining of Fallowe Deare, with a lardge Warren of Conyes, not far

207

from the house, lying between East Haddon and Long Bockbye. Aboute the house are greate store of Hares. And above the rest is especially to be noated with what industrye and toyle of man, the garden have been raised, levelled, and formed out of a most craggye and unfitable lande now framed a most pleasante, sweete, and princely place, with divers walks, many ascendings and descendings, replenished also with manie delightful Trees of Fruite, artificially composed Arbors, and a Destilling House on the west end of the same gardens, over which is a Ponde of Water, broughte by conduite pypes out of the feyld adjoyninge on the west, quarter of a myle from the same house.'

The most fugitive part of Holdenby is its interior. Thorpe gives its plan, but little is known about its decoration. The features most commented on in the few surviving descriptions were the three obelisks or 'pyramids' in the hall. These took the place of a screen, and were decorated with the arms of the Northamptonshire nobility and gentry. One of them survived well into the eighteenth century, and figures prominently in depictions of the ruins. In 1600 a foreign visitor described 'some beautifully made fireplaces: one shows Apollo, one the Muses, and another Athene and Mercury, all carved in stone.' These have long since disappeared; today the only identified survivals of the interior decoration are in the church and the library of the present house.

The remains in the church are extremely interesting. According to Emily Hartshorne (whose *Memorials of Holdenby* (1868) is a valuable source of references to the house) they were brought in by Daniel Amyand, the rector from 1691 to 1750. The main portion was set up as a chancel screen. At some period (possibly during Gilbert Scott's restoration of the church about 1868) the upper half was taken down, and re-erected as the entrance to the vestry in the tower (Pl. 188); it has recently been replaced in its former position. The main screen is a handsome and sober piece of Doric design. The arch of the superstructure is flanked by vigorously carved lions and scrolls decorated with grotesque heads, and stylistically suggests the influence of France rather than Flanders, and of Du Cerceau rather than Vredeman de Vries (Pl. 189).

There is little doubt that this woodwork came from the chapel in Holdenby House. The hall had no screen; but Thorpe shows a screen, of identical arrangement to that in the church, between the chapel and the lobby. Confusingly, the scale is different; the church screen is about seventeen feet wide, the screen shown by Thorpe measures twenty-eight feet. But Thorpe is seldom reliable over details.

The arch between the attendant lions may have been purely ornamental; but it looks as though it was intended to open into or out of something. It is tempting to see

188. The chancel screen in the church, which probably came from the chapel in Holdenby House.
189.(right) A detail of the screen.

it as the remains of a first-floor gallery, originally above the screen. Galleries looking down through arched openings into chapels survive at Hatfield and Knole. If this was the original purpose of the woodwork in the church, it is probably only a surviving portion of something more elaborate.

Other remains in the church and house lend support to this idea. The reredos at the east end of the church is made up of panels of the same design as those on the screen, but with different proportions. There are more of these panels incorporated in the library fireplace. This is flanked by large Doric columns of identical dimensions to those on the screen and decorated with smaller, attenuated columns similar to those between the big columns in the screen, but of different proportions. According to the article on Holdenby in *Country Life* in 1912, 'the panels and pillars of the library chimney-piece are portions of the old work, but strangers to their present position'. The wording suggests a clever nineteenth-century make-up of old fragments, rather than an original sixteenth-century chimney-piece.

Hatton died in 1591. The huge house, built by a bachelor for a queen who never came, immediately became a white elephant. Hatton had left debts owed to the Crown of about £42,000, an immense sum in those days; in effect he had used his farm of the first fruits and tenths as a source of loans as well as income. Elizabeth's refusal to write off the debt is said to have hastened his death.

His heir was his nephew, Sir William Newport, who took the name of Hatton, and started selling property and possessions almost immediately. Two sets of tapestries were bought by Bess of Hardwick for her new house. They are still at Hardwick; antlers were added to the Hatton golden hinds to turn them into Cavendish stags. Holdenby stood empty and deserted. Finally, in 1608 it was sold to James I; Sir William Newport-Hatton's widow (who married Sir Edward Coke, the great lawyer) lived on in the Dairy House.

This essay is not concerned with Holdenby's short life as a royal palace, or with Charles I's imprisonment there in 1647. In 1650 the trustees for the sale of crown lands sold Holdenby to Adam Baynes, a Parliamentary soldier and M.P. from Yorkshire. He paid £22,299 6s. 10d. for it, pulled most of it down, sold the materials and fitted up the kitchen wing for himself. A puzzling survival of his period is the archway that leads to the forecourt of the present house. It is dated 1656, but it looks Elizabethan, and an arch is shown in or near that position in the Elizabethan surveys. The explanation may be that Baynes altered the date when he fitted up the kitchen wing for himself.

Holdenby reverted to the Crown at the Restoration, and thereafter passed through several hands, by grant or purchase. In 1675 Evelyn described it as 'showing like a Roman Ruine, shaded by the trees about it, one of the most pleasing sights that ever I saw of state and solemn'. Baynes's house became a farmhouse; in about 1872-6 it was converted and enlarged by its then owner, the 4th Viscount Clifden, first for his mother and then for himself. The house was further enlarged in 1887-8. The architect was R.H. Carpenter, in partnership with William Slater (who died in 1872) and then with Benjamin Ingelow. The façades were largely rebuilt, in the Elizabethan style; but the original chimneys still rise evocatively on the skyline. Holdenby House now belongs to James Lowther, the great-great-nephew of Lord Clifden.

210

190. (right) Detail of the painting of Chatsworth, Derbyshire, by Richard Wilson after Siberechts.

4 THE GHOST OF ELIZABETHAN CHATSWORTH

Elizabethan Chatsworth was a famous and splendid building. If the Cavendishes, like the Cecils, had decayed instead of flourished in the days of the Whig hegemony, it would probably have survived up till the present day and become as celebrated an example of its period as Hatfield. The evidence for its appearance is infuriatingly incomplete, but still considerable. The entrance front is shown in a copy by Richard Wilson of a painting of 1680 (Pl. 190), and in an Elizabethan needlework picture (Pl. 191), both now at Chatsworth. The layout of the house and its surroundings are shown in a survey of 1617. An engraving by Kip and Knyff gives a bird's-eye view when the house had been half remodelled by Talman. There are a number

of references in contemporary letters, and a fragmentary but invaluable collection of accounts and other building papers at Chatsworth. Finally, the inventory attached to Bess of Hardwick's will is also at Chatsworth, and describes both Chatsworth and Hardwick room by room as they were in 1601.

The inventory is perhaps the best tool with which to start an attempt at reconstruction. One can restore the plan from it with reasonable certainty as to its main lines, though of course none at all as to its details. Like most inventories of the time it was made by going round the house from room to room and floor to floor, in this case starting from the top and working downwards. The accompanying sketch plans (Pls. 192-4) were worked out by applying the 1601 inventory and all other available information to the plan of Chatsworth in *Vitruvius Britannicus* (1717), showing it as remodelled by the 1st Duke of Devonshire. Plan and inventory fitted together remarkably easily, considering that the house had been completely remodelled in the interval between them. The fit is at first sight surprising, until one remembers that the 1st Duke's remodelling was a piecemeal affair carried out range by range over twenty years, so that of necessity the layout of the new rooms was conditioned by the ones they replaced. The remodelled house fitted almost exactly the same space as the old one, and probably concealed rather more of the Elizabethan fabric than Francis Thompson suggests in his history of Chatsworth.

At any rate, armed with the plans and inventory, let us attempt to penetrate beyond the façade shown in the needlework and Wilson views.

> The noble front of the whole edifice
> In a surprising height is seen to rise ...

212

191. Elizabethan Chatsworth, as depicted in a contemporary embroidery.

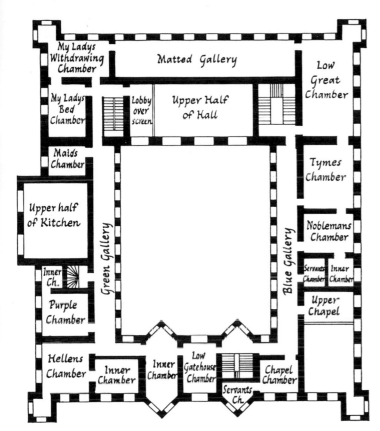

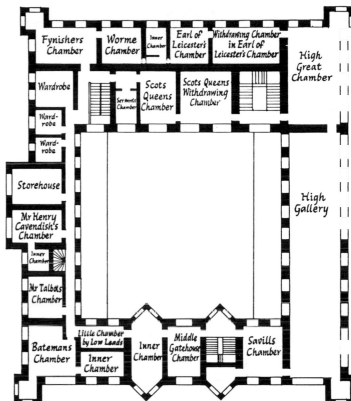

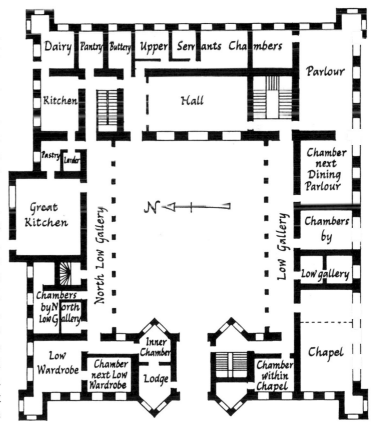

as Charles Cotton wrote in his *Wonders of the Peak* of 1681. But Cotton saw the house as in Wilson's view, when the Elizabethan glazing had recently been replaced by sash windows; the original mullions, transoms and leaded lights are shown in the needlework picture.

The house was entered, as it continued to be until the mid-eighteenth century, by means of an archway leading through the gatehouse into the central courtyard. Asymmetrically across the court was the porch to the great hall; to north and south were two storey galleries, their upper floors glazed and the lower floors probably open to the courtyard. The porch opened into the hall, occupying much the same space as the Painted Hall today, and, as today, the principal staircase led off the end of the hall to the state rooms up on the second floor. The high great chamber filled the same position as Talman's great dining chamber; to one side of it, filling the space now occupied by Talman's other state rooms, was the high gallery. The great window lighting the west end of this occurs prominently in the

213

192-194. A reconstruction of the first, second and ground floors of Elizabethan Chatsworth.

needlework picture and shows that these state rooms were high enough to allow a mezzanine floor to be inserted on the entrance front. To the other side of the high great chamber the state suite in which the Earl of Leicester was put up in 1578 and the rooms occupied by Mary Queen of Scots filled the upper floor of the east range. On the floor below, the high great chamber was exactly echoed by a low great chamber. A second long gallery, the Matted Gallery, joined this to the Shrewsburys' own suite in the north-east corner and filled the space later occupied by the 1st Duke's long gallery (which the 6th Duke converted into the library). To the other side of the low great chamber a series of rooms led to the gallery of the two-storey chapel, which occupied the same space as the chapel today. On the ground floor the lion's share was taken up by the lower half of the hall, chapel and kitchen, and by a great parlour under the low great chamber.

The Chatsworth estate was bought by Sir William Cavendish in 1549, at the instigation of his wife Bess of Hardwick. An existing house on it was demolished. A payment made on 24 December 1551, and recorded in the first surviving account-book (November 1551 to March 1552: 'geven Roger Worde my Mrs mason for drawing my mrs platt XXs') has been reasonably assumed to be for the plan of the new house. In 1555 Cavendish wrote to Sir John Thynne at Longleat that 'my hall is yet onmade' and asked for the loan of a 'connyng plaisterer'. In 1555 he died and in 1559 Bess made her third marriage, to Sir William St Loe, a wealthy West Country courtier. Accounts survive for the year October 1559 to October 1560 for money 'payd to workmen that have wrought on the worke abowte the new bylding'. They give no detail, but show that the labour force varied from about twenty to thirty, and included masons, carpenters, joiners, plumbers, glaziers and slaters. In April 1560 Bess wrote to Longleat asking Thynne to 'spare me your plasterer' for work at Chatsworth.

St Loe died in 1565 and in 1568 Bess made her final and most brilliant marriage, to George Talbot, 6th Earl of Shrewsbury, the richest man in England. Work, if it had ever stopped, started up again soon after the marriage, and in August 1573 Lord Burghley sent his regards to Bess 'wishing myself with hir at Chattesworth when I thynk I shuld se a gret alteration to my good likyng'. The next surviving accounts only cover the years 1577 to 1580. They show operations going on on a much more

195. The Hunting Tower at Chatsworth.

lavish scale, with a labour force varying from eighteen in the winter to a maximum of eighty-two in the summer of 1577. They give the impression of covering the final stages of a considerable operation; there are references to a new screen in the hall, a chimney-piece and panelling in the bedrooms and parlour, and work on walls, turrets and gates for the entrance court, turrets at the 'bridge end' and on the mount, and much 'tarriss' (parapet) for the fish ponds and elsewhere.

The inventory also refers to two further 'turrets', in the south garden, an 'arbour' and a 'stand'. A contract survives for the plasterwork of the 'turrets in the mount'; it seems in fact to have consisted of a central room and four corner turrets, and James Both contracted to work frieze and cornice for the turrets by April 1581, to moulds supplied by Abraham Smith, a plasterer who reappears at Hardwick. The 'stand' is the building now better known as the Hunting Tower, on the then treeless hilltop above the house (Pl. 195). It has a similar plan to the 'turret in the mount' and three of its little turrets have plasterwork of great liveliness and charm, probably worked by Abraham Smith (Pl. 196). The Hunting Tower can confidently be ascribed to the early 1580s, and is one of two surviving Elizabethan buildings at Chatsworth. The other is the building known as Queen Mary's Bower, a parapeted enclosure surrounded by water and approached by a bridge. Its water surround is in fact the furthest and only survivor of a string of fish ponds that once ran north-west from the house to the river.

The house that emerged from this thirty-odd year building history had one especially curious feature. If the top floor, with its great chamber, long gallery, and state suites for important guests had been removed, it would still have been a completely equipped Elizabethan house, for there was another great chamber, another long gallery, and another state suite on the first floor, the usual position for such rooms in houses of this date.

The following building chronology can tentatively be suggested to explain this peculiarity and fill the gaps in the documentation. The original house built to Roger Worde's platt was a courtyard house only one room thick and two storeys high, with no courtyard galleries and no range of rooms to the east of the hall. In the second stage, perhaps during the St Loe marriage, the west range was doubled in thickness to provide a long gallery, a feature then increasingly coming into fashion. In the third stage, during the Shrewsbury marriage, a complete extra storey was added to contain splendid new state rooms, the courtyard galleries were built, the corner turrets may have been added and the hall enlarged, and there was much refitting of the existing rooms, and a lavish provision of outbuildings and garden works.

196. Plasterwork in one of the turrets of the Hunting Tower.

Although only a hypothesis, this has its advantages, apart from explaining why the house ended up with a double provision of state rooms. It makes the house expand at an equivalent rate to Bess's own fortunes. The piling of a new floor of state rooms on top of the old would explain why by the 1680s (according to the evidence of the 1st Duke's auditor, James Whildon, in 1706) the structure was found to be 'decaying and weake'. And it can be paralleled by the Earl of Shrewsbury's work at Worksop Manor, where in the 1580s he built no fewer than two floors of splendid new rooms on top of an existing early sixteenth-century hunting lodge.

However it emerged, there is no doubt that Elizabethan Chatsworth exerted a powerful influence both on the seventeenth-century Chatsworth that succeeded it and on the new house that Bess built at Hardwick. In particular the new Chatsworth inherited the position of its state rooms high up on the second floor, an arrangement that was unusual in the Elizabethan period, highly eccentric by the late seventeenth century, and found increasingly inconvenient by subsequent generations; the rooms only survived because the 6th Duke kept them as historical curiosities when Wyatville designed his magnificent new low-level state rooms in the early nineteenth century.

But at the time Bess was clearly delighted with them, and repeated the arrangement both when she remodelled her family house at Hardwick in the 1580s and when she built the new house there after her husband's death in 1590. The long and stately ascent from the entrance hall to the great rooms on the second floor and the dramatic extra height given to the house externally clearly appealed to an ostentatious, extravagant or possibly even romantic element in her nature. New Hardwick, in particular, is modelled in some respects very closely on old Chatsworth, with high great chamber, long gallery, withdrawing chamber and best bedchamber on the second floor, and low great chamber with easy communication to her own suite on the floor below — a floor for state and a floor for use. But at Hardwick, redundant rooms, like the second long gallery, are done away with, and the house has no internal courtyard.

The memory of Elizabethan Chatsworth survives at Hardwick not only in its plan but in its contents. From the very beginning, fittings and furniture were being transferred from Chatsworth to Hardwick. The 1601 inventory makes clear that, although Chatsworth was the larger and grander house, Hardwick was more fully and richly furnished. The explanation probably lies in Bess's personal history. She had moved to Hardwick in the first place because the ownership of Chatsworth was in dispute between her and her husband after their marriage broke up in 1583. After her husband's death she had undisputed ownership of Chatsworth, but it was only on a life tenancy and she knew that it would go to her eldest son, Henry, who had taken her husband's side and whom she disliked; whereas Hardwick was earmarked for her favourite son, William (who later bought the reversion of Chatsworth as well, but this she could not foresee).

So a good deal of the contents of Chatsworth were shipped over to Hardwick and are down in the inventory as to 'remayne and contynewe' there. Almost all the plate went, and all the pictures. The great embroidered panels of the virtues, their embodiments and their opposites, which are now one of the glories of Hardwick (Pl. 197), were made in the 1570s for Chatsworth, out of medieval copes belonging to Sir William St Loe; but by 1601 they were in the withdrawing chamber at Hardwick. The famous long table inlaid with musical instruments and Talbot and Cavendish arms,

and the inlaid chest with the initials *GT* on it (for George or Gilbert Talbot?) were almost certainly originally at Chatsworth.

What remained at Chatsworth was, above all, the fittings, including the panelling. One of the most interesting aspects of Chatsworth, as revealed by the 1601 inventory, is that room after room was filled with intricate and magnificent panelling, to which there was no equivalent at Hardwick. The following list gives the more elaborate examples:

High Great Chamber	verie fayre waynscotted with coloured woodes markentrie and set fourth with planetes
High Gallerie	verie fayre waynscotted with coloured woods markentrie and pelasters fayre set foarth
Savills Chamber	verie fayre waynscotted or seeled with coloured woodes markentrie pelasters and carving

217

197. Detail of *Faith and her Contrary, Mahomet,* one of a set of embroideries originally at Chatsworth and now at Hardwick.

Round Turrett	verie fayre waynscotted and with alablaster blackstone and other devices carving
Another turrett	fayre waynscotted with coloured woods and piramides
Matted gallerie	fayre waynscotted to the height markentrie with portalls
My Ladies withdrawing chamber	verie fayre waynscotted deep french panel markentrie
My ladies bedchamber	verie fayre waynscotted to the height with coloured woodes
ffynishers Chamber	fayre waynscotted markentrie

Compared to this, Hardwick has only low panelling stencilled in imitation of marquetry work. All the evidence goes to suggest that in the 1590s Bess did not have craftsmen capable of elaborate joinery at her disposal. The only elaborate panelling at Hardwick is in the high great chamber and this was certainly not there when the inventory was made in 1601.

The traffic of goods from Chatsworth to Hardwick continued after Bess's death, even if for different reasons. The first important influx came, not surprisingly, when the 1st Duke started to remodel Chatsworth in the late seventeenth century. The accounts show that many of the fittings of the Elizabethan house were carefully stored. Two payments relate directly to Hardwick. In March-April 1690 George Cowley was paid 'for helping to Remove wainscote and sending it to hardwick and setting ye rest up againe 2 dayes'. In October-November 1691 Edward Whilldon was paid for '1 day makeing 3 boxes to carry a chimney piece in, to Hardwick'.

Can the panelling be identified today at Hardwick? There are in fact a number of possibilities. One is the high great chamber panelling, with its elaborate carved pilasters. As already stated, this is not in the 1601 Hardwick inventory, when the room had panelling only three feet high; so it is tempting to identify it with the panelling with 'pelasters' in the high gallery or Savills Chamber at Chatsworth. The argument against this, however, is that this Chatsworth panelling is described as being 'markentrie', and the Hardwick high great chamber panelling has no inlay but is painted and decorated with coloured prints glued to the woodwork. So perhaps it is more likely to have been an addition made after 1601.

198. One of four inlaid panels now on the north staircase at Hardwick, but probably brought from Chatsworth.

But there is one set of panels which almost certainly came from Chatsworth, though not necessarily in 1690. These are the four remarkable panels of architectural scenes, one at least derived from contemporary engravings, which now hang in semi-darkness on the second stairs at Hardwick (Pl. 198). They are described in the 6th Duke's handbook to Hardwick as 'four very curious panels of coloured inlaid wood long ago discovered in the ruins of the old house'. They must originally have come from Chatsworth; they are not in the inventory of the Old Hall and one of them is dated 1576, at which period work was in full spate at Chatsworth, while Hardwick Old Hall was still a decaying manor house bought by Bess in that year from her indigent brother James. Another fragment which can reasonably be surmised to be a relic from Chatsworth is the panel inlaid with a splendid interlacing design, now incorporated in the wooden enclosure round the chapel altar, a fitting made up of various fragments, probably in the nineteenth century.

A mysterious payment in the building accounts for 9 December 1577 may show who was responsible for the inlaid panelling at Chatsworth. It runs: 'Payd to Tayler the inlayer aforhand VLi toward the payment of VIIILi for tow years wadge to beginn at candlemas contwilvmonth which shalbe in XXIreq years' (that is to say February

219

199. Detail of Apollo and the Muses, an overmantel brought from Chatsworth to Hardwick in the eighteenth century.

1579, in the twenty-first year of the Queen's reign). Nothing else is known about Tayler, but the payment suggests he had already been at Chatsworth and that Bess was paying a retainer to ensure his return after he had completed a fourteen-month contract elsewhere.

To turn to the chimney-piece, the 1691 reference is quite certainly not to the splendid overmantel panel of Apollo and the Muses (Pl. 199) in the withdrawing chamber of Hardwick, though this was equally certainly originally at Chatsworth. It was brought to Hardwick by the 6th Duke, having in his time been the over-mantel in the steward's room there, and then, in his words, 'for many years buried in the wooden packing case on the way to, and stumbled over by, all who approached the offices and kitchen'. It was probably made for the 'Muses' Chamber', a description used in the 1601 inventory as an alternative either for the high great chamber or the withdrawing chamber to the Earl of Leicester's chamber.

The only chimney-piece at Hardwick which could conceivably have come from Chatsworth in 1691 is the one in what is now generally known as the Blue Bed-chamber, with its alabaster panel of Tobias and the Angel (Pl. 200). This bears no rela-tionship to anything at Hardwick, and moreover the overmantel appears to have had its entablature removed to fit it to the ceiling height. Both it and the 'Muses' panel are capable works, well above the Elizabethan average, though probably not by the same hand. In general, the surviving remains at Hardwick combine with the documentary evidence to suggest that Eliza-bethan Chatsworth, though far less inventive architecturally, was both more magnificent than Hardwick and rather more sophisticated in much of its craftsman-ship. Bess at Chatsworth in the 1570s was, after all, not only even richer but, which was more important, closer to the centre of power than as a formidable widow at Hardwick in the 1590s.

200. The 'Tobias and the Angel' chimney-piece in the Blue Bedchamber, Hardwick, which may origi-nally have been at Chatsworth.
201. (right) Morris dancers on the Dixton Manor estate, Gloucestershire. Detail from an anonymous painting of c. 1725-35.

5 COUNTRY-HOUSE PICTURES

Two very different images foster the cult of the country house. One is an upstairs-downstairs image, the image of complex communities organised in hierarchies and spreading out from the family and the many grades of servants in the house itself to gardeners, grooms, lodge-keepers, estate workers and tenantry. Such communities are far enough from most people's experience to seem exotic, but close enough to be imaginable, they give an impression of ordered security that can be comforting to those who feel they are living in a troubled world.

The other image derives from an inside-outside relationship rather than an upstairs-downstairs one. It is an image of Elysium, which makes each country house, protected by its park and encircling belt of trees, seem the enchanted abode of glamorous and beautiful people. The downstairs element fades to a blurred background of faithful or admiring figures; it is the upstairs world that counts. To outsiders one of the attractions of this world is that it is remote but not entirely inaccessible. There is always a chance of receiving that nod, that smile, that little note of invitation that will transmit the longed-for message 'come and be one of us'.

202. (top) *Prospect of Littlecote*, English *c.* 1710. Artist unknown.
203. (bottom) View of the park from Petworth House, from the painting by J.M.W. Turner.

One image derives from a way of life that has largely disappeared; the other, in so far as people are still living in country houses, has a link with the present. One feeds off curiosity and nostalgia, the other off romanticism and snobbery. With four such emotions behind it, it is not surprising that the cult flourishes.

Both images can be found in the numerous pictures of country houses painted from the sixteenth to the twentieth century. Such pictures are a source both valuable and neglected. They have been neglected because too little has been known about them. A pioneering account by John Steegman and Dorothy Stroud was published in 1949; in the past twenty years or so Paul Mellon has been the first person to collect pictures of this type on a large scale; but there was no thorough and authoritative study before John Harris's *The Artist and the Country House* (1980). This features 118 artists, ranging from Canaletto, Gainsborough and Turner to artists like Thomas Bardwell, who advertised in the *Norwich Gazette* in 1738: 'History, Landscapes, Signs, Shew-Boards, Window-Blinds, Flower-Pots for Chimneys, and House Painting in imitation of all sorts of Wood, Stone and Mahogany, to such Perfection, as is not practised in this part of the Kingdom.' Small beer, one might say; and yet Bardwell's paintings are among the most attractive in a book that is full of pleasures and surprises.

The country house as the centre of its neighbourhood, rather than as a secret world apart, comes across most strongly in those aerial views of country houses that were popular from the mid-seventeenth to the mid-eighteenth century (Pl. 202). Such views are extraordinary in the richness and variety of scene that they depict. They show houses, gardens and deer parks, but also stables and farms with their yards, duck-ponds, vegetable gardens, orchards, drying yards with linen hanging on lines, or laid out on the ground, timber yards, fields, woods, villages and churches. A coach-and-four with attendant horsemen lumbers up the avenue; the master of the house and his friends hunt in the deer park; the meadows are crowded with horses and cattle, hay-makers make hay, hay-carts trundle through the fields, milkmaids are milking. In a panoramic view of the great hayfield at Dixton Manor, Gloucestershire (Pl. 201), taken at harvest time, morris dancers, gaily decked out with blue and red sashes, leap in line and hold handkerchiefs in each hand. In the immediate neighbourhood of the house, grooms ride horses out to exercise or fondle dogs in the stable yard; peasants and peasant women bring provisions in baskets carried on their heads or slung on poles across their shoulders; pedlars approach with pack-horses; the gardens are crowded with strolling couples, gardeners roll the lawns, and groups play bowls on the bowling green.

In contrast are the views, usually taken from ground level, in which the house floats or glows in a setting of Arcadian parkland or spacious lawns, peaceful and empty except for a herd of browsing deer or cattle (Pl. 203), or a solitary gardener or ploughman, or, very often, the owner of the house and a privileged group of family or friends, riding or driving through the enchanted solitudes of their domain. With a few exceptions the teeming panoramic views date from the late seventeenth and early eighteenth centuries, the empty idyllic ones from the late eighteenth and early nineteenth centuries; in the intermediate period the bird's-eye view gradually went out of fashion, but the emerging ground-level views still tended to be crowded with people.

Clearly, the pictures, quite apart from their decorative or pleasure-giving qualities, are valuable documents, supplying evidence not only (especially the earlier ones) of the appearance, setting and activities of country houses, but of the values and attitudes of their owners. But like all documents they need to be interpreted with caution, and checked against other sources. As far as buildings, parks and gardens are concerned, one can never be absolutely certain, without other evidence, that the artist is showing what was there rather than what the owner hoped would be there shortly. Moreover, although the pictures clearly teem with information about field enclosures, household economy, the management of deer parks, decoys and woodland, methods of farming, and so on, one is always left with a doubt as to where the artist got his information from; how many of the details derived from what actually happened in and around the houses, how many were studio props, filled in by the artist in his city painting room?

Attempts to interpret the owner's attitudes from the pictures are probably even more subject to pitfalls, without supporting evidence. The panoramic views certainly seem to have had more behind them than pride of possession; like the country-house poems written a little earlier by Ben Jonson and others, they suggest a deliberate attempt to project country houses as the hospitable centres of a fruitful countryside. But was this really one of their aims? Or is their teeming life depicted more through convention than conviction, following the accepted realism of Dutch landscape painting, to which school, in terms of art history, the pictures peripherally belong?

The changeover from populated bird's-eye views to empty ground-level ones partly resulted from changes which can be precisely documented. It reflects a notable change in country-house surroundings. Parks (as the bird's-eye views make abundantly clear) were originally by no means inevitable appendages of a country house, and were often at some distance from the house, or attached to one side or one corner of it; they were there to supply deer for hunting, rather than to be a setting for the house. But in the eighteenth century their role changed: their main function was to set off the house, and deer became an optional extra, kept for decoration rather than sport. The change came with the development of landscape gardening and the cult of the picturesque; another result of which was that bird's-eye views went out of fashion in favour of views taken from accessible viewpoints and chosen because they were striking rather than because they conveyed the maximum information.

The resulting contrast between seventeenth or early eighteenth-century houses, where the weave of the countryside, and the public roads that formed part of it, went right up to the houses, and the late eighteenth and early nineteenth-century houses, protected from what one is tempted to call the real world by park, drives, lodge-gates and woods, is very striking; it was, incidentally, the reason why Constable said 'a gentleman's park is my aversion; it is not beauty because it is not nature'.

But did the change express more than an aesthetic change? Or did it, even if aesthetic in origin, affect the attitude to life of the families living at the end of the drives? Prince Pückler-Muskau, who toured England in the 1820s, thought that the English upper classes were heading for trouble just as the French aristocracy had been in the mid-eighteenth century. But his English hosts would have denied that they were any more out of touch with their tenants and the surrounding countryside than their predecessors; beyond the Arcadian unreality of their parks (under which lay the ghost of many a demolished village) their estates were undoubtedly better farmed than they had ever been. After all, there was no English Revolution. And yet, and yet — were the siren charms of the English country house entirely innocent?

224

204. (right) Congreve's monument on the island in the lake at Stowe, Buckinghamshire, from the drawing by John Piper.

6 THE MAGIC OF STOWE

Stowe has always fascinated me, because it exists on so many different levels. One can walk around the house and gardens at any time of the year and enjoy them in the simplest and least critical way, for their beauty. But one can also start trying to find out what lies behind them, aided by the work of those who have loved and written about Stowe, especially Christopher Hussey, pioneer and founder of all studies of the English landscape garden, and George Clarke, who is still perceptively disinterring its meaning and history. Stowe then becomes a magic box, from which one can pull out layer after layer of meaning, or a diamond which flashes and sparkles in a different way, depending on the angle from which one looks at it.

To begin with, the whole history of the eighteenth-century garden is there, phase superimposed on phase, so that it can be read like a palimpsest, with the semi-formal script of Bridgeman and the Rococo twirls of William Kent still distinguishable beneath the smoothly flowing hand of Capability Brown. The original formality, it is

true, has largely disappeared, but it can still be sensed in the straight avenues which border the gardens, in the Boycott Pavilions guarding the approach like twin watchdogs, and above all in the great axial vistas (Pl. 205) to north and south of the house, the latter crossing the avenue beyond the lake at an exact right angle and pursuing its inexorable way up and down hill to Buckingham, nearly three miles from the south portico.

In the Elysian Fields Kent's genius at creating an intimate informality of secret glades and streams, surveyed by exquisitely sited buildings, can be enjoyed better than anywhere else in England, except perhaps at Rousham in Oxfordshire. Here is that 'new taste in gardening', described as having 'the appearance of beautiful nature', which startled and delighted Kent's contemporaries in the 1730s; and although the passage of time has mellowed and to some extent changed the layout, one can still get a vivid sense of how revolutionary it must have seemed to those accustomed to the pleached hedges, parterres and formal vistas of the gardens of the time. But a few steps out of the Elysian Fields brings one out on to the lakes and the huge south lawn; and one can appreciate in an instant the second stage of the landscape garden and the boldness with which Capability Brown (but probably even more his employers Lords Cobham and Temple) elided and enlarged the intricacies of earlier generations into the breathtaking simplicity of grass and water.

Architecturally too, Stowe is an epitome, almost a museum, of Georgian styles; where else can one savour Vanbrugh, Kent and Gibbs, and move to and fro from Baroque to Palladian, Gothick to Neoclassical, so freely and enjoyably within a few square miles? Or pass so easily up and down the diapason of scale, from the miniature gaiety of the Shepherd's Cove to the triumphant grandeur of the south front? There is much to intrigue and delight in the garden buildings at Stowe, but the garden front is perhaps the one piece of architecture there which could be described as a work of genius (although whose genius is a subject for architectural historians, for its evolution was a complex one). It seems now to preside so effortlessly over the whole of Stowe that one tends to forget how late it arrived on the scene. While the gardens gradually

226

205. One of the set of views of Stowe by Jacques Rigaud, engraved in 1739.

evolved towards greater and greater perfection, the garden front of the house remained a vast anticlimax, an inadequate centre with two long and disjointed wings sprawling to either side of it. Remodelling it was the last project of Lord Temple, the second creator of Stowe, and it was only finished within a few years of his death in 1779. It must have been an inspiring moment when the scaffolding was removed and he saw that the design had come off, that the keystone had dropped into place, anticlimax had become climax, and his and his uncle's life-work had achieved its centrepiece and culmination (Pl. 206).

But Stowe is more than a collection of buildings, or a splendid house in a beautiful setting. It is also a statement of political, social and personal attitudes. Lord Cobham and his nephew and heir, Lord Temple, put their whole lives into it in rather more than the usual sense of the word. Their friends, their pets, their politics, and their passions are all there, glorified by a column or a temple, distilled into an epitaph or a poem. The Home Park was dedicated to love and pleasure, and presided over by Bacchus and Venus. Bacchus had his own temple, and his statue in the Rotunda looked down to Venus's temple by the lake; both statue and Temple of Bacchus have gone, but Kent's Temple of Venus remains one of the most beautiful of the garden buildings at Stowe. On a lesser scale, the Shepherd's Cove suggests pastoral swains, and Dido's Cave commemorates the meeting-place of two of the most famous of classical lovers. On the other side of the garden, to the east of the central vista, the mood changes to a more serious one; the theme is friendship and virtue. Busts of Lord Cobham's political friends were in the Temple of Friendship, full-length statues of selected classical

227

206. The south front of Stowe, as drawn by John Piper.

heroes were in the Temple of Ancient Virtue, and the serried ranks of his English heroes still look across the Elysian Fields from the Temple of British Worthies. The Ladies' Temple had none of the amorous innuendoes which filled the Temple of Venus at the other end of the gardens; it was decorated with pictures of 'Ladies employing themselves in Needle and Shell-work' and 'Ladies diverting themselves with Painting and Music'. The scene suggested is one of wives amusing themselves while their husbands were discussing politics in the adjacent temples and glades. This side of the gardens is vibrant with eighteenth-century politics. Stowe was not a place of retirement. To begin with, it was a hotbed of the opposition, dedicated to bringing down Walpole and ending jobbery and corruption; then it became a mainstay of the government, pursuing honour and glory under Lord Temple's brother-in-law William Pitt. It was nothing less than the British Empire that was being hatched by the young men who fished, joked, drank and walked among the temples of Stowe.

The inscriptions on the Temple of British Worthies bristle with innuendoes about the latest scandal or crisis in politics at the time when they were composed. It was an approach that could lead to problems, when an alliance crumbled or a policy was abandoned; inscriptions had to be erased, monuments demolished or renamed. But the main lines remained consistent. The Gothic Temple stands for the medieval foundations of British law and liberty; its neighbour, the Temple of Concord and Victory, suggests Britain's role as the heir of the Roman Empire, and celebrates the victories of the Seven Years' War; from its portico one looked across to the obelisk in honour of General Wolfe, and the 'Naval Column' in honour of Lord Cobham's nephew Captain Grenville, killed fighting the French under Admiral Anson. Indeed, the great garden front of the house can be seen as a celebration of glory and victory, looking out to the Triumphal Arch between 'military columns' at the top of the hill, the steps to its portico flanked by British lions, and the oval saloon behind the portico decorated with a sculptured frieze of figures, representing the triumph and sacrifice of Victory.

But besides acting out a moral and political allegory, the gardens at Stowe were also there for recreation, enjoyment and entertaining. They were not designed for driving or riding; the park was for that. They were for walking in; and as such they could solace, divert or intrigue almost anyone, from the huge crowds of tourists who came to visit at all times of the year to Lord Temple himself, out for a solitary stroll with his dog in the evening. They contained two obvious circuits, which could be taken singly or together. Either or both could be used to divert a house party after the early dinners of the eighteenth century, and keep them wandering in groups from temple to obelisk, and fountain to pillar, reading the inscriptions, admiring the ever shifting views of one feature from another, and being entertained by refreshments or a meal in one of the bigger temples on the way. The great lawn before the south front was big enough for the biggest of garden parties, or for a 'Grand Promenade and Military Concert', such as was given in 1840, in honour of Queen Adelaide, sitting benignly under the orange trees which then adorned the portico, watching the crowds on the lawn before her. The valley of the Elysian Fields could be used for more intimate and romantic entertainments. Dips could be taken in the Cold Bath; there was fishing in the lakes and ponds; the greyhound Fido coursed up and down the long glades and ended up with a monument and long inscription of his own: 'Reader, this

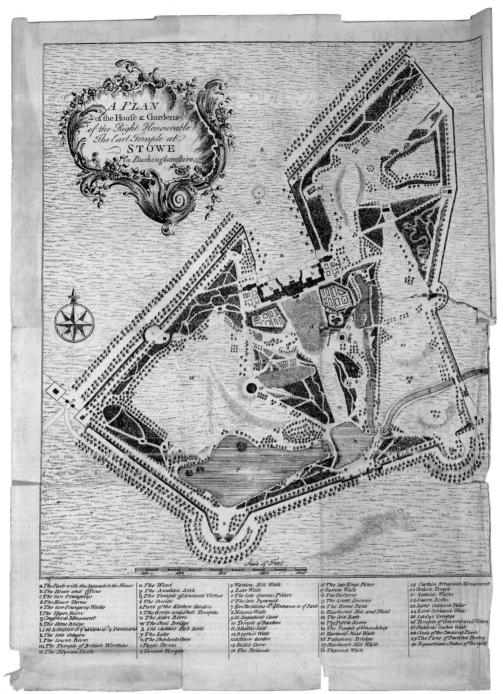

Stone is guiltless of Flattery, for he to whom it is inscrib'd was not a Man but a GREYHOUND.'

A great deal is known about the reactions of the tourists who came to Stowe in the eighteenth century; numerous descriptions of their visits survive in letters and journals of the day. Much less has come to light about how the gardens were used by the family and their guests; much has to be surmised. What, if any, Bacchanalian or Paphian revels went on in the Temple of Bacchus, or below the vanished frescoes of the Temple of Venus, depicting Spencer's Malbecco peeping from behind a tree to watch his wife 'revelling with a beastly herd of Satyrs'? All that is recorded is that Princess Amelia, George III's daughter, once took refuge there from the rain. We know that

229

207. Plan of Stowe and its gardens, from the 1773 edition of Seely's *Guide*.

Pope fished in the lakes; but did Congreve fish there too? It would be nice to think that his monument, perhaps the most delightful of the smaller monuments at Stowe (Pl. 204), commemorates a favourite fishing spot of his, for it was on the edge of one of the canals until, in the changes of the later eighteenth century, it was left hidden on its own secret island on the edge of the east lake.

One would swap half-a-dozen of the many surviving descriptions of Comings of Age, Tenants' Balls, Royal Visits and other jollifications at Stowe in the nineteenth century, for a few more descriptions of similar events in the eighteenth. Much the best of those that have survived is the account of the entertainment given to Princess Amelia in 1764. It took place at night-time, before the grotto in the upper part of Kent's Elysian Fields. 'All day a number of people were preparing the grotto and garden for Her Highness and company to sup there ... At ten the gardens were illuminated with above a thousand lights, and the water before the grotto was covered with floating lights. At the farther end of the canal on the ship, which was curiously figured with lights, was a place for the music, which was performed all supper-time ... Her Highness walked down to the grotto at half-past ten, and was pleased and delighted with the grand prospect which was presented to her view; nothing was seen but lights and people, nothing was heard but music and fireworks, and nothing was felt but joy and happiness.'

The outdoor entertainments and events at Stowe in the early nineteenth century were on a much grander scale than Princess Amelia's candle-lit supper and seem to have taken place mainly in the vast and somewhat arid open spaces of the park to the north of the house. But their splendour in fact marked the beginning of the most disastrous chapter in the history of Stowe; for Stowe not only played its part in national dramas, it was the scene of a family drama awesome in its scale and comprehensiveness, a Greek tragedy of success leading to pride, pride to arrogance, arrogance to disaster. Once one knows the story, it becomes an inescapable element in the atmosphere of Stowe, adding a melancholy undertone to its splendours. It is the story of the great debacle of 1848, which shattered the family's image, emptied the house of its contents and, ultimately, stripped the temples of their statues and paintings.

In the seventeenth century the Temple family of Stowe had been prosperous country gentlemen. In the eighteenth century Lord Cobham and Lord Temple made Stowe a place of national importance, both politically and because of its gardens and buildings; it was on the centre of the stage, and played an honourable and even splendid part there. But Lord Temple, although a high-principled and able man, was also a proud and touchy one: the impression of overpowering arrogance that exudes from Allan Ramsay's portrait of him had a basis in reality. Over the next three generations the abilities grew less, but the pride and pretensions grew greater. The family climbed to a marquessate and a dukedom, but although they were still a power to be reckoned with, Stowe was gradually slipping out of the mainstream. The 1st Duke of Buckingham had a good eye for pictures and an informed interest in archaeology, but also what is described as 'a ludicrously exaggerated notion of his own capacity and consequence'. The 2nd Duke brought nothing to the house of any interest, except a series of water-closets disguised in cupboards surmounted by his coronet and ducal coat of arms. But his parties were superb. They culminated with his son's Coming of Age in

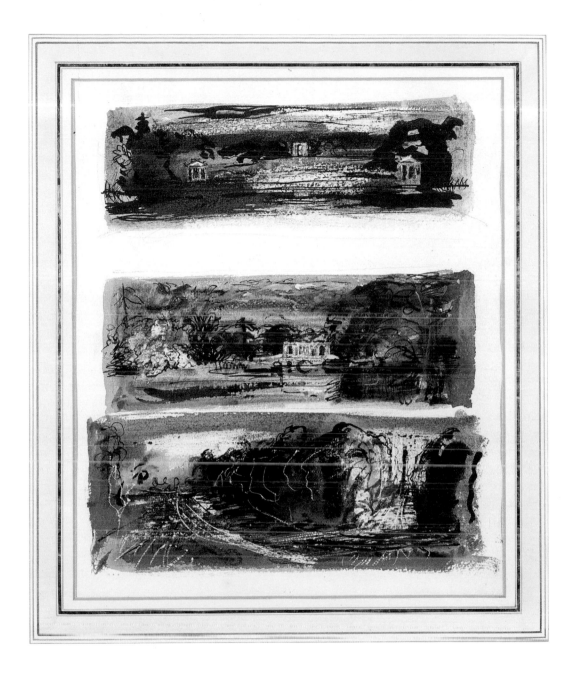

1844, and the visit of Queen Victoria and Prince Albert in 1845. Seldom if ever can one English family have given two such lavish entertainments within two years. The Queen was welcomed by three bands brought from London, 500 mounted tenants wearing scarlet rosettes, 500 farm labourers in white smocks and green ribands, and an entire regiment of Yeomanry. Both entertainments were crowded with balls, dinners, roastings of oxen, fireworks, fire-balloons, bonfires and illuminations.

It was all a sham. The Queen had never wanted to come, and was furious at having been pressured into the visit by her ministers; she was in a temper throughout the visit, and kept making remarks to the effect that the Dukes of Buckingham lived much more splendidly than she did. In fact they had been living above their means for fifty years; the 2nd Duke had inherited a debt of £200,000 and had got it up to a million in

208. The Grecian Valley, the Palladian bridge and the Lake Pavilions at Stowe, drawn by John Piper.

five years. Finally in 1848 almost all the contents of Stowe came under the hammer, and were auctioned in 5,000 lots in a sale which lasted for nearly eight weeks. The Duke handed over what remained to his son, and retired to the arms of his mistress, and to death thirteen years later in the Station Hotel at Paddington. His descendants lived on in, by ducal standards, shabby gentility at Stowe; but the inevitable end came in 1921, when the house and what remained of its surrounding estate and contents were sold. Then came sudden and unexpected rescue when the house was bought to be a school — in its way an equally extraordinary story.

And so the owners of Stowe left their paradise, driven out of it by the hubris of their ancestors. There is a little more to this than metaphor. Of all the aspects of Stowe, and other great landscape gardens of the eighteenth century, one of the most interesting is their role as a re-creation of Paradise, Arcadia, Elysium, the Garden of Eden, the Golden Age — or whatever other name human beings have used to label their vision of an ideal world, beyond and above the imperfections of actual life. Stowe takes its place in a long tradition. All through the Middle Ages it was widely believed, not only that the Garden of Eden was an actual place, rather than a myth or a metaphor, but that it still existed. It was generally identified with Paradise. Strictly speaking, Paradise was distinct from Heaven; but since Heaven tended to be called Paradise too, it was sometimes distinguished as the Earthly Paradise. Paradise was the place on earth where the good dead waited in a state of blissful happiness until they ascended to Heaven at the Day of Judgement. The consequences of the Fall did not hold in it. It was always summer there; trees carried perpetual flowers and fruit at the same time, and animals of all kinds lived happily together. The image gradually attracted other, related, images; it became associated with the classical Elysium, or Elysian Fields, or Isles of the Blest, with the Garden of the Hesperides and with the enclosed garden of the Song of Solomon.

In the sixteenth century, belief in the actual existence of the Earthly Paradise began to melt away, but it was replaced by another one. The contents of Paradise had been scattered over the world at the Fall, but if they were assembled again in one place, it might be possible to re-create Paradise on earth, complete with continuous blossom, greenery and summer; moreover, the produce of this re-created Paradise might provide a diet which would enable men to surmount disease and at least delay death.

Ideas of Paradise gradually collected a series of visual images. The main medieval one was of a grassy enclosure thickly sown with flowers and scattered with trees, surrounded by a wall or wattle fence; from the outside it appeared as a walled enclosure, with trees rising from behind the walls. In the seventeenth century the image tended to be expanded, and Paradise became a park-like landscape of woods and glades in which animals of all breeds lived peaceably together. Landscapes of this sort were shown in numerous paintings and engravings, and are the basis of Milton's description of the Garden of Eden in *Paradise Lost*. But Milton kept elements of the medieval image when he surrounded his 'delicious Paradise' with a 'verdurous wall', above which rose a circuit of trees. Inside were groves, lawns, downs, grazing flocks, lakes, streams, shady grottoes and perpetual spring.

In the eighteenth-century landscape garden, the Christian Paradise and the classical Elysium or Arcadia were fused together with Platonic theories of the ideal. Its designers

232

saw themselves as returning to nature, but by this they meant, not what they called the 'common nature' of the world around them, but ideal nature. Whether this was seen in terms of a Platonic abstraction, or of Elysium, or of Nature before the Fall, that is to say of Paradise, did not matter very much. Paradise tended to figure less prominently because the eighteenth century was so overpoweringly conscious of Greece and Rome; hence the temples, Elysian Fields and Vale of Tempe at Stowe, and all over England a conscious imitation of idealised or sacred Roman landscapes, such as the gardens of Hadrian's Villa, with their multitude of little buildings, or the temple-dominated valley of Tivoli, visited by all English tourists to Rome. But Paradise was always there in the background — most obviously, at Stowe, in the 'verdurous wall' which circumscribed the gardens and figures prominently in all eighteenth-century plans. Admittedly, this consisted, not of a medieval-style stone wall or paling, but (suitably enough, since Lord Cobham was a field marshal) of a circuit of bastions and earthworks, reinforced by belts of trees. This circuit had the advantage that those inside could look out into the surrounding countryside; but outsiders were also effectively prevented from coming, or even seeing, in, except at controlled points.

So Paradise and Elysium joined together to create the Golden Age. When Mrs Montagu wrote in 1744: 'Stowe is beyond description. It gives the best idea of Paradise that can be; even Milton's images and descriptions fall short of it', she was not just a gushing lady, she was expressing one facet of Lord Cobham's pursuit of the ideal. Whether he, or Lord Temple, or anyone else actually believed that there had been such a time as the Golden Age, or such a place as Paradise or Elysium, was and is irrelevant; by the eighteenth century they had acquired a force or magic of their own, regardless of any relationship to actual places or events. Perhaps the fact that they retain their power today is one reason why Stowe has such a strange intensity; one needn't know anything about its background to feel transported into a secret and enchanted world as soon as one crosses its boundaries.

But something else has been added. Stowe owes its character, not just to its surviving eighteenth-century buildings, or to the design of the gardens in which they stand, or to the strength of the ideas and images behind them, but also to the way in which buildings and design have been and are being worked on by time and nature — not ideal eighteenth-century nature, but actual nature. In the mid-eighteenth century it was expected that natural forces and the passage of time would clothe and soften the lines of a landscape design, but it is unlikely that anyone anticipated how far the changes would go, or that Lord Cobham or Lord Temple would necessarily be pleased if they came back and walked round Stowe today. It is we, with the Romantic Movement between us and them, who can appreciate the miracles which nature has worked and continues to work at Stowe. This is not to say that the gardens should be left alone; at the very least, trees have to be replanted and buildings repaired, and much has been achieved in the last twenty-five years. But when one thinks of Stowe one thinks always of a combination of the ideal and the changing; of the Palladian bridge rising from the weed- and lily-encrusted lake, of the Temple of Ancient Virtue half concealed by foliage, of lichened stonework set off by tangles of mare's-tails, of inscriptions half effaced and the Temple of Friendship so sadly and beautifully a ruin, of a building suddenly transformed by a low sun or a black sky, of trees swaying and

sighing in the wind and buildings standing immovable among them — and yet seeming to have their own secret and intense life, and to be signalling to each other across the landscape.

Considering its fame, Stowe has been less drawn or painted than one might have expected. There are, however, three series of views showing it in Georgian days. The set of engravings after drawings by Jacques Rigaud (Pl. 205) are as evocative and beautiful as any series of depictions of an English country house and its setting. But they date from about 1733, when the gardens were still largely formal; they show canals, trimmed hedges, straight avenues, all thronged with people. For the house and gardens at the time when their fame was at its height, in the mid-eighteenth century, there is little except George Bickham's engravings, and, pleasant though these are, their subject deserved something better. Finally comes an exciting recent discovery of the series of 105 drawings made in 1805-9 by J.C. Nattes. These vividly re-create the character of Stowe when the planting was beginning to mature, an Arcadian world where elegant Regency ladies wander under parasols from temple to temple, and flocks of sheep graze in the Grecian Valley (Pl. 209).

Then, in the 1930s, when the trees were at their prime and the buildings at that magical moment of romantic decay before repair became necessary if they were to survive, John Piper first came to Stowe. It was a piece of good fortune, for few English artists have been so sensitive not just to buildings, but to buildings as worked on by Nature. But Stowe as it appears in his drawings (Pls. 204, 206, 208) is very different from the gentle, rather bland Stowe of Nattes. It has acquired an edge of drama and intensity, the drawings shimmer with a life of their own, the buildings seem living presences in the ghostly groves. The unique and unforgettable atmosphere of a secret kingdom, so hard to describe in words or even illustrate in photographs, is invoked with extraordinary intensity. And yet it is not just a mirror of Stowe that is presented in this wonderful series of drawings; it is Stowe re-created by the vision of the artist, at once recognisable and transformed, *John Piper's Stowe*.

209. Captain Cook's Monument and the Grenville Column, from the drawing by J.C. Nattes.
210. (right) The garden front of Mount Clare, Roehampton.

7 WHAT IS A VILLA?

When I was a London child in the 1930s, I used to go to the annual hay party given by Lancelot Smith, a bachelor stockbroker who lived at Mount Clare, near Roehampton. This was an exquisite classical villa, built in 1770, probably to the design of Sir Robert Taylor, and embellished by Placido Columbani ten years later. To one side broad lawns stretched to where Richmond Park billowed away into the distance; to the other, between the house (Pl. 210) and Roehampton Lane, there was enough space for a swimming pool, a neatly manicured kitchen garden, a couple of meadows, a small herd of Jersey cows, and thatched farm buildings, deliciously rustic. There were no other houses in view, no hint of Piccadilly Circus six miles or so away. For the hay party, the lawns before the house were scattered with cocks of hay. Children from thoroughly nice London nurseries were let loose to jump in the hay or throw it at each other, watched by indulgent nannies. When they seemed sufficiently exhausted there was a Punch and Judy show in another part of the garden, followed by strawberries and cream in the house.

The hay parties remain my liveliest personal experience of the villa tradition: of the villa as a rural retreat for prosperous city dwellers; of the architectural model of the Italian villa, as developed in eighteenth-century England; and of the rustic play-acting which leads Professor Ackerman to say that 'the villa accommodates a fantasy which is impervious to reality'.

But 'villa' is a tricky word. What is a villa? One can deal with the term in three ways. One can investigate it in terms of usage: what buildings have actually been called villas, since Roman days? Or one can apply it to a social phenomenon, whether or not called 'villa' at the time: houses built in a rural setting, as places of retreat, recreation or relaxation for the well-off. Or one can use 'villa' to describe a specific architectural type. Summerson's influential article 'The Idea of the Villa' was concerned with a particular group of compact English houses, the architecture of which derived from villas designed by Palladio. But, as he pointed out, many of these houses were not called 'villas' when they were built.

Mount Clare falls into all three categories. In 1780 it was called 'an elegant new-built villa'; its architectural design is influenced by that of Palladio's villas; its modest twenty-three acres clearly make it a rural retreat, rather than a full-blown 'seat'. This kind of triple fit is by no means invariable. What the Romans called villas were not necessarily just for recreation. Rich Romans built luxurious retreats around the Bay of Naples and elsewhere, but many provincial villas were the centres of agricultural kingdoms, often of such importance that in France the word 'villa' developed into the word 'ville'. In Italy there is a considerable range between villas on the edge of Rome or Florence, in which the recreational element predominates, or villas in the Veneto, designed by Palladio and others, which had one function as places of retreat but an equally important one as centres of agricultural investment, incorporating granaries, barns and farm-stables, and the larger and more bombastic seventeenth or eighteenth-century villas, which speak of power much more strongly than of pleasure or profit.

In Europe, outside Italy, houses were built in the country for purposes of recreation from at least the early sixteenth century. Many of them owed little to Italian examples

211. Wothorpe House, Northamptonshire, built *c.* 1610, and one of the most memorable of Elizabethan and Jacobean lodges.

or Italian architecture, and most of them were not called villas: they were 'lodges', 'maisons de plaisance', 'lusthause', 'lustplaatse', 'jagdschlosse', and so on. In early eighteenth-century England such houses began to be called 'villas', mainly because they imitated Italian models. It was not until about 1770 to 1840, however, that 'villa' became the standard term for rural retreats of all sizes in England, even though by then a high proportion of them owed nothing to Italy.

The term 'villa' dropped out of fashion in England and America largely because it had become vulgarised. Lancelot Smith, whose route from Mount Clare to the City was close-packed with rows of Victorian or Edwardian villas, would never have thought of applying the term to his own house. After about 1850 American houses in the country of any pretensions ceased to be called villas. Specialist types were known as 'cottages' or 'camps' but the generic term became 'country house'. The term, in an American context, may grate on English readers, for in England (but only within the last fifty years or so) 'country house' has acquired a specialist meaning, as describing the seats of an aristocracy and landed gentry, whose power, prestige and, to a considerable extent, income derived from their ownership of tenanted farmland around their houses. Such houses barely existed in America after the mid-nineteenth century; the attempts by the Vanderbilts at Biltmore to create one, and a deferential tenantry to go with it, ended in fiasco. An American could well indignantly disagree with an Englishman who claimed that all so-called American country houses were really villas. Both would be right: it all depends on what is meant by 'country house' or 'villa'.

Even if one confines treatment of villas to the 'villa as social phenomenon' rather than the 'villa as description' or the 'villa as architectural type', it is difficult to draw a hard line between it and the country house. There is, it is true, a clear conceptual distinction between a house to which its owner goes in order to re-create himself in the country and a house from which he organises or oversees the sources of his wealth and power — between rural retreats and country seats. The distinction necessarily produces different symbolic languages. Since retreats must, by definition, retreat from something, they tend to contrast with whatever place or way of life is being withdrawn from. Ackerman, in his classic study of the villa, compares the simplicity and prismatic purity of early Renaissance villas with the formidable grandeur of town palazzi; and the modest scale and ingeniously innovative geometric plans of Elizabethan lodges (Pl. 211) contrast with the size and traditional apparatus of courtyards and gatehouses in great Elizabethan houses.

Contrast could also lie in the setting. The desire to get in touch with nature informed nearly all rural retreats. But what is 'nature', and how does one get in touch with it? City dwellers could relish agricultural landscapes improved and made fruitful by man, as well as nature in its wilder or purer aspects; landowners, all too familiar with farmland, retreated to grouse moors or deer forests. Alternatively, both classes could prefer nature-as-it-ought-to-be to nature-as-it-is and create their own Arcadian landscapes.

Fantasy was important, both a generalised fantasy of belief in the good country as opposed to the wicked city, or the desire to play specific roles. American tycoons could see themselves as farmers, cowboys, robber barons, hunters, Southern gentlemen, or country squires on an English or French model; they removed accordingly

from their downtown offices to neo-clapboard farmhouses in New England, ranches or castles in California, inflated log cabins in the Adirondacks (Pl. 212), colonial-style mansions in Virginia, or Tudor manor houses and Louis Seize chateaux on Long Island.

Rural retreats, in short, could imitate country seats. But country seats could also imitate rural retreats. Conceptually different though they may be, in practice it is impossible to separate one from the other. A medieval castle may be concerned entirely with power, and a week-end cottage with recreation, but there are numerous gradations in between. Almost all country seats were planned to cater for the entertainment and recreation of their owners and their guests. They picked up ideas from rural retreats which, being less tied by precedent, were freer to innovate. The compact plans of Elizabethan lodges were imitated in great houses such as Hardwick and Hatfield. The landscape garden, the origins of which, as John Dixon Hunt has shown, can be found in Italian villas, reached its apogee in the great country mansions of Georgian England, collecting ideas from Pope's villa at Twickenham and Lord Burlington's at Chiswick on the way.

The Arcadian beauty of the resulting Georgian parks, shut off from the outside world by encircling belts of trees, provided relief from the tame criss-cross of surrounding farmland, profitably enclosed by the owners of the parks. But they also added to their power. Who can read the description of Little Lord Fauntleroy's arrival at Dorincourt Castle without being made aware that the dreamy two-mile approach through parkland contributed as much to the haughty Earl's aura as the towers and battlements of his castle? It is part of the complexity of the story that the same symbols were used for different ends.

238

212. Sagamore Lodge, an American holiday house in the Adirondacks.
213. (right) Sir George Beaumont and Joseph Farington sketching a waterfall in the Lake District, from the drawing by Thomas Hearne, c. 1770.

8 THE HOUSE AND THE NATURAL LANDSCAPE:

A Prelude To Fallingwater

A drawing by Thomas Hearne (Pl. 213) shows Sir George Beaumont and Joseph Farington sketching a waterfall in the Lake District, some time in the 1770s. Waterfalls were being visited and sketched all over the British Isles at this period. But although gentlemen of taste sketched waterfalls, they did not build houses by them, still less over them. None the less, there is a connection between Sir George Beaumont, sketching his waterfall in the 1770s, and Edgar J. Kaufmann, commissioning Frank Lloyd Wright to build Fallingwater in the 1930s. Between them lies a gradual development of the romantic imagination, and of attitudes to the natural landscape and to the problem of how buildings should, or should not, be fitted into it.

In the eighteenth century, when English travellers first began to appreciate natural scenery, and to tour the mountains, lakes, rocks, waterfalls and wild places of the British

Isles, their attitude was by no means uncritical. For them 'nature' was the supreme arbiter, but by 'nature' they understood a Platonic ideal that actual natural scenery did not necessarily live up to. They had come to their appreciation by way of art and poetry, and travelled with minds conditioned by the way in which artists had painted wild landscapes, or poets had written about them, in both cases selecting and adjusting in order to compose a picture or a poem. A guide to the Lake District, first published in 1778, set out to take tourists 'from the delicate touches of Claude, verified in Coniston Lake, to the noble scenes of Poussin, exhibited on Windermere-water, and from there to the stupendous romantic ideas of Salvator Rosa, realized in the Lake of Derwent'. When looking at a view, travellers would pass judgement on it, and mentally readjust it if necessary.

Scenery was condemned for being too simple or too bare. A landscape of heather and rocks needed trees to break its outlines and give it light and shade. 'Mere rocks', wrote Thomas Whately in his *Observations on Modern Gardening* (1770), 'may surprise, but can hardly please; they are too far removed from common life, too barren and inhospitable, rather desolate than solitary, and more horrid than terrible.' Rocks were improved by water falling over or running through them; this produced a broken light and a broken sound that was both picturesque and pleasing. Trees, rocks and water joined together in the right proportions made up a picturesque composition.

Conventions developed about what did, or did not, go with particular views or features. Some types of buildings harmonized with waterfalls: Whately, for instance, described with approval 'an iron forge, covered with a black cloud of smoke, and surrounded with half-burned ore' next to the 'roar of a waterfall' on the River Wye. It suggested 'the ideas of force or of danger' and was 'perfectly compatible with the wildest romantic situations'. But a regular house next to a waterfall was a solecism: it

240

214. Culzean Castle, Ayrshire, as painted by Alexander Nasmyth in the early nineteenth century.

spoiled the picture because it had the wrong associations. Looked at the other way, a wild landscape coming right up to a house spoiled the house. 'And while rough thickets shade the lonely glen, Let culture smile upon the haunts of men', wrote Richard Payne Knight in his poem *The Landscape* (1795). A house of any size needed a park, and a park, while it should never be formal, had 'a character distinct from a forest; for while we admire, and even imitate, the romantic wildness of nature, we ought never to forget that a park is the habitation of men' (Humphrey Repton, *An Enquiry into the Changes in Landscape Gardening*, 1806).

So it came about that when eighteenth-century devotees of the picturesque painted or drew 'the romantic wildness of nature' they depicted it without domestic accompaniments; when they imitated it, they imitated it out of sight of their houses; and when they went to live in it, they inserted a zone of culture and cultivation between house and wilderness. Hafod in Wales, for instance, which was the most famous wild demesne in eighteenth-century Britain, was renowned for its waterfalls. But none of these was in sight of the house itself, which was built in a more pastoral setting of greensward and grazing cattle.

Country-house owners whose property did not happen to contain waterfalls not infrequently constructed artificial ones. At Bowood, in Wiltshire, Lord Shelburne made one at the end of an artificial lake, after the model of a picture by Poussin. Lord Stamford's new cascade at Enville in Staffordshire was described with enthusiasm by Joseph Heely: 'I think I never saw so fine an effect from light and shade, as is here produced by the gloom of evergreens and other trees, and the peculiar brightness of the foaming water' (*Letters on the Beauties of Hagley, Envil and the Leasowes*, 1777). But neither fall was in sight of the house. The most that was considered suitable to embellish a waterfall was a statue or inscription, perhaps to a departed relative or friend, suitable to the mood of gentle melancholy induced by the sound of water, or a seat from which to admire it. The latter had to be in the right mode, however, like that at the Leasowes, near Enville: 'a rude seat, composed of stone, under rugged roots'.

Unlike ordinary houses, castles, especially ruined castles, were also considered appropriate features in wild scenery. They had the right romantic connotations. But sometimes castles were still lived in, and sometimes they needed to be rebuilt. Culzean Castle in Ayrshire, for instance, was an old fortified house on a cliff-top over-looking the sea. Its position was superb, its family associations were valued, but as a house the building failed to meet late eighteenth-century standards of accommodation and comfort. Between 1777 and 1792 it was rebuilt to the designs of Robert Adam, but in his own individual version of a castle style, in sympathy with its site (Pl. 214). The new house rose straight from the cliffs, like the old one.

Culzean pioneered a fresh approach, based on the idea that the architecture of a new house could be adapted to fit it to a wild situation. In the early nineteenth century a number of such houses were built, on dramatic sites or in wild settings, even when

241

215. Dunglass, East Lothian, built to the designs of Richard Crichton, 1807-11.

there had been no house there before. Normally they were built in a castle manner, but some, like Dunglass in East Lothian, were in the classical style, though on an asymmetric plan and with a broken outline, to fit the site (Pl. 215). In the 1860s and 1870s Richard Norman Shaw established his reputation by designing Leyswood in Sussex, and Cragside in Northumberland, on dramatic rocky sites to which the houses played up with fragmented plans, soaring verticals and picturesquely broken roofs (Pl. 218). Shaw was consciously continuing the picturesque tradition, but, on the whole, new houses in this kind of position were built comparatively seldom in the British Isles.

When clients or architects did opt for a wild site it was usually an elevated one, with the house rising out of wild nature rather than melting into it. This was partly because such houses were built for people of position, who wanted their place of residence to have a degree of importance; but also because houses on higher land had a view, and enclosed low-lying situations were thought to be unhealthy. It was probably for these reasons that houses down by waterfalls were a rarity.

There was one building type, however, that could appropriately be designed to melt into its surroundings. This was the cottage. An interest in natural scenery had almost inevitably led to an appreciation of the way in which nature worked on and weathered man-made structures. Ruins appealed to eighteenth-century eyes in part because they were usually overgrown with moss and creepers. Artists on the look-out for picturesque effects also began to take an interest in old cottages, particularly when they were so dilapidated that nature seemed to be taking them over, to the delight of the artist if not of the inhabitants. 'Moral and picturesque ideas do not always coincide', as William Gilpin put it (*Observations on Several Parts of England*, 1808).

216. The Swiss Cottage, Cahir, Co. Tipperary, built in about 1812, perhaps to the designs of John Nash.

From the mid-eighteenth century onward similar effects, suitably adapted to cope with problems of keeping out wind and weather, began to be incorporated into new buildings. Thatched roofs, rough undressed stonework, and creeper-clad porches and verandahs made of untrimmed branches, often with the bark left on them, were especially popular. To begin with, these elements were confined to buildings such as grottoes, hermitages and bathhouses, which were built as features in a park rather than to be lived in. But by the end of the eighteenth century they were being used for residential cottages. These included elaborate 'cottages ornées', designed for the residence of ladies and gentlemen themselves, especially when they were on holiday by the seaside, or in retreat from the responsibilities of an active life. In such situations dignity and importance were not called for; people went to live in a cottage ornée specifically in order to feel that they were escaping from the conventions of society and tasting something of the rural innocence that poets had always associated with cottage life: 'the insinuating effusions of the muse, that true happiness is only to be found in a sequestered and rural life,' as William Heely put it.

Perhaps the most alluring cottage ornée ever built is the so-called Swiss Cottage at Cahir, in southern Ireland (Pl. 216). It was designed, possibly by John Nash, for the Earl of Glengall in about 1812. Its position is a singularly beautiful and peaceful one, on a low rise above a reach of the River Suir. The cottage was, and is, almost swallowed up by the woods that envelop it, and by its own thatched roofs and rustic verandahs. Inside, however, a selection of highly fashionable French wallpapers kept Lord Glengall in touch with metropolitan society.

The Swiss Cottage is worth comparing with the 'cabin' built for or by Jean-Jacques Rousseau near the chateau of Ermenonville, where he spent the last years of his life. The cabin, as described in an anonymous *Tour to Ermenonville* (1785), was 'built against the rock and thatched with heath. Within, besides a plain and unornamented fireplace, we found a seat cut out of the rock, and covered with moss, a small table and two wicker chairs.' On the door was the inscription 'It is on the tops of mountains that man contemplates the face of nature with real delight. There it is that, in conference with the fruitful parent of all things, he receives from her those all powerful inspirations, which lift the mind above the sphere of error and prejudice.'

The cabin clearly related to rustic hermitages in English parks, but it related with a difference. For one thing it was not in a park; it was on a hilltop in what contemporaries called a 'desert', a stretch of completely unimproved heath a mile or two from the chateau. Round the chateau itself its owner had created conventionally picturesque grounds in the English manner, complete with an artificial cascade and a monument to Rousseau, erected after his death on an island in a lake. The English visitor was struck by the contrast between all this and the adjacent 'desert'. Rousseau himself had used the cabin on 'excursions, during which he loved to read the great book of nature, on the tops of mountains, or in the depths of some venerable forest'.

A new note is being struck, the note of the Romantic Movement, which grew out of appreciation of the picturesque, overlapped it, but was essentially different from it. Wild natural scenery ceased to be looked at with a critical eye, as something to be enjoyed but also improved, in the light of a literary or artistic tradition; the simple life ceased to be seen as a form of agreeable play-acting. Nature, in the sense of actual

wild landscape, not a lost ideal, was now to be approached with reverence, as a means of regeneration and a source of mystical experience. Rousseau was a pioneer, but in the first half of the nineteenth century the attitudes he had helped to inaugurate spread through the Western world.

The idea of the picturesque had inevitably come to America, but its American devotees were at a disadvantage. America had no ruined abbeys, castles or temples, no landscapes rich with suitable associations. For a time Americans felt deprived when they looked at their own scenery. The Romantic Movement reversed the situation. 'All nature is here new to art', Thomas Cole wrote of the Catskill Mountains in the 1830s, in celebration, not in a mode of despondency. 'No Tivolis, Ternis, Mont Blancs, Plinlimmons, hackneyed and worn by the pencils of hundreds, but primeval forests, virgin lakes and waterfalls' (quoted by Charles Rockwell, *The Catskill Mountains*, 1873). 'Here', wrote Washington Irving in *Home Authors and Home Artists*, 'are locked up mighty forests which have never been invaded by the axe; deep umbrageous valleys where the virgin soil has never been outraged by the plough; bright streams flowing in untasked idleness, unburthened by commerce, unchecked by the mill. This mountain zone is in fact the great poetical zone of our country.'

As early as 1823-4 the hotel known as the Catskill Mountain House was built on the edge of a cliff in the heart of the range. Forty years later it was still going strong, and being celebrated in verse by Charles Rockwell:

> There it stands, to bless the pilgrim
> From the city's heated homes.
> Worn and weary with life's contest
> To this mountain height he comes.

By the middle decades of the century spreading railways and growing cities were bringing more and more visitors to mountainous or wild country all over America. Its

217. The Catskill Mountain House, from the painting by Thomas Cole, *c*. 1830.

By the middle decades of the century spreading railways and growing cities were bringing more and more visitors to mountainous or wild country all over America. Its apparently inexhaustible wealth of wild landscape was accepted as one of its chief glories; so was the role of this landscape as a source of cleansing, refreshment, and spiritual recharging for tired city dwellers.

The summer rush to the wilds brought architectural problems. A tent and a camp-fire may have been the ideal equipment with which to commune with nature, but more permanent forms of settlement inevitably developed, even if they continued to be called 'camps'. What were these to look like, and how could they best be fitted into wild surroundings? Any idea that wild nature could or should be 'improved' had been jettisoned, nor was there any desire to interpose a barrier of cultivation between dwelling and surroundings. The Catskill Mountain House seemed to have been dropped on the edge of its precipice in an almost unaltered landscape. But the hotel itself was a porticoed Neoclassical building, such as could have been found on the edge of dozens of American cities. Thomas Cole, in his superb picture of hotel and mountains, had to paint the hotel narrow-end on, in order to keep it from being too obtrusive (Pl. 217).

For a time, experiments were made with the Swiss-chalet style, as on occasions in England. Later on in the century Norman Shaw's houses exerted a powerful influence on American seaside and holiday architecture, mainly on the strength of the brilliant drawings with which they had been illustrated in English architectural magazines. The rocky settings of Cragside and Leyswood were not all that different from the rocky coastline of New England; both Shaw's architecture and the style of draughtsmanship with which it was presented are immediately recognisable in Eldon Deane's drawings of summer cottages at Manchester-by-the-Sea in Massachusetts. One of them was even called Kragsyde (Pl. 219).

But in these and other summer cottages up and down the coast Shaw's architecture was already undergoing a process of simplification, designed to make it more 'natural'. Boulders were incorporated into foundations as well as left littered over the surrounding ground. Detail was eliminated and the houses covered with a skin of shingles that rapidly weathered to a colour in harmony with their setting. Inside, Shaw's great inglenook fireplaces were simplified until they became caves of rough-hewn stone. An extra repertory of forms was drawn from America's brand of natural architecture, the log cabin. It was a form of construction that both made sense in practical terms and had the right connotations; it became especially popular for camps in the Adirondacks and other mountain districts.

By the early 1900s there were local and individual variations, but a brotherhood of plan, materials, motifs and descriptive language united holiday houses and camps in country all over North America. 'The outside will weather to nature's gray, which, combined with the natural effect of the porch and the rough stonework will cause the building to blend into the landscape.' The description (from W.T. Comstock's *Bungalows, Camps and Mountain Houses, 1908*) is of a holiday house on the St Lawrence River, but similar descriptions were being applied to Adirondack camps, or weekend cottages on Signal Mountain in Tennessee. Boulders or rough-hewn stonework were de rigueur for fireplaces as well as for foundations and chimneystacks, especially for

the great stone fireplace that invariably dominated the living-room (Pl. 220). Walls were normally of timber, either shingle-clad or of exposed logs, carrying the marks of the adze or sometimes with the bark left on them.

Occasionally cottage-ornée techniques were revived, and porches, verandahs and even furniture were made of untrimmed roots, trunks and branches. The oddest example of this was the New Inn in Estes Park, Colorado, built *c.* 1906-10 by Enos A. Mills, naturalist and pioneer of national parks. Every conceivable detail, inside and out, was made from the bleached and twisted remains of an adjacent stretch of fire-killed forest. It looked (according to Sunset: *Pacific Monthly*, May 1921) as though 'it had been shaped by the same slow-acting elemental forces that had shaped the region'. The main bedroom in Kamp Kill Kare in the Adirondacks is almost as strange (Pl. 221): the bed incorporates an entire tree, with a stuffed owl perched on its branches, and the fireplace looks like a mountain cairn with a hole in it. Such features were occasional eccentricities, but other furnishings suited to the simple life became commonplace: rocking chairs, built-in benches, simply patterned hangings, bedcovers and cushions made from Indian or other native textiles, native pottery, and huge iron cooking-pots and traditional kitchen cranes, to embellish the living-room fireplace.

The planning and disposition of the houses had to live up to two sets of standards. They had to cater to a life ostensibly 'dominated by nature and its ways'. Easy access

218. (top) Leyswood, Sussex, by Richard Norman Shaw, 1868-9.

219. (bottom) Kragsyde, Manchester-by-the-Sea, Massachussets, by Peabody and Stearns, *c.* 1882.

to water, for boating, fishing or swimming, was almost invariable, as was a verandah set with rocking chairs and overlooking water or forest; in the William A. Read camp in the Adirondacks there were two, one cantilevered out into the treetops (Pl. 222), one over the water. Uncovered balconies were a popular feature, on which to savour the 'perfect joy of a night under the canopy of stars' (*Craftsman*, May 1911). But houses were also expected to cause the minimum disturbance to their setting, to be 'of the woods woodsy, seeming a part of their natural surroundings' (*Country Life*, December 1923). Contemporary descriptions mention with approval efforts to 'leave the grounds in the natural rough state' and to cut down the minimum of trees in order to fit in the requisite accommodation. This attitude was often symbolised by a tree left standing within inches of a wall or window, or even growing through a verandah. In order to minimise their impact, camps were often broken up into a number of smaller units, sometimes joined to each other by a covered way. Tact was necessary because the bigger camps could include accommodation for sixty or seventy guests, along with a complex back-up of servants and services. The Vanderbilts, Morgans

Huntingtons who holidayed in the Adirondacks did not want the simple life to be too simple. A description of an evening at Kamp Kill Kare in the winter of 1899 captures the atmosphere. 'Inside the bright fireplaces blazed from great stone fireplaces, and the table was spread with all the delicacies one would expect to find at Delmonico's' (Craig Gilborn Durant: *The Fortunes and Woodland Camps of a Family in the Adirondacks*, 1981).

The conventions of camp and cottage life had been set by 1910, and changed remarkably little in the 1920s. They were still going strong in the 1930s, when Frank Lloyd Wright designed Fallingwater. To a considerable extent he and the Kaufmanns worked within them. Fallingwater incorporates open terraces that could be used for sleeping out, and covered ones from which to enjoy woods and water exposed to fresh air but sheltered from sun. Chimneystacks and fireplaces are of rough stonework; the *in situ* boulder that projects as a hearth through the living-room floor could be seen as Wright's development of the traditional boulder fireplace. There is a cooking pot, a crane and plenty of Indian fabrics and pottery. Existing trees were disturbed as little as possible, and a beam was cast with a kink in order to leave a large one growing un-touched in front of the entrance. There is no garden by Fallingwater; any new planting was carefully designed to merge into the forest surroundings. Guest accommodation is in a separate building, joined to the main one by a covered way. The use of concrete instead of timber was unusual, but not unique; a fishing lodge built of stone and concrete, in order to be fireproof, was featured in the *Craftsman* of May 1911. Even the language in which Fallingwater is sometimes described ('it seems part of the rock formations to which it clings', etc.) follows the conventions.

248

222. Verandah of the Adirondack lodge of William A. Read, photographed in 1907 for *House and Garden*.
223. (right) Ono Falls, by Hokusai, formerly in the collection of Frank Lloyd Wright.

In fact this kind of description is not especially apt; and Fallingwater is on a different creative level from Adirondack camps or the great majority of holiday cottages. However, this is not because it rejects the conventions that lay behind them but because it transforms them, through new technology, the injection of a second tradition, and the working of a creative imagination. The second tradition is that of China and Japan, where wild landscapes had been appreciated centuries before the Picturesque Movement got under way in Europe. Moreover, in China and Japan, unlike Europe, houses were frequently built in natural settings next to waterfalls, as places from which priests or scholars could commune with the spirits that were thought to live in wild places. Such combinations were depicted in Chinese and Japanese prints and drawings that Wright both knew of and owned (Pl. 223). They may have influenced the siting of Fallingwater.

But the style in which such landscapes were depicted was probably as important for Wright. In *The Japanese Print: An Interpretation* (1912) he analyzed what he called, for lack of a better word, conventionalization: the way in which, in Japanese and other arts, natural forms were transformed through knowledge and love into another medium, without being killed through imitation. It was an approach that can be savoured in his own perspective drawing for Fallingwater (Pl. 224). It enabled him to get away from the 'natural' approach epitomized at its most naive by walls of boulders or bark-encrusted verandahs, and poise a clearly man-made structure in perfect harmony above a waterfall.

250

224. (above)   A perspective view of Fallingwater, largely drawn by Wright.
225. (right)   The Assembly Room at Bury St Edmunds, Suffolk.

226. (right)   Chawton Cottage, Hampshire, in which Jane Austen lived from 1809 until 1817.

1 THE GEORGIAN HOUSE

Jane Austen's unfinished novel *The Watsons* starts off on the day of the first winter Assembly in the small country town of D. From various directions the characters foregather in the assembly room in the White Hart. Mr and Mrs Edwards, a family of comfortable private means, drive with their party in their own coach from the best house in the town, 'higher than most of its neighbours, with two windows on each side the door, the windows guarded by posts and chains, the door approached by a flight of stone steps', and the door opened by a powdered footman.

Mr Tomlinson, the banker, and his wife and two sons come in from their new house on the edge of the town, with its shrubbery and sweep, the only rival to the Edwardses' more old-fashioned dignity. The Edwards family are accompanied by Emma Watson, the novel's heroine. Her widowed father, 'a man of sense and education', has too many children and not enough money. He lives three miles from the town and does not own a carriage, so on assembly days one or more of his daughters go in early to the Edwards family, and stay the night there. Emma's brother Sam, an apprentice surgeon, is in love with Mary Edwards, but her parents do not think a surgeon good enough for her; her other brother is a successful attorney in

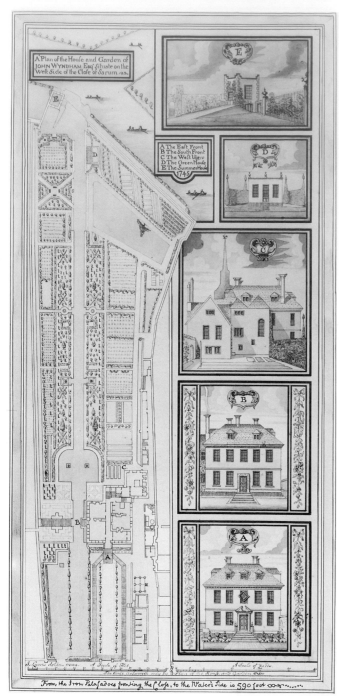

Croydon, where his rather pretentious wife 'gave genteel parties and wore fine clothes' in 'a very smart house'.

'I dare say it will be a very good ball', Emma's sister says to her, 'and among so many officers you will hardly want partners.' Officers are there in plenty; so are unspecified families who have driven in from their country houses. Tom Musgrave, the brash local lady-killer who has a private income of eight or nine hundred pounds a year, has ridden in from his house in the country, and is spending the night in the White Hart. He hangs around in the corridor, waiting for the local grandees, the Osbornes of Osborne Castle, to arrive, so that he can walk into the assembly room with them and their party: Lady Osborne, her daughter, and her daughter's friend, her son Lord Osborne, who was only there 'because it was judged expedient for him to please the borough', Mr Howard, Lord Osborne's tutor, to whom he had presented the living of the church next to the castle, and Mr Howard's widowed sister and her little boy.

Jane Austen writes about the world she knows, and in which she had been brought up. The more one gets to know about late-Georgian society, the more one appreciates her exquisite social sense; she is always spot on target. Her touch is as sure for houses as it is for people, even though she never describes houses in detail, and often leaves one to infer them from the way in which people move about in and use them. One recognises immediately the Edwardses' 'best house in the town'; it is one of those early eighteenth-century houses, of stone or red brick, like houses in the Close in Salisbury (Pl. 227), or Pallant House in Chichester, exquisitely symmetrical, like an enlarged doll's house, with a pedimented door, two rows of small-paned sash windows, a bold cornice, dormers in a hipped roof, panelled rooms and a straight-legged staircase with barley-sugar balusters. The banker's new house on the edge of the town is equally recognisable, in the same group as the 'neat, new-built' rectories which feature in many of her novels: stone or stucco with its own short drive and gravel sweep, big panes, big windows down to the ground, and no basement (Pl. 228). A grade below come neat, box-like houses, like Barton Cottage in *Sense and Sensibility,* the lowest level at which a family with pretensions to gentility could be expected to live: a central hall, a

254

227. Arundells, in the Close at Salisbury, from a survey of 1745.

parlour sixteen foot square to each side, four bedrooms upstairs, and servants' bedrooms in the attics. But as a cottage, Barton Cottage was 'defective', as Jane Austen puts it, with a side look at the fashionable 'cottages' that came into vogue in the late eighteenth century as holiday houses, or houses for up-and-coming young-marrieds. It lacked a thatched roof, green shutters and honeysuckle growing up the walls, in contrast to the modish cottage in which the young Musgraves live in *Persuasion,* 'with its viranda, French windows and other prettiness'.

The people whose lives and houses Jane Austen portrayed belonged for the most part to what was known at the time as polite society. This was a powerfully unifying factor in eighteenth-century England, and distilled common values throughout the country. Polite people talked alike, behaved alike and built alike. They abhorred extremes, or what they called 'enthusiasm'. They were incurably social, believing that men and women civilised each other by meeting in society. They visited constantly at each other's houses, and met in public places, at assembly rooms, theatres and race meetings, or on public promenades, in their home towns, in London, or in Bath and other resorts. Their houses reflected their shared values: they expressed the classical language, as distilled for their use by London architects and spread by books, engravings and travel, to such good effect that a Georgian house in Newcastle is often indistinguishable from one in Truro, apart from variations in material.

Polite society was in fact made up of hundreds of individual societies, influenced by the society of London and Bath, but rotating locally around a particular town and the assembly room in it. Most of these towns had their own neighbouring great house or houses, like Osborne Castle in *The Watsons.* 'The Osbornes are coming, the Osbornes are coming' was the refrain at Jane Austen's assembly in the town of D, as that

228. Ridgebourne, Kington, Herefordshire, refronted in 1806 by Edmund Watkin Cheese, solicitor and partner in the Kington and Radnorshire Bank, from the lithograph of 1846 by W.L. Banks.

family's carriage disgorged its contents outside the Rooms. The arrival of people like the Osbornes at social events was always a matter of excitement, for during much or even most of the year they were away, attending Parliament or the Season in London, visiting Bath or one of the other resorts, staying at country houses in other parts of the country, or touring on the Continent.

The round-the-year basis of local assemblies was provided by less grand families living in the town or in the smaller houses in the country. The latter consisted of modest country houses and manor houses on the one hand, and rectories on the other — like the rectory of Steventon where Jane Austen was brought up, and from which she and her sisters would go over to stay with friends at a country house a mile or two outside Basingstoke, in order to attend assemblies in the Angel Inn there.

Some of these country-house owners also had a house in their local town. It is a widely held belief that the majority of the good eighteenth-century houses in country towns were built or occupied by such families as their second houses, just as the grander country-house families built or occupied town houses in London. In fact the extent to which this happened — outside a few towns, of which York is the best example — has been much exaggerated. Even when such houses had a connection with a country-house owner, it tended to be of a rather different nature. Their widows retired to them, their elder sons lived in them while waiting for their fathers to die, they themselves often practised as doctors or lawyers in the town, in order to supplement their income; a few lived mainly in the town, and used their country houses as little more than holiday homes.

Many, if not most, of the best houses in country towns have quite different origins. They were built by a town establishment, of doctors, attorneys, clergymen, bankers, merchants, rich shopkeepers and people of private means, all of whose main houses were in the town, though they sometimes had a subsidiary one in the country. Attorneys were inescapable in country towns. They were the predecessors of today's solicitors, but had their fingers in many more pies, and often had reflected glory through being the local representatives of great families, whose estates and political interests they looked after.

Towns had their resident parish or cathedral clergy, and in addition, in the eighteenth century, rectors of country parishes often lived in neighbouring towns for most or even all of the year, until a determined campaign was waged in the late eighteenth century to make them live in their parishes: no fewer than forty non-resident clergymen are said to have been flushed out of Louth, for instance, by the Bishop of Lincoln in the early nineteenth century. This is the reason why so many of the most agreeable English rectories date from this period, and Jane Austen is accurate, as always, in describing these in her novels as new-built, or in course of improvement. She is similarly accurate in making Mr Tomlinson, the banker in *The Watsons*, live in a new house, for bankers scarcely existed in country towns before the later eighteenth century. Banking developed as a sideline of the business of attorneys, or brewers, or the clothiers whose substantial houses still line the main streets of former clothing towns such as Frome, Bradford-on-Avon or Painswick in the West, or Norwich in East Anglia.

Every town had its own pattern of snobbery, the test of which was, who was, or was not, admitted to its assemblies. 'Trade never agreed with us ladies', declared Mrs

Barnes, the bossy and snobbish lady who managed the Derby Assembly, in 1748, and in 1790 the chambermaid at the George Inn at Knutsford boasted to a visitor that 'none but gentility — and on no account any tradesman' — were admitted to its assembly rooms. These and other towns — like Ludlow or Richmond or the resort towns — acquired a reputation as good places for genteel people of modest but adequate private means to retire to, and widows, spinsters and retired people of all kinds of different backgrounds were attracted to them, and tended to be snobbish about 'trade', not least if their own money ultimately derived from it. But in working towns this kind of snobbery was impossible, and social life was dominated by the money-makers — merchants in Hull and Bristol, shipowners and ship-builders in Whitby, and clothiers and wool-staplers in the numerous textile towns such as Norwich in East Anglia, Wakefield and Leeds in Yorkshire, and Frome, Bradford, Painswick or Trowbridge in the West Country or the Cotswolds. All these built handsome houses, and were sufficiently prosperous, cultivated and confident to marry into local country families, and ultimately to merge with them.

Besides acting as a social centre for polite families, assembly rooms conditioned the plans of the houses in which they lived. Although there was a good deal of hospitable giving of dinners, taking tea and playing cards in private homes, the numbers involved were small; the main social events were the assembly room balls, especially those at the time of the local race-week or the Assizes, which the grander country families attended in force. Up till the end of the eighteenth century private balls or other entertainments involving large numbers of people were comparatively rare in the bigger country houses, and even more so in the smaller ones, both in country and in town. Because of this their rooms were usually not at all large; their size was often found constricting from around 1800 onwards, leading to two rooms being knocked together, or a big room being added on.

The diaries of James Woodforde, who was rector of Weston Longueville, near Norwich, in the late eighteenth century, give a good picture of social life at the level of a reasonably prosperous clergyman, on visiting terms at neighbouring country houses. There is a great deal of giving of dinners, including the practice of 'rotation' dinners, an arrangement by which five or six local clerical families dined at regular intervals in rotation at their various vicarages. The dinners normally involved from eight to a dozen people; dinner was inevitably followed by tea and coffee, served at the same time, and then by cards.

In July 1785 Woodforde gave the nearest he ever came to a dance. There were only ten guests, and the party lasted from three in the afternoon until three in the morning. It started with dinner at three — a choice of pike, fried sole, boiled beef, ham, fowls and goose, followed by puddings. Then coffee and tea in the garden, after which 'the Ladies and Gentlemen got to dancing, and danced and sang till supper time'. Supper ended at twelve, and there was more singing and dancing until three. 'Upon the whole we spent a very agreeable, merry and cheerful day.'

Woodforde called this party a 'frolic'. He gave another 'frolic' of a different nature every year just before Christmas, in the form of a dinner for the farmers of the parish when they came to pay him their tithes — which formed a considerable portion of his income. In 1782 twenty-three farmers were entertained. It was an all-male party;

Woodforde's niece, who kept house for him, always ate her dinner in another room. All present, including Woodforde, normally ended the worse for drink. Men-only parties were a common feature of eighteenth-century life, at all levels. Many took place outside the home, in the form of dinners given by town corporations or guilds, or meetings of an endless variety of clubs, usually held in a private room at an inn. But it was common enough for a husband to ask his men-friends to dinner, and entertain them at home, apart from his wife.

The minimum provision for modest social life of the kind lived by Woodforde was two parlours, a common parlour for everyday, and a best parlour, for company (Pl. 229). Parlours were always on the ground floor, often to either side of the entrance hall. Slightly more capacious houses had a study or library for the owner, and a drawing-room off the best parlour. After dinner (which was normally served about three o'clock), the women retired into the drawing-room to brew up the tea and coffee, and were ultimately joined by the gentlemen. While both sexes were imbibing, the servants cleared the parlour and set up the inevitable card-tables. An agreeable alternative in the summer months was to serve tea and coffee in the garden, either out of doors, or in a garden temple or one of the gazebos which form such a pretty adjunct to many town houses of the date.

But in a number of both town and country houses up till the mid-century, the main reception rooms for company were on the first floor, and consisted of a room known either as a dining-room or a dining chamber, and a withdrawing room off it. The arrangement went back to medieval times, and had the advantage of impressing visitors with a preliminary ascent up a handsome staircase. It tended to be found in larger houses, but they were not necessarily very large. Handel, for instance, lived in London in a medium-sized house off Bond Street, which still survives. He had a

229. The Fothergills of York in their parlour, from a lost painting by Philip Mercier, c. 1740.

dining parlour and study on the ground floor, and a drawing-room and dining-room on the first floor. He lived comfortably and shabbily on the ground floor; although his bedroom was on the second floor, he used his study as a dressing-room, and kept a shaving mirror and stands for his wigs in it. The first-floor rooms were more grandly furnished for entertaining, with gilded mirrors and candle brackets, his two Rembrandts, his harpsichord and house-organ, and numerous card-tables.

Besides tea and card parties Handel, not surprisingly, gave musical parties, often to launch a new composition; guests continued to sip their tea and coffee, but listened to music provided by Handel and a small group, instead of playing at cards. Such parties were a common feature all over eighteenth-century England, the music usually being provided either by a group of amateurs, or by mixed amateurs and professionals.

In the remote and rather old-fashioned setting of Woodforde's Norfolk rectory, an invitation to tea and coffee was inevitably accompanied by an invitation to a meal. An invitation to the former only was reserved for people of straightened means — as Mrs Gaskell demonstrated, with her coterie of ladies in Cranford serving tea, bread-and-butter and sponge-biscuits to their friends. But in London, where social life was much busier, and people's circles of acquaintance likely to be much larger, such invitations were found by the fashionable to be a good way of getting rid of social obligations. In the early eighteenth century comparatively small numbers were involved, but the numbers grew larger and larger in the course of the century, until several hundred people could be invited to what became known as a 'drum', with a squash of people in one room, card-tables in another, and tea being served in a third. From London the fashion spread over the provinces, until it provided an alternative to public assemblies. In *Persuasion,* Jane Austen is accurate, as usual, when she describes the Eliots at Bath as having abandoned the Assembly Rooms, so that their 'evening amusements were solely in the elegant stupidity of private parties'. These were predominantly card parties, to judge from the diaries of Mrs Lybbe Powys, who spent a few weeks at Bath every year in the 1780s and 1790s. Private parties first appear at Bath in her diaries in the 1790s, and one can watch them getting bigger year by year; seven card-tables in 1798 (but the hostess apologises for the fact that 'she had hardly any company'), ten in 1799, sixteen in 1801. In addition to those playing cards, the guests included numbers who did not. 'How unfashionable I am in disliking these immense parties I keep secret', confessed Mrs Lybbe Powys.

One result of bigger parties was the appearance of the double drawing-room, connected by folding doors, on the first floor of town houses, and the disappearance of the first-floor dining-room as a result. Double drawing-rooms seem to have evolved for card parties, but were soon being used for dances, which became increasingly popular in the more fashionable houses. In general, both in town and country, reception rooms grew bigger, to allow for entertaining on a larger scale, as private families began to imitate the kind of event they had become accustomed to in assembly rooms. In the country, too, another noticeable change took place, the result of a growing desire to relate houses, especially their living-rooms, to their surrounding parks or gardens.

First-floor reception rooms disappeared altogether; all living-rooms were on the ground floor and often opened directly through French windows on to the garden. In general both windows and window panes grew bigger, sills lower and sash bars thinner, all of which helped to break down the barrier between inside and outside. In town houses where space was expensive, as in London and the bigger towns, houses remained stacked up floor on floor, and it was impossible to get all the reception rooms on the ground floor. But at least the drawing-room windows could be dropped to floor level, and made safe by the interposition of a balcony, giving views on to the trees in the square, and enabling the occupant to emerge from hot summer dances to take the air.

What about the rooms other than the living-rooms, the furniture and furnishings which filled them, and the servants who serviced them? Parson Woodforde employed a footman, a cook-housemaid, an undermaid-cum-dairymaid, a boy, and a farming-man, who occasionally lent a hand in the house. His was a modest household, but that of Henry Purefoy, a comfortably-off squire living in a Buckinghamshire manor house in the mid-century, was not all that much larger: a footman, who also worked in the garden and drove the cart in to market with the coachman; a coachman who occasionally took a hand with the plough or worked in the house; a gardener, who similarly served at meals on occasions; a cook-maid; a housemaid-cum-laundrymaid; a dairymaid, who helped out with the laundry; and a charwoman. The staff seems large enough by the standards of today, even if the combination of functions is a little bizarre; but by 1850 the number of servants in equivalent households would have approximately doubled, and they would not have been taking a hand in the garden or on the farm.

Servants normally slept up in the attics, and ate in the kitchen — a servants' hall, in moderate-sized houses, was a rarity. The family slept on what was known as the chamber-floor — usually the first floor in the country, and the second floor in London. Many bedrooms up till the mid-eighteenth century had a little room off them, known as a closet, in which the owner of the bedroom kept books and, sometimes, clothes, and into which he or she retired to read, pray or be private. Such a room was a popular amenity because bedrooms tended to function as bed-sitting rooms, and had much less of an aura of privacy than they were to acquire in the next century.

A delightful drawing of about 1750 shows the bed-sitting room of an unidentified artist, probably a chaser of watch-cases (Pl. 230). It is one of the very rare drawings of the time that give one the feel of actually being in the room. The artist and two friends are drinking tea together around a folding table. His tools are spread out on a ledge under the window, his bed, in the opposite corner, has a canopy angled to fit the slope of the roof. The room is furnished with good upholstered or rush-seated chairs, and a handsomely framed mirror or picture, but there are no curtains or carpets, and a pleasantly untidy litter of objects and little pictures, framed and unframed, are scattered over a chest of drawers and the wall behind it.

Of course this is not at all a grand room; it is an attic bed-sitting room, probably in London lodgings. Even so, it displays tastes and habits that were common at all levels, all through the eighteenth century. Everything was much more fluid than in Victorian days, and also simpler and less cluttered. Not only did footmen help in the garden, and dairymaids lend a hand with the beds. Sitting-rooms doubled up as bedrooms, dining parlours as living-rooms, studies as dressing-rooms, day nurseries as

night nurseries, kitchens as servants' halls. Houses were also places of work, at all levels. Weavers kept their looms behind specially large windows in their attics; lawyers and bankers had their offices off their front halls or attached to their houses; merchants walked down to their warehouses at the bottom of their gardens.

To suit the fluid nature of rooms, furniture was easily movable, and often dismountable. Folding tables were set up for both cards and meals, wherever they were needed. Lightweight tables and chairs were moved over to the window, to benefit from the daylight, or the fire, to enjoy its warmth. When not in use, chairs and tables were lined up against the walls, and the centre of the room left open. There was little in the way of upholstery. Handel's house had only one chair which could have been described as comfortable, an easy chair in his study. His study and bedroom were the only rooms with curtains. None of the rooms had carpets. Uncarpeted and uncurtained rooms were common at all levels of society in the early eighteenth century. In the course of the century carpets came increasingly into use in living-rooms, in middle-class houses as well as the grander ones. But they were by no means invariable, and bedrooms often remained uncarpeted. Matting or painted floor coverings were common as a cheaper alternative. It was not until about 1830 that curtains became an invariable

230. A London bed-sitting room in about 1750, from the drawing by Louis Philippe Boitard.

feature of all genteel rooms; canopies and curtains on beds were for functional reasons, to keep the light out.

In the early eighteenth century the standard finish for all but the most utilitarian rooms in houses of all grades was panelling: painted deal panelling in the less grand rooms, unpainted oak sometimes varied by tapestry and enriched by carving in the grander ones. In the course of the century panelling was replaced by silk brocade, wallpaper, or plain plaster enriched by stucco decoration. Wallpaper, which had been a rarity in the early eighteenth century, became a common-place in all middle-class homes. In general, rooms were growing prettier, more varied and more comfortable.

They were still, however, recognisably in the same tradition. It was between about 1820 and 1840, when furniture grew heavier, more comfortable (or, at least, more upholstered) and less movable, room arrangements and uses became fixed, plans grew more complicated, and room shapes less regular, that the long supremacy of the classical tradition finally gave way to a free-for-all and the Victorian house emerged.

What is the secret of smaller Georgian houses? It is certainly neither variety nor originality. They are, for the most part, totally predictable, inside and out. The same details, the same arrangements of windows and treatment of interior, are repeated over and over again. They are as unadventurous as the modest people for whom, for the most part, they were built, people moving in the limited circles of small-town society or country neighbourhoods, their monthly recreation a trip to meet the same two dozen families in the local assembly rooms, their annual excitement a visit to Bath or Brighton.

And yet they are constantly and unfailingly pleasurable. They rest on the secure basis of a tradition which had found that certain formulas worked, and did not hesitate to repeat them. They knew from experience that rooms of a certain proportion were pleasant to be in, that cornices and mouldings reduced the monotony of box-like rooms and increased the apparent size of small ones, that sash bars and deep window reveals broke and reflected the light so that it flowed gently and pleasurably through the interiors of their houses. They used an easily understandable vocabulary of ornament, published in pattern-books which were accessible to everyone from country gentlemen to small-town craftsmen, but used it sparingly, to make a door or a fireplace into an enjoyable object. In the design of their houses, just as much as in the polite manners of their assembly rooms, they avoided exaggeration, and aimed to please.

Their success is made clear by the subsequent history of their houses. These have always inspired affection. Even Street, Butterfield, Pearson and Waterhouse, the great and at their best glorious mastodons of the Victorian Gothic revival, lived, worked and designed their chunky, multi-gabled, multi-coloured villas and vicarages behind the tall sash windows and simple stockbrick façades of late eighteenth-century terrace houses in the neighbourhood of Oxford Street. Today smaller Georgian houses have never been more popular. All over England sleek BMWs purr up and down the drives of Georgian rectories — or rather Old Rectories, for the rector himself has long since been removed by the Church Commissioners to a little villa half a mile up the road.

NOTES

The great majority of articles republished in *Town and Country* were originally printed without footnotes. I have footnoted those on Slaughter's Coffee-House, the Haynes Grange Room, and Waterford, but otherwise have only provided notes on the principal sources used.

Some articles have been slightly cut, in others I have restored sections which were cut to make them fit. I have made occasional minor corrections and alterations. The current level of reproduction fees have made it impossible to reproduce more than a handful of the photographs originally used in a number of the articles and they have been replaced by new photographs, or photographs from other sources. The place of publication is London, unless otherwise stated.

COFFEE AT SLAUGHTER'S

Originally published in three sections in *Country Life* on 13 and 27 January, and 3 February 1966. These have been much the most influential of my articles. They stimulated (although they certainly did not create) an interest in English Rococo which culminated in the exhibition held at the Victoria and Albert Museum in 1984; the influence of the articles can be seen in, for instance, the allotment of separate introductory sections of this to 'Gravelot and Printmaking', 'Hogarth and St Martin's Lane' and 'Vauxhall Gardens'.

The exhibition catalogue, *Rococo: Art and Design in Hogarth's England* (Victoria and Albert Museum, 1984; referred to in the footnotes as *Rococo*), contains a mass of material to do with the style and period, and a full bibliography. Much else of relevance has been published since 1966, and I have tried to include references in my footnotes. The original articles were a pioneering study, and an excursion outside my usual field, and have inevitably been amplified and corrected by subsequent work; in particular, the alignment of Burlingtonian Palladianism with the government, and of St Martin's Rococo with the opposition, was certainly an over-simplification.

1. George Vertue *Notebooks* III (Walpole Society XXII), p. 91.

2. Ephraim Hardcastle (pseudonym for W.H. Pyne) *Wine and Walnuts* (1823) I, pp. 72-87.

3. John Thomas Smith *Nollekens and his Friends* (1828) II, pp. 95-6.

4. Joseph Farington *The Farington Diary* (ed. J. Greig) III (1924), pp. 267-8; Vertue III, p. 91.

5. Vertue III, p. 67.

6. *Ibid.*, p. 105.

7. John Pye *Patronage of British Art* (1845), p. 56. For Gravelot's design work, see also the statement in d'Anville's funeral elegy, published in the 1774 volume of *Le Necrologe des Hommes Celebrés de France*: 'Il y joignait beaucoup de goût dans l'ornement, et à des formes propres à les pieces d'orfevrerie et à des bijoux.'

8. For a discussion of the meagre material concerning the St Martin's Lane Academy, see Michael Kitson in Walpole Society XLI (1966-8),

pp. 64 *ff*, and R. Paulson *Hogarth: His Life, Art and Times* (New Haven and London, 1971) I, pp. 369-75; II, pp. 137-44.

9. Vertue III, p. 127.

10. *Ibid.*, p. 150.

11. W. Wroth 'Tickets of Vauxhall Gardens', *Numismatic Chronicle* 3rd series XVIII (1898), pp 73-92.

12. *Dictionary of National Biography*, quoting Hawkins *Life of Johnson*, p. 516. Many of the song sheets and other Vauxhall material were engraved by George Bickham, sometimes working to Gravelot's designs; Gravelot also designed decoration for George Bickham Senior's *Universal Penman*, issued in sheets between 1733 and 1741.

13. 'Follower' would be preferable to 'protégé'; Wale's documented connections are with Hayman and Grignion, rather than Gravelot. For Wale and the Hayman connection, see Brian Allen *Francis Hayman* (New Haven and London, 1987), p. 58.

14. John Lockman 'A Sketch of the Spring-Gardens, Vauxhall' in *A Letter to a Noble Lord* (1751).

15. *Champion*, 5 August 1742, reprinted *Gentleman's Magazine* XII (1742), p. 418; *Amelia* (1751) Bk IX, Ch. 9. A full earlier account in the *Scots Magazine* (1739) was not known to me in 1966; it is quoted in David Coke's useful introduction to the Vauxhall Gardens section of *Rococo*, pp. 75-81.

16. *Remembrancer,* 7 October and 29 November 1749.

17. According to A. Blum *La Gravure en Angleterre du XVIIIme Siècle* (Paris, 1930).

18. Documented and signed works by Roubiliac are listed in Rupert Gunnis *Dictionary of British Sculptors 1660-1851* (1953).

19. *Remembrancer,* 29 July 1749.

20. For the attribution of Woodcote and Belvedere to Ware, see John Harris 'Clues to the Frenchness of Woodcote Park' *Connoisseur* (May 1961).

21. Smith *Nollekens* II, pp. 206-20, listing Ware, Gravelot, Gwynn, Hogarth, Roubiliac, Hudson, M'Ardell, Luke Sullivan, Theodore Gardell, Moser, Wilson ('not a regular customer'), John Parry, T. Rawle, and Smith's father and informant (and Roubiliac's apprentice) Nathaniel. There is a further account of Slaughter's habitués, including Richardson, Fielding, R.E. Pine and Folkes, in Pyne *Wine and Walnuts* I, p. 113.

22. Vertue VI (Walpole Society XXX), p. 170.

23. For Cheere and Roubiliac, see Smith *Nollekens* II, p. 94; for his visit to France, Vertue III, pp. 141-2.

24. Chimney-pieces documented as by Cheere, and a book of his

chimney-piece designs in the Victoria and Albert Museum (D715-1887), enable numerous others to be attributed to him with reasonable confidence, the one formerly at Woodcote among them.

25. Vertue III, p. 157, and article by Terence Hodgkinson *Victoria and Albert Museum Bulletin* I, no. 4 (October 1965), pp. 1-13 (Handel *modello*); Smith *Nollekens* II, p. 93 (Roubiliac caryatids); Vertue III, pp. 161-2 (Italian visit). For Hudson in general, see the catalogue of the exhibition at Kenwood, *Thomas Hudson 1701-1779* (GLC, 1979).

26. There is a useful general account of Folkes in the *Dictionary of National Biography*. He is mentioned in Pyne *Wine and Walnuts* as a frequenter of Slaughter's (I, p. 113), and as a friend and patron of Hogarth's (I, p. 118). In my original article I suggested that he was the sitter in the National Portrait Gallery portrait by Hayman formerly catalogued as of Hayman painting Sir Robert Walpole, but Allen *Hayman*, p. 95, identifies the sitter as Grosvenor Bedford.

27. W.T. Whitley *Artists and their Friends in England 1700-1799* (1928), p. 89; Tessa Murdoch 'Roubiliac as an Architect? The Bill for the Warkton Monuments' *Burlington Magazine* CXXII (1980), pp. 40-6.

28. For Gainsborough's relationship with Hayman, now securely documented, see Allen *Hayman*, pp. 39-44; John Hayes *The Landscape Paintings of Thomas Gainsborough* (1982) I, p. 34.

29. For Collins, see Gunnis *British Sculptors,* and *Rococo*, pp. 307-8. The fact that he is mentioned by Smith *Nollekens* II, p. 313, as 'famous' for modelling tablets similar to those on Cheere chimney-pieces, and exhibited them at the Society of Artists from 1760 onwards, suggests that before that date he may have been working for Cheere. His friendship with Hayman can be deduced from Pyne *Wine and Walnuts* I, p. 177; I cannot trace my source for saying that he was friendly with Gainsborough.

30. See Jersey's brief entry in Howard Colvin *Biographical Dictionary of British Architects* (1978).

31. *Gentleman's Magazine* LIX (1789) II, p. 1153. The statement that he studied at the St Martin's Lane Academy as a young man comes from a late source, Wyatt Papworth's *Dictionary of Architecture*, but his stylistic development and documented links with Hayman make it convincing. For Paine in general, see Peter Leach *James Paine* (1988).

32. Smith *Nollekens* II, pp. 222-3. Paine's house was next door to Slaughter's.

33. I. Ware *Complete Body of Architecture* (1756), pp. 300-1.

34. He had a drawing school at the Sign of the Pestle and Mortar, James Street, Covent Garden, according to Whitley *Artists and their Friends*, p. 94, probably drawing on contemporary newspapers.

35. Alexander Gilchrist *Life of William Blake* (Everyman ed., 1942), p. 18. Basire told the story to Blake, who was his pupil.

36. E. Edwards *Anecdotes of Painting* (1808), p. xxi; Vertue III, p. 76.

European Magazine 42 (August 1802), p. 89 (the second of a series of articles entitled 'Vestiges', by George Michael Moser's son).

37. For Moser, see Richard Edgcumbe's introduction to the section on 'Gold-chasing' and subsequent catalogue entries in *Rococo,* pp. 126-36.

38. Pyne*Wine and Walnuts* I, p. 177. The list was drawn up in consultation with Hayman's pupil John Taylor. Linnell has now been very fully treated in H. Hayward and P. Kirkham *William and John Linnell: 18th Century London Furniture Makers* (2 vols., 1980).

39. For the Hallett portrait, see Allen *Hayman*, pp. 38, 103-5.

40. Nicholas Sprimont, manager of the Chelsea factory, stood godfather to Roubiliac's daughter Sophie in 1744, but the extent of Roubiliac's involvement, if any, with the factory remains uncertain. See *Rococo*, p. 66.

41. J.A. Rouquet *The Present State of the Arts in England* (1755), p. 22 (Hayman); p. 62 (Roubiliac); p. 85 (Moser); p. 104 (Gravelot); p. 13 (Vauxhall).

42. *Ibid.*, p. 85.

43. 'Of the Proportion of the Orders' in Ware *Architecture* II.1.II .

44. Preface to J. Paine *Plans, Elevations and Sections of Noblemen's and Gentlemen's Houses* (1767) I.

45. For the embellishment of the Foundling Hospital courtroom, 1745-8, by a group of artists to an iconographic scheme devised by Hogarth, see Benedict Nicholson *The Treasures of the Foundling Hospital* (1972).

THE BAITING OF BURGHLEY

This was first published in *Country Life* of 31 May 1990. The main archival sources were the back numbers of the *Stamford Mercury*, available in its library at its premises in Stamford; the election broadsheets, poems and other literature in the Phillips Collection in the Town Hall, Stamford; the entries on Newcomb, Noel and others in the biographical card index in the Stamford Museum, Broad Street; and the 1919 sale catalogue of the Newcomb estate, also in the Museum. Books consulted included the Royal Commission on Historical Monuments, England *The Town of Stamford* (1977); the entries in the relevant volumes of *The House of Commons* (ed. L. Namier *et al.*) for details of elections and candidates; the entry on Drakard in the *Dictionary of National Biography*; J.L. Gilbert Wansford's *Paper Mills: Their History and Romance* (published by the author, Wansford, 1974); and E.J. Till *A Family Affair: Stamford and the Cecils 1650-1960* (Rugby, 1990), which Dr Till kindly let me see in typescript.

COUNTRY-TOWN PORTFOLIO

Originally published as 'A Country-Town Portfolio' in *Country Life* on

7 December 1989, and largely based on papers still in the possession of the Chubb family. Other material used included Mary Chubb 'A Forbear and his Hobby' *The Countryman* (Winter 1963 and Spring 1964); T. Bruce Dilks *Charles James Fox and the Borough of Bridgwater* (Bridgwater Booklets 6, 1937); and election lists of voters in the possession of Bridgwater Public Library. The article owes much to the help of Miss Mary Chubb.

LOCAL GOVERNMENT IN SPITALFIELDS

This first appeared as a chapter in *The Saving of Spitalfields*, a collection of essays published by the Spitalfields Historic Buildings Trust in 1990. It is very largely based on the Minutes of the hamlet of Spitalfields, and the vestry Minutes of its successor, the parish of Christ Church, Spitalfields. Also consulted were the *House of Commons Report of the Committee on Select and Other Vestries* (John Cam Hobhouse, Chairman, 1830); Beatrice and Sidney Webb *English Local Government* I (1906); the text of the relevant local Acts of Parliament; *The Survey of London* (ed. F.H.W. Sheppard) XXVII; *Spitalfields and Mile End New Town* (1957).

'WHAT A PLACE IS WHITBY GROWN'

First published in *Country Life* on 5 and 12 May 1988, and mainly based on the Rev. George Young's admirably thorough *A Picture of Whitby and its Environs* (2nd ed., 1840), supplemented by Lionel Charlton *History of Whitby* (1779). Other material consulted included Richard Weatherill *The Ancient Port of Whitby* (Whitby, 1926); F.R. Pearson *The Abbey House, Whitby, under the Cholmley Family* (Whitby, 1983); T.H. Woodwark *The Quakers of Whitby* (Whitby, 1926); Robert T. Gaskin *The Old Seaport of Whitby* (Whitby, 1909, reprinted 1985); and manuscript material, directories, guidebooks, etc., in the comprehensive Whitby collection in the library of the Whitby Literary and Philosophical Society, Whitby Museum, Pannett Park. Twistleton's poem can be found in *The Whitby Repository* 2 (1826), pp. 350-1.

THE BIRTH OF A SEASIDE RESORT

Originally published in *Country Life* on 19 and 26 August 1971. The main sources were back numbers of the *Norfolk Chronicle* and the collection of photographs, books, press-cuttings and other material assembled by the late C. Crawford Holden, and now in the Cromer Museum. Other material used included various editions of the *Guide to Cromer*, and other local guidebooks and directories; *Memorials of Hannah, Lady Buxton* (1883); Ellen Buxton *Journal 1860-4*; the first octave of Compton Mackenzie's *Autobiography*; Victoria Glendinning *A Suppressed Cry* (1969); C. Crawford Holden *Cromer: The Cutting of the Gem* (Leicester, 1967); and A.C. Savin *Cromer: A Modern History* (1936; reprinted Holt, 1950).

PIPE-DREAMS IN MANCHESTER

First published in *In Search of Modern Architecture: A Tribute to*

Henry Russell Hitchcock (ed. Helen Searing, New York and Cambridge, Mass., 1982). Based on Ogden's own books and biographical information, references in periodicals, etc., generously communicated by Stuart Evans. Copies of Ogden's books are hard to find, but there is a complete set in Manchester Public Library. His references to Peter Ogden and the Peterloo Ogden come from anonymous manuscript comments written by someone who knew him in the Manchester Public Library copy of *Manchester a Hundred Years Ago*. His will was reported in *The Times* of 24 April 1926.

A COUNTRY-HOUSE CHILDHOOD

First published as 'Memories of an Eccentric World' in *Architectural Digest*, Spring, 1987.

BELVEDERE AND THE WICKED EARL

First published in *Country Life* on 22 and 29 June 1961. Apart from sources cited in the text, material used includes W.H.G. Bagshawe *The Bagshawes of Ford* (1886: Caldwell quotes p. 334); Arthur Young *Tour in Ireland* (1780); entries under 'Belvedere' in G.E. Cokayne and V. Gibbs *Complete Peerage* (1910, etc.); C.P. Curran *Dublin Decorative Plasterwork* (1967). Belvedere House is now the property of Mullingar District Council.

MISS SMITH COMES TO TIPPERARY

Originally published in *Country Life* on 8 and 15 September 1988, based on papers, photographs, albums, scrapbooks, etc., then at Newtown Anner and now at Hatfield House in the custody of the Marquess of Salisbury, great-nephew of the 12th Duke of St Albans. Other material used includes Charles Smith *The Antient and Present State of the County and City of Waterford* (1746); Catherine Isabella Osborne *Memorials of the Life and Character of Lady Osborne* (Dublin, 1870) I; entry on Ralph Bernal in *Dictionary of National Biography*; article by T.H.S. Escott on Ralph Bernal Osborne, *Fortnightly Review* 42 (1884), p 535. The account of Lady Osborne's marriage and first years in Tipperary comes from a manuscript account in the Newtown Anner papers.

MODERNISING AN IRISH COUNTRY HOUSE

First published in *Country Life* on 23 and 30 December, 1971, and almost entirely based on papers still at Tullynally Castle.

THE NOBLEST QUAY IN EUROPE

Originally published in *Country Life* on 8, 15 and 22 December 1966, when the centre of Waterford, like that of other Irish towns at the time, seemed scarcely altered since 1900. The articles were a record of the town as it was at the time, and it seemed a mistake to try to bring them up to date. I have made a number of corrections of fact, kindly sent to me by Mr Julian Walton, and at the end of the footnotes have added a short list of demolition or alterations made since the articles were published. The articles drew heavily, especially for the early history of Waterford, on Charles Smith's *Antient and Present State of the County and City of Waterford* (1746) and Edmund Downey's *The Story of Waterford: From the Foundation of the City to the Middle of the Eighteenth Century* (Waterford, 1914, 2nd enlarged ed. 1919).

1. Edmund Spenser *Faerie Queene* IV.II.43.

2. 853 is the traditional date, but archaeologists now suggest 914 as more likely.

3. See article on Holy Ghost Friary and Hospital by the Rev. P. Power in *Journal of the Waterford and South East of Ireland Archaeological Society* I, p. 202.

4. So the Holy Ghost deeds show. Information from Julian Walton, who has also supplied some corrections to Power.

5. Richard Stonyhurst 'Description of Ireland' printed in Vol. I of Holinshed's *Chronicles* (1577).

6. Downey *Waterford*, p. 144. Downey's dramatic account is an exaggeration. The 950 in the census are now thought to have been heads of households, and the surviving Catholic population included a number of men of substance.

7. *Waterford Arch. Soc. Journal* I, p. 51.

8. *Ibid.* XIII, p. 1, quoting Ramsey's *Waterford Chronicle*.

9. Downey *Waterford,* p. 312, quoting Corporation Council Minutes.

10. *Ibid.*, p. 134 (Mason reminiscences); Corporation Council Minutes, 24 September 1773.

11. William Tighe *County of Kilkenny* (1802).

12. The vaulted undercroft below the eighteenth-century Deanery, next to the cathedral, is probably a survival from a medieval merchant's house, rather than of ecclesiastical origin.

13. Council Minutes, 13 July 1773.

14. For John Roberts, see the article on the Roberts family in *Waterford Arch. Soc. Journal* II (1896), pp. 98 *et seq.* Roberts's date of birth is there given as 1712, but parish registers prove it to have been 26 January 1714.

15. *Waterford Arch. Soc. Journal* II, pp. 98 *et seq.*

16. Council Minutes, 17 October 1783.

17. *Ibid.*, 29 June 1781.

18. *Ibid.*, 13 March 1782.

19. *Ibid.*, 14 January 1784.

20. *Ramsey's Waterford Chronicle*, 13 December 1787 and January 1788.

21. Council Minutes, 22 January 1813. The lease was brought from Mr Thomas Scott.

22. At the King's Birthday Ball in June. *Waterford Arch. Soc. Journal* XII, p. 166.

23. Council Minutes, 5 May 1792.

24. At various dates during the nineteenth century the sanctuary was extended, the apse added, and (after 1892) the present west front built.

25. There is a genealogy of the Morris family under 'O'Connor Morris of Gartnamara or Mt Pleasant' in *Burke's Landed Gentry* (1898 ed.).

26. 'Hon. George Ponsonby's list of Waterford incomes, 1775', published in *Waterford Arch. Soc. Journal* XVI, p. 49.

27. For the Chamber of Commerce, see Des Cowman *The Role of Waterford Chamber of Commerce 1787-1987* (Waterford Chamber of Commerce, 1988).

28. For Newport's Bank, and Waterford banks generally, see the article in Vol. XII (1910) of the *Journal of the Institute of Bankers in Ireland.*

29. Quoted Downey *Waterford*, p. 84.

30. There are useful articles on Waterford glass in *Country Life* (30 August and 6 September 1946). The Penrose genealogy is given in *Burke's Irish Landed Gentry* (ed. H. Montgomery-Massingberd, 1976), under 'Penrose-Welsted'.

31. *Waterford Arch. Soc. Journal* I, p. 1.

32. Council Minutes, November 1782.

33. e.g. advertisement in *Ramsey's Waterford Chronicle*, 29 September 1789, referring to William and Samuel Penrose of Adelphi Terrace.

34. There is a brief account of the Wyse family at the beginning of the full entry on Sir Thomas Wyse (1791-1862) in the *Dictionary of National Biography.*

35. For the Wyses' commercial activities, see Charles Ryland *Topography and Antiquities of the County and City of Waterford* (1824), pp. 269, 273, etc. See also Downey *Waterford*, p. 350, quoting Bishop Pococke's *Tour* (1752).

36. Edward McParland *James Gandon* (1985), pp. 146-9, Pls. 2, 158-60.

37. Dr Maurice Craig has established that the architect of the Court House was Joseph B. Keane of Cork.

38. See *A Short History of the Waterford Savings Bank* (Waterford, 1916), with illustration of the Bank before the cupola was removed.

39. Although Waterford has escaped the full trauma of ring-roads and wholescale redevelopment experienced by many English towns and cities, it has suffered a good deal from piecemeal demolition or insensitive alteration since the articles were first published in 1966. Buildings demolished include Adelphi Terrace, the former County Club, Mason's School in Lady Lane, and the Widows' Apartments; in general, the feeling of a close around the Protestant Cathedral has been much eroded. The fittings of St Olave's Church have been removed by Mr Ambrose Congreve and others to churches elsewhere in the diocese, and the church is now used as an indoor tennis court.

THE HAYNES GRANGE ROOM

The article was written as one of a series presented in typescript to Professor Peter Murray on his sixtieth birthday in 1980. It was the basis of a lecture given at a seminar at the Society of Antiquaries on 1 March of that year, but has not been published before.

1. They appear to be doves or pigeons, but are sometimes described as ducks. For their original colouring, see *Architectural Review* XXIV (1908), pp. 8-16. In the re-erected room the ceiling was a modern one, presumably based on squeezes of the original, and the background was white.

2. For the history of the room from 1908 to 1928, see H. Clifford Smith *The Haynes Grange Room* (1935), pp. 10-11, 26-7. The prefatory note acknowledges 'above all' the help of Professor A.E. Richardson.

3. Clifford Smith *Haynes Grange Room*, pp.21-2.

4. The originals are at Woburn. The elevations of the north and west fronts are reproduced in J. Harris, S. Orgel and R. Strong *The King's Arcadia: Inigo Jones and the Stuart Court* (Arts Council Catalogue, 1973), pp. 109, 110.

5. Donaldson's plans are in the RIBA Drawings Collection.

6. The plans are now in the Bedfordshire County Record Office.

7. See, for instance, the monument to Lady Cotton at Norton-in-Hales, Shropshire, designed, as John Newman has established, by Jones *c.* 1611.

8. Harris, Orgel and Strong *King's Arcadia*, pp. 141-2. John Summerson had dated the drawing 1608, but Harris thinks this impossible and suggests *c.* 1620.

9. M. Girouard *Robert Smythson and the Elizabethan Country House* (New Haven and London, 1983), p. 30.

10. In *Chronologia Architectonica*, the fourth section of his MS *Monumenta Britannica*, Bodleian Library, MS. Top. Gen. c. 25, pp.152-79.

11. The archway is engraved in Scribonius's account of the entry, *Cincq Arches Triumphaulx*, published in 1550.

12. The panels are shown in an elevation of the front, one of a set of measured drawings made prior to demolition in 1774 and now in the Department of the Environment Library.

13. See Martin Biddle 'A "Fontainebleau" Chimney-piece at Broughton Castle' in *The Country Seat* (ed. H. Colvin and J. Harris, 1970), pp. 9-12, and H.G. Slade's article on Broughton, *Archaeological Journal* 135 (1978), pp.138-94. Slade suggests that the chimney-piece may originally have been intended for the Duke of Northumberland's new building at Dudley Castle, Staffordshire, left incomplete owing to his fall from power.

14. W.J. Hemp 'The Dormer Tombs at Wing' *Trans. Mon. Brass Soc.* VI (1910-14), pp. 59-74, and E. Mercer *English Art 1553-1575* (Oxford, 1962), pp. 222-3, Pls. 76a, 79a.

15. John Shute, for instance, still remains an almost entirely mysterious figure. The source of the elaborate figurative sculpture engraved in the *First and Chief Groundes of Architecture* (1563) has, to the best of my knowledge, never been investigated.

16. J.P. Roberts 'English Wall Paintings after Italian Engravings' *Burlington Mazagine* LXXXVIII (1941), pp. 86-92.

17. Anthony Wells-Cole's forthcoming monograph on the engraved sources of Elizabethan and Jacobean design will throw a flood of light on the subject. The identification of the Hardwick panel is due to him. My *Country Life* article on Elizabethan Chatsworth is reprinted on pp. 211-20 of this book.

18. *Country Life* 10 December 1953 (Burghley); Mercer *English Art*, pp. 230-1, Pl. 82 (Gresham Tomb); *Country Life* CLXVI, pp. 1286-9, 1398-1401 (Holdenby), reprinted pp. 197-210 of this book; Girouard *Smythson*, Pl. 70 (Heath).

19. There are measured drawings of the chimneys in J.A. Gotch *Early Renaissance Architecture in England* (2nd ed. 1914), p. 143. Buck's engraving of the abbey shows them in their original position. They appear to derive from column chimneystacks at Somerset House, of which measured drawings survive (see note 12); these, however, had coffered shafts in a curious variant of the Tudor Gothic fashion. There are or were Elizabethan column chimneystacks at, for instance, Burghley, Moreton Corbet and Wollaton; at Longleat and Aston Court, Bristol, they have stone hoods or caps, of the type shown in Philibert de L'Orme's *Architecture* (1567).

20. For Longleat, see Girouard *Smythson* pp. 39-76, and 'The Development of Longleat House between 1546 and 1572' *Archaeological Journal* CXVI (1961), pp. 200-22.

21. For Chalcot, see Girouard *Smythson*, p. 63 and Pl. 26.

22. John Humphreys 'Elizabethan Estate Book of Grafton Manor' *Birmingham Arch. Soc. Trans.* XLIV (1919) pp. 1-24. The porch is illustrated in the Worcestershire volume of the *Buildings of England* series.

23. The best account of Caius's work remains that in R. Willis and J.W.

Clark *Architecture of the University of Cambridge* (1880) I, pp. 165-86.

24. R.H. Gretton *Burford Records* (1920), pp. 265-8. Harman was surgeon to Henry VIII and one of the witnesses to his will.

25. For the attribution of these monuments to a fictitious 'Thomas Kirby', see the note by Jon Bayliss in International Society for the Study of Church Monuments *Bulletin* 7 (1982), where possibly related monuments are also listed. I would surmise the hand of an unidentified sculptor of French origin, working in the Midlands, perhaps also identifiable in the staircase, hall chimney-piece and other details at Burghley. It is perhaps worth noting that low-relief 'square and circle' ornament, similar to that on the staircase at Burghley, appears on soffits in the Haynes Grange room.

26. 'The Smythson Collection' *Architectural History* V (1962), p. 77; Girouard *Smythson*, Pls. 49, 50. There are similar flaming balls on the tomb of Dean Nicholas Wotton (d.1567) in Canterbury Cathedral.

27. In the Pantheon the motif occurs eight times, in alternation with screens of columns and the four arched alcoves which are the dominant features of the interior, apart from the dome.

28. For Slaugham Place and the Covert Tomb, see *Country Life* (9 January 1964); J.H. Cooper 'The Coverts - 2' *Sussex Archaeol. Coll.* XLVII, pp. 129-30.

29. I am most grateful to Nicholas Barker for his comments on the lettering.

30. There is a useful account of Peter Osborne in the *Dictionary of National Biography*. An interesting full-length portrait of Edward VI, a variant on the well-known portraits at Windsor and Petworth, is still in the Osborne collection and was presumably acquired by Peter Osborne. The spelling of the family name was later changed to Osborn.

31. R.C. Barnett *Place, Profit and Power: A Study of the Servants of William Cecil* (Chapel Hill, N. Carolina, 1969), pp. 40-1, 46, 110-12.

32. F.B. Williams *Index of Dedicatory and Commendatory Verses in English Books before 1641* (1962).

33. Caius made Parker his literary executor (*Dictionary of National Biography* under 'Caius'), and their friendship seems to have survived the difficulties caused by Caius remaining a Catholic.

34. So stated in early entries in Burke's *Peerage and Baronetage*. The Osborn papers have been removed from the Bedfordshire County Record Office, and I have not had access to them.

35. *Victoria County History: Bedfordshire*, II, pp. 271-5 (Chicksands); pp. 341-2 (Haynes). Haynes Grange is within a few hundred yards of Hawnes Park (Hawnes is the alternative and earlier spelling) but the two properties have always had separate ownerships.

36. A crude sketch plan showing the ground floor in the early seventeenth century is reproduced in *Victoria County History* , p. 274.

37. See S. Houfe 'The Builders of Chicksands Priory' *Bedfordshire Magazine* XVI (1978), pp. 185-9, 228-31.

38. *Op. cit.*, p. 117.

39. The reason for the doves remains to be established. They appear to have no relation to the coat of arms or crest of the Osbornes or any other local family. Possibly they symbolise the liberated soul, in sympathy with the inscription.

40. Rooms lined rather than panelled with wood, but without the elaborate detail of the Haynes Grange room, are found at approximately this period in Scotland, for instance at Culross Palace. The use of pine is common in Scotland from the sixteenth century onwards, but in England no other identified example appears to be known dating from earlier than the late seventeenth century. There is no evidence or likelihood that the Haynes Grange woodwork was ever painted.

41. I am grateful to Roger Ward and the R.A.F. Commandant at Chicksands for arranging access to Chicksands, and to Roger Ward for information about the house.

42. In an article published in *Country Life* on 9 May 1991, I suggested that the panelled room from Sizergh Castle, at present on display in the Elizabethan gallery of the Victoria and Albert Museum, should be returned to Sizergh and the Haynes Grange room brought out of storage to take its place.

SOLOMON'S TEMPLE IN NOTTINGHAMSHIRE

Originally published in *Country Life* on 3 October 1991. The bibliography of Koberger's version of Nikolaus de Lyra's notes on the Bible, and the accompanying engravings of the Temple, is complex; it appeared in numerous editions, either inserted page by page into actual Bibles, or published separately. Bernard Lamy's reconstruction is in his *De Tabernaculo Foederis de Sancta Civitate Jerusalem et de Templo eius* (Paris, 1720). Josephus's descriptions of Solomon's and Herod's temples are in Books VIII and XV of his *Antiquitates Judaicae*. A useful account of Temple reconstructions, with numerous illustrations, is Helen Rosenau's *Visions of the Temple: The Image of the Temple of Jerusalem in Judaism and Christianity* (1979).

For Wollaton and the Willoughbies in general, see M. Girouard *Robert Smythson and the Elizabethan Country House* (New Haven and London, 1983), pp. 81-108, and Alice Friedman *House and Household in Elizabethan England: Wollaton Hall and the Willoughby Family* (Chicago, 1989). The seventeenth-century catalogue of the Wollaton library is in the Manuscripts Department of Nottingham University Library, Middleton I 17/1; Martin Hill's and Stanton's sermons are Middleton LM 33 and O 16/28 in the same place.

RECONSTRUCTING HOLDENBY

Originally published in *Country Life* on 18 and 25 October 1979. Of the visual material used, the Thorpe drawings are in the Soane Museum

('I'182-4) and were published with annotations by John Summerson as editor of the *Book of Architecture of John Thorpe* (Walpole Society XL, 1966), pp. 93-4, Pls. 84-5; the two Holdenby surveys are in the Northamptonshire Record Office; the Thornhill drawings in the Center for British Art, New Haven; the Thomas Eayre drawing in the Prints and Drawings Collection, British Museum. Most of the printed sources used are available in Sophia Hartshorne's *Memorials of Holdenby* (1868). Much help with both visual and printed material was given by James Lowther.

THE GHOST OF ELIZABETHAN CHATSWORTH

Originally published in *Country Life* on 22 November 1973, and mainly based on building accounts at Chatsworth and the inventory of the contents of Hardwick and Chatsworth attached to Bess of Hardwick's will, which was made in 1601. The original is with her will in the Public Record Office (Prob 10/275); there are contemporary copies also in the PRO (Prob II/III/Fo.23) and in the archives at Chatsworth, and a twentieth-century manuscript copy in the National Trust office at Clumber Park, Nottinghamshire. The Hardwick portion of the inventory was edited by Lindsay Boynton and Peter Thornton for the *Journal of the Furniture Historical Society* VII (1971). The relevant Elizabethan accounts were edited by Basil Stallybrass in 'Bess of Hardwick's Builders and Building Accounts', *Archaeologia* LXIV (1913), but I have also drawn on accounts at Chatsworth which are not in Stallybrass.

COUNTRY-HOUSE PICTURES

Originally published in the *Times Literary Supplement* on 29 February 1980, as a review of John Harris's *The Artist and the Country House* (1979).

THE MAGIC OF STOWE

This grew out of a week-end spent with John and Myfanwy Piper in the Gothic Temple at Stowe. It was written as the introduction to *John Piper's Stowe*, a limited edition of John Piper's drawings and watercolours, published by the Hurtwood Press in conjunction with the Tate Gallery in 1983.

Christopher Huxley wrote about Stowe in *English Gardens and Landscapes 1700 1750* (1967). George Clarke's many writings on Stowe include 'The Gardens of Stowe', part of a special number, 'The Splendours of Stowe' *Apollo* (June 1973); jointly with M.J. Gibbon the comprehensive 'History of Stowe', published in 26 instalments in *The Stoic*, March 1967 to July 1977, and, as editor, *Descriptions of Lord Cobham's Gardens at Stowe 1700-1750* (Buckinghamshire Record Society no. 26, 1990). The description of the fête for Princess Amelia appears in *The Grenville Papers* II (ed. W.J. Smith)(John Murray, 1852) pp. 407-8. The Nattes drawings were reproduced as *Drawings of Stowe by John Claude Nattes in the Buckinghamshire County Museum* (ed. C.N. Gowing and G.B. Clarke)(Buckinghamshire County Museum and Stowe School, 1983). There are accounts of the 2nd Duke's bankruptcy and sale in *Apollo*, *op. cit.* above (by Paul Whitfield), and the *Stoic History* Part XXVI (by M.J. Gibbon).

WHAT IS A VILLA?

Originally published in the *Architectural Review* as a review of James Ackerman's *The Villa: Form and Ideology of Country Houses* (London and Princeton, 1990).

THE HOUSE AND THE NATURAL LANDSCAPE

This was written on the invitation of Edgar Kaufmann Jr. as an introduction to his *Fallingwater: A Frank Lloyd Wright Country House*, published by Abbeville Press, New York, in 1983.

The main sources are given in the text. I am indebted to a most comprehensive bibliography of literature on American country retreats, camps, cabins, etc., prepared in typescript by Alfred Willis, at Edgar Kaufmann's request.

THE GEORGIAN HOUSE

Written in 1989 for an abortive special issue on the English House in the *Sunday Times Magazine*.

The two assembly-room quotations come from *Letters from Lady Jane Coke* (ed. Mrs A. Rathbone, 1899), p. 8, and the *Torrington Diaries* (ed. C.B. Andrews, 1934) II, p. 175; the inventory of Handel's house is printed in Otto E. Deutsch *Handel: A Documentary Biography* (1955); for the Purefoy servants, see *The Purefoy Letters 1735-1753* (ed. G. Eland, 1931), pp. 126-56..

PHOTOGRAPHIC CREDITS

Mark Girouard: 1, 2, 5, 8, 9, 15, 21, 26, 42, 53, 54, 58, 59, 60, 62, 63 (photograph by Geremy Butler), 70, 74, 75, 76, 77, 78, 79, 80, 81, 82, 85, 94, 135, 141, 146, 147, 151, 156, 164, 170, 179, 182, 184, 188, 192, 193, 194, 195, 204 (photograph by Geremy Butler), 207, 208 (photograph by Geremy Butler), 211, 218; Peter Burton and Harland Walshaw: 3, 20, 22, 24, 25, 50, 52, 55, 56, 57, 64, 72, 84, 93, 94, 95, 96, 99, 100, 101, 104, 111, 127, 128, 129, 133, 136, 137, 138, 139, 142, 143, 144, 145, 153, 168, 183, 189, 191, 196, 197, 198, 200, 210, 225, 226; the British Museum: 4, 17, 130; by courtesy of the Board of Trustees of the Victoria and Albert Museum: 6, 16, 18, 166; National Portrait Gallery: 7; Country Life Ltd.: 10, 97, 98, 103, 105, 106, 132, 134, 140, 174, 199, 215; by courtesy of Lord Courtenay (photograph by Col. Delforce): 11; the Courtauld Institute of Art: 12, 152, 157, 177, 185; by kind permission of the Marquess of Tavistock and the Trustees of the Bedford Estates: 13; Stamford Town Council: 23, 27; Lincolnshire County Council (Stamford Museum): 28, 29; courtesy Mary Chubb: 31; courtesy Nicholas Chubb: 30, 32, 33, 34, 35, 36, 37, 38, 39, 40, 41; Simon de Courcy Wheeler: 45; private collection: 48, 49, 102, 108, 109, 110, 112, 113, 228; Whitby Literary and Philosophical Society: 51; Scarborough Public Library: 61; Norfolk Museums Services (Cromer Museum, Norfolk): 65, 66, 67, 68, 69, 71, 73; Mary Durlacher: 86, 87, 88, 89, 90, 91; Thomas Pakenham: 114; Patrick Rossmore: 115, 116, 117, 118, 119, 121, 122, 123, 124, 125, 126; John Searle: 120; Waterford City Corporation: 131; National Monuments Record: 154, 155, 158, 161, 162, 163, 165; the Warburg Institute: 159; Walter Scott (Bradford): 160; Yale Center for British Art: 167, 230; the British Library: 169, 171, 173, 175, 176; the Paul Mellon Centre, London: 178; Northamptonshire Record Office: 186, 187; John Harris: 201, 205; the Board of Trustees of the Royal Armouries: 202; the Tate Gallery, London: 203; Buckinghamshire County Museums: 209; Mark Fiennes: 212; the Wordsworth Trust: 213; the National Trust for Scotland: 214; Michael Boys: 216; Courtesy of Sotheby's, Inc., New York: 217; New York Public Libraries: 219, 222; Adirondack Museum: 220 (photograph by R.T. Stratton), 221 (photograph by Richard Linke); Art Institute, Chicago: 223; Frank Lloyd Wright Memorial Foundation: 224; Royal Commission on Historic Monuments (England): 227; Courtesy W.L. Banks: 228; Courtesy John Ingamells: 229.

INDEX